LEGENDS OF LINCOLN

Tall Tales & Legends of The Life & Times of Abraham Lincoln

By Michael John Joseph Del Toro

For

Michael John Joseph Del Toro

Mom & Dad,

Vicky

&

My Gloria

TABLE OF CONTENTS

Preface   6

Introduction   8

Captain Abraham & Daniel Boone   12

The Captain & The Indians   22

The Courtship of Abraham & Mary   31

Abraham's Battle Against A River   40

America's Pioneering Spirit   52

Pa Brings Us A Momma   64

Abe & The Rule of Three   72

To Kill A Hog   80

The Eyes Of Desperation   87

No Way To Make An Entrance   96

The Chains of Bondage   103

Thirst For Knowledge	109
A Way With Words	117
America's Hercules	125
The Bounty of the River	134
All In A Day's Work	141
An Abe of All Trades	151
Cash or Kind – The Frontier Economy	159
Fun & Games of Abraham Lincoln's Youth	167
Duty, Honor, Faith & Family	176
The Winter of The Deep Snow	186
Honest Ambition & Compassion	194
Loves Won And Lost	211
Tussling With Onions & Mosquitos	220
Fight of the Century	226
The Inspiration of America's Martyr	245

A Final Word   259

Select Bibliography   260

PREFACE

The first seed of an idea to create this book came during my long research on the Civil War. Abraham Lincoln was obviously the seminal figure in that titanic struggle for America's future identity. The strength of mind, perseverance of will, his sagacity and political acumen, willingness to adapt and utilize every means necessary were the dynamic features that allowed him to succeed where so many others may very well have failed.

How a man of supposedly the most meager means was able to overcome his birth, childhood and every other obstacle facing him up to and through the war I found extremely intriguing. I felt a desire to study his history trying to unmask the extraordinary man.

I quickly began to find that beneath all of the stories of his from the start of his career as an adult in Illinois up to his death there lay the mystery of his childhood. All the stories that we know didn't come close to explaining who he really was. This led me on a quest to part the mists of time and find what made Lincoln tick.

What I thought would be a few months diversion turned into a decade long pursuit. Through that time the distraction turned into an idea to create a history dealing solely with his youth then evolved into making the novel a series of short stories about his youth.

I struck a snag in that so many of the stories were hearsay so there was no way to really make a definitive history of Abraham Lincoln's childhood that could stand the test of critical analysis. There were a few certainties separated by huge gaps of myth and legend, in some cases more akin to fantasy than history.

At first I thought this was the end of my short lived book idea but it was only the beginning because it gave me an epiphany. I had learned through my initial research was that there were many different perspectives on Lincoln from those who knew him deeply or as an acquaintance. There were as many different ideas about why Lincoln was the way he was as there were people in his world.

To each of them Lincoln was unique and in some ways a reflection of their ideals. I realized that to fully understand Abraham Lincoln, how he became who he was and how he viewed the world, I needed to study not only him but the people around him and America as it was before he was born, when he was young, as a young man, in his prime and up until his death.

This course led me in the end to expand the premise of the book from a series of short stories of Lincoln's youth to one of his time, the culture of America as he grew into a young man, and from the perspective of his many friends, family and acquaintances, what he was like as a man all the way through his untimely death. While for the most part this book will deal with his youth there are several chapters that will discuss the characteristics that made him who he was all through the medium of tall tales, legends and perspectives.

I would to take the opportunity to thank my mom, Theresa and my pop Michael for a mother's faith and confidence in what I was trying to do and a father's critical analysis and constructive advice in tempering my overconfidence and ambition.

I want to acknowledge the unwavering support from Vicky over the course of the many years we spent wandering around America from the midwestern states of Lincoln's exploring the region of his birth and youth, from his home to his haunts, to the deep south and southwest to gain new perspectives of American culture during the 1800s.

I've had a lot of help from friends and professional writers to try and give constructive feedback on how to present a historical narrative in the style of a tall tale. Special thanks go to Rachel and Timothy in always being available and for their advice and support.

I want to especially thank Gloria for her patience and understanding over the past three years as I secluded myself in my office for hours on end in order to compile the myriad of information sources and mesh them with my thoughts then forcing her to listen to me recite the stories each night, and for the inspiration and discipline she gave me to finally complete this work.

This book, like I believe most do for writers, became a journey through time and discovery. I learned far more than I believed I ever would when I first took up the challenge and I earnestly hope that whoever reads this learns a little about the time and country in a real sense through those who lived it, but all within the traditional framework of American myth and legend.

INTRODUCTION TO THE LEGENDS OF LINCOLN

This novel work will entice those who have an interest in general history, American History and English Literature. It is also valuable as an educational tool for teachers of the above disciplines. This historical content is presented as a series of stories will put a fresh take on these moments in time, sort of like a number of snapshots of history. The different writing styles, required in a book of this kind, will appeal to those who enjoy English Literature.

This book will work well for teachers looking for a different way to present their subject to students. With over two dozen chapters, students can be assigned a chapter each, either by choice or designation, and be asked to provide a brief summary of the tale and their views on the material. This works for classes of up to, or over, 30 students, allowing for some overlap with larger classes. The chapters studied by more than one student can be compared and contrasted to help illuminate the class on perspective and assist in providing points of interest or introspection the class might not have perceived upon first reading.

Abraham Lincoln was a dynamic individual who rose from humble beginnings to become elected to the highest position possible in American politics, to navigate the perils this election caused and to be considered one of the great, if not the greatest, Presidents in American History.

This book is meant to present the great man in a different light than normally depicted. It isn't meant to provide an answer to the many questions surrounding his youth and character, though some attempt is made to draw a distinction between the myths that surround his experiences before he made his way onto the political scene and place the history surrounding this time on more solid footing. That task is nigh impossible due to the inadequate records of the period and the intentional distortion of this history, at times by Lincoln himself, for political purposes.

Lincoln's past and for the most part his background was placed firmly under the myth that he came from nothing and everything he had or achieved was due to himself and him alone. Over the last couple of decades this myth has begun to crack.

I hope not to shatter it completely but to put it on a more realistic footing. He did achieve much through individual effort but all of that was on a firm foundation of his family heritage, his father and both his mothers and the communities in which he lived.

When I read many of the older biographies about Tom; Abe's father, I didn't think much of him and I thought little more of either of his mothers. Basically, it was that his father was a good for nothing while his mothers were a little smarter and the main thing they did for him was impart in him the value of learning.

They did far more. It was when I was traveling through Texas and then Louisiana that I gained a new found respect for the pioneers of America. I learned there how much they had to actually know in the practical arts and how much they taught themselves and their children. I saw firsthand through recreations the evolution of their homes from simple homesteads to large more modern houses and plantations.

It was there also that I discovered the integral part the women and young girls played in keeping and managing a household and the family, much like I learned in my travels through Europe and Asia.

Therefore, some effort is made to provide an alternative perspective of the family life that was often painted of the great man. He had a loving family and, except for a brief period of time, had a mother and father throughout his youth and long into manhood. His father was not the aimless drifter so often portrayed and that young Lincoln was a bit of a rascal and quite the prankster, evidence of which is amply provided in his antics in later life.

These sketches draw upon many sources to attempt to provide a vivid picture of the United States at the time prior to his birth through the time around his death. It uses many historical figures of his time, sometimes in fictional settings and circumstances, to describe incidents in his life in fuller detail, if not in absolute fact. Drawing absolutes in Lincoln's youth and through much of his adult life in our day would be fruitless, as one cannot look through the lens to the past without the tint of time, and it was nigh impossible to draw absolute truth of Lincoln's life even in his own day.

This is not meant to be a comprehensive biography of Lincoln's entire life or even his youth. It is meant to cover in a very general fashion both the generation prior Abraham Lincoln's birth and after his assassination. His life and times are covered through the eyes of Lincoln and contemporaries. His youth is covered in much more detail and with it the culture in which he was raised but there will be large holes, much like it was during Lincoln's life.

I suspect much of the missing details could have been filled by Lincoln himself but he may not have wanted his past to be dissected just like many modern politicians would rather keep that part of their lives buried. Abraham Lincoln was undoubtedly one of the greatest Americans, which is a major reason I felt he would be an ideal subject for this sort of novel but even he had a few unsavory episodes he might want to wash under to table or keep in its respective closet.

A man of Lincoln's wide influence would understandably call forth a myriad of emotions and I attempted to portray these as vividly as possible within the context of his time and the storyteller's own background and experience, as well as in the tradition of tall tales and legends of America. If there is any fault with the narration it is entirely my own and I hope you can understand the effort of worthy of my goal in displaying this, in many ways, unique individual.

For many and for their own reasons Lincoln was placed on a pedestal until he became, much like the Founding Fathers of America more myth than man. This is at once a blessing and a curse which befalls most great men over the course of time. As the ancient Greeks and Romans came to believe in classical times, if one's achievements reached high enough the only course left to man was to ascend to the realm of gods. It is a fate that few reached, the Alexanders, the Julius Caesars, the Augusti of their day.

As the centuries passed the facts of their lives blended with the myths and legends and became one. They achieved the status of heroes and gods, either rightly or wrongly. Over the subsequent centuries, others have reached this exalted level. King Arthur, Charlemagne & Genghis Khan to name but a few.

In the American pantheon there is George Washington, Thomas Jefferson, Benjamin Franklin and James Madison among others but at the top of the pedestal for most Americans stands Abraham Lincoln alone. For the others their faults are usually downplayed or swept under the carpet but are still readily apparent on close inspection. This is not the case for Lincoln.

What I try to do through these stories is to humanize Abraham Lincoln. I believe that this may cause him to descend from the highest echelons of the American Pantheon of Deities but in doing so I will elevate him as a Man.

I tried to impart all of this into these stories for they are all important parts of the fabric woven into the American psyche, which blends much of the Old World into the New to create that dynamic American culture that has come to influence much of the world today.

The focus of this fictional narrative is to give insights into President Abraham Lincoln's youth and later life through the eyes of his contemporaries and the generation following his death. My desire is it will give us all some ideas, some keys, into what made this man so great, and to provide some inspiration to us all.

I know it has for me. I hope it does for you as well.

** on a few occasions where I have obviously deviated from certain facts in order to embellish an event in true "tall tale" fashion I do add in Notes at the end to offer a truer account to explain the deviation. I haven't marked the specific possible contradictions, nor have I listed every instance because I want the reader to enjoy the story as it is first and not feel compelled to go and look to see a fuller explanation or added context for every little incident.

You may often see that the perspective of the storyteller may color his recollection of the past in a positive or negative way. I also hope the reading of these stories will inspire curiosity to look further into the history of Lincoln and see how perspectives of different authors and how the environment and times the author writes these histories influence their recording of the events.

I suspect it will be understood that as second or third person retellings, this sort of "error" or "inadvertent omission" should be expected and go without saying. I hope any scenario that doesn't coincide with anyone's belief in how things happened will respect this aspect of the story. Thank you. **

CAPTAIN ABRAHAM & DANIEL BOONE

President Lincoln leaned back against the plush chair within the warm confines of the White House, his long legs sprawled out seeming to reach into the very corners of the spacious room. It was mid-September of 1861, a mere six months into his Administration, and the President was alone with his young son William, one of the few moments he was to spend alone as President with the boy. The country was at war with itself and the President was busier than any of his predecessors had ever been. Each moment he could spare, as few and far between as they may be, he would spend with his children, especially his favorite, Willie.

This was a most trying period for President Lincoln. The war had taken a turn for the worse. The disastrous battle of First Bull Run had taken place a little over a month ago, and the city was still ill defended, the government under constant threat of attack by the rebels directly across the river, their fortifications in plain view along the hills to the south of the Potomac River bordering Washington DC. Troops had been pouring in from all across the North but were untrained, as green as grass, and there was acrimony amongst the top Union Generals. The dashing young, charismatic Commander of the self-styled Army of the Potomac, Major General George B. McClellan was at loggerheads with the General-in-Chief, the legendary, yet aging First Soldier of the Republic, Winfield Scott. Lincoln was hard pressed to maintain his composure under the strain, and he took much comfort with any time he could with his family, his wife Mary, young Tad, and of course, Willie. His eldest son, Robert was attending Harvard College.

Willie was a precocious child, who loved poetry, animals, reading, theatrics and religion. He was a sweet tempered young boy, aged ten, who's most endearing trait was his compassion. He had a talent for mathematics and one of his favorite activities was drawing up railroad timetables. Willie was very conscious of his surroundings and of all Honest Abe's children, was most like his father.

The day had been hectic as usual but in the evening things had quieted down enough for the President to take the opportunity to read poetry with his young son. Both of them enjoyed poetry immensely and the duo spent a couple of precious hours reading and discussing them together before Willie became interested in hearing stories of their family's past. This brought a wistful smile from Abraham as it allowed him to recall a simpler time, some with hardship and pain, but none with the immense prolonged strain of the last six months.

The room was well protected against the ravages of the autumnal weather outside and young Willie was content as ever sitting on the knee of his father, in awe of his dad and his legendary storytelling skill. Neither father or son could know that in less than half a year the boy would be resting eternal in the same chamber, stricken down by sickness, and father and mother mourning the death of their beloved son. Oblivious to this somber fact Honest Abe began his tale, his high pitched voice, incongrous with his large frame, filling the room and drawing his son into the world of his father's memory and imagination.

"The stove was blazing as young Abraham Lincoln's mother," began the President, "prepared the evening meal while bold Thomas Lincoln sat upon a wooden stool entertaining his two young children. The rudimentary three walled house was open on one side, a rude cloth tarp, the only protection besides the fire, against the elements of a Kentucky spring." Honest Abe would often depict himself in the third person in his stories to lend authenticity and present a detachment that would allow others to express their full emotions to the morals of the tale. Abe's stories almost always had some moral or point. It might take some time to draw it out but it was there.

"Little Abe sat atop his father's knee, much like you dear boy," the President continued, "while his sister Sarah sat cross-legged on the coarse wooden floor. A smallish bed upon which the whole family slept was set in one corner of the tiny cabin, while on the other side was the stove, next to which was a shelf and cabinet containing all the possessions of the Lincoln household. Thomas took up most of the bed and though not a tall man, he was thick in bone and rough-hewn, as stout as any tree. Ole' Tom's wife, Nancy, was seated upon a well worn but finely crafted chair knitting a pair of socks while absentmindedly listening to her husband."

"Both the children were rapt with attention upon their father, their eyes' aglow as he spun his tale, weaving words as only he could, the epitome of a storyteller of the old West. Little did the young Abe or Sarah, much less their parents know, their mother would be dead come fall and brother and sister would be forced to fend for themselves for six whole months while their father went east to find a wife."

"It was 'nother drenching day in ole' Virginia, way back when our country was first fighting for the right to govern themselves. This was a little over a year after the great winter that General Washington and his troops spent at Valley Forge, when Daniel Boone returned from one of his many adventures in the wilds of the west", Thomas began. The sights and sounds around them slowly receded until all their attention was centered on Thomas and his tale, who brought his listeners to exotic faraway places in the distant past and into the mind of a stranger.

Thomas continued as if he was Daniel Boone. Now Thomas Lincoln liked to present his story from the mouth of another. This gave it a freshness and personal touch unavailable from a third person narrative. *"The spring rains are here again in the old counties. Awash with rain the country roads are flooded, and the farms look like little islands amidst the man-made plains dotted here and there with a wooded glen or dell. Well could I imagine how this valley may have looked a generation earlier when the native Indians trod the land and only a handful of the White Man had ever spied its magnificent beauty. How I miss the Kentucky district. The untamed lands, waiting for Civilized Man to settle, and the untold riches abounding within its midst.*

The road, or what could be called a road, more like a muddy track, much used by wagon, beast and man, began to take on a more familiar hue. Looking up from my broad brimmed hat, in use today over my usual coonskin cap, for the benefit of keeping my face free from the incessant rain, I could barely see ahead of me, my old friend Abe's home. Nestled in the western reaches of Virginia proper on a lush farm in the Shenandoah Valley, Abe had become something of a patriarch of the community. My friend was deemed a moderately wealthy man and had many of the creature comforts you would find in a well to do house in the more developed eastern part of the State or in even the motherland of England itself.

Not that Abraham was a traditional patriarch. True he was a wealthy man amongst these parts, and had a rich bounty in children and relatives, here and in his family's home in Massachusetts. He was a mainstay in this county, imbedded in the community, a leader affectionately called 'The Captain'.

Abraham received this nickname from his time as a captain of the local militia company during the Revolutionary War, which was still being contested between the Colonies and Mother England under the thumb of the wicked King George, and was much loved by his men. Not that I cared for any of these things at the moment. I was cold, wet and hungry and my destination was near at hand. It would be good to spend some time with the creature comforts I have sorely missed dur-

ing my time pioneering the untrammeled region of Kentucky County, Virginia.

My mission required I not enjoy the luxuries of modern living too much for I had a serious purpose here. To move a man who had done well for himself, acquiring all the success one could wish to achieve, out from his comfortable living and into an uncertain future would take all the persuasiveness I might have, and more. But I didn't come here to fail and if my past accomplishments were anything to go on, I could be persuasive indeed.

The last half mile proved uneventful and soon I was in front of the large yet, modest front door of the house of one Abraham Lincoln, one of the wealthiest landowners in this part of Virginia and a friend to boot. After a quick knock and short wait, an elderly well-dressed black man answered the door and after I introduced myself, I was led inside. I was brought through the foyer into the main living room where Abraham was sitting legs outstretched entertaining a number of guests, as was his wont.

Old Abe was a congenial fellow and loved to string a yarn a mile long if given the opportunity, and with his melodious voice and never ending bounty of antidotes he was ever a source of amusement and fun for anyone lucky enough to hear him. Thus his home always had a few neighbors or travelers that found themselves drawn there in the evenings, after The Captain had finished his work in the fields, waiting for the merry time when Abe would sit back, draw on his pipe and bring his guests into his world of fun and frolic. If there was ever a man with the gift of gab, it was Captain Abraham Lincoln. Often he would sit in his great chair, next to the fireplace with sprite little Tom upon one knee and weave a tale that could last hours while leaving all who listened wanting more. Little Tom would sit upon the knee of his father, gazing at him, only half understanding the words but filled with wonder at the jovial face drawing all around him into his own world with his story. There was a sense of power for the storyteller to be able to entrance his listeners, having them eagerly anticipating each word of the tale and enthralled by their voice and gyrations.

Often at the end of one of these evenings, Tom would be curled in the Captain's lap and would be carried upstairs into his room into his inviting bed the young boy shared with his siblings.

There Abe sat in the midst of one of his spellbinding tales when he spied me, old Danny boy, in my scruffy garb, wet and unkempt, but with a proverbial grin and positive air. Immediately Lincoln stopped his tale, rose to his feet and rushed to greet his old friend. We Boones and Lincolns go back a long way and many of my relations married into the Lincoln family and vice versa. The Captain was born not a day's journey from my own birthplace and my own dear cousin, Anne, was married to Abraham's father John's half-brother.

"Danny Boy!", The Captain exclaimed. "Back from your never ending forays into the wilds yonder?" Abe clapped me on my back. While not a tall fellow, The Captain was as sturdy as they come and with immense strength earned in the toils of farming his land. His friendly slap on my back hurt even one such as me, accustomed to the hardships of living alone in the wild for months at a time. Turning to the others he continued his introduction, "Well folks, this here, if you don't know, is the legendary Daniel Boone himself, tamer of the Wilds and pioneer of the yonder lands that to us yeomen are mere legend. What brings you to my humble abode my dear friend?"

Smiling wincingly, I returned his greeting with a few murmurings meant to disarm those around us and quell any questions towards myself. I then excused myself to wash up, not wanting to spoil his fun and the attention of the locals. I was led by the servant and went off through an adjoining room then into a smaller one that abutted the kitchen. The room had some odds and ends in it with a large basin in the middle. I undressed while the servant drew a bath, when he finished I entered slowly dipping my feet into the warm, welcome water. How long it had been since I enjoyed a drawn bath! I felt the grime separating from me and basked in the long-neglected feeling of being clean. I took the time to enjoy the bath and some of the small luxuries of civilized life while my boon host entertained his guests for a bit before bidding them good night. My talk would be more persuasive if delivered alone.

The two of us settled down, after the others had been long gone, with a glass of imported wine from the vineyards of France, some rare stuff indeed. Old Abe was certainly not sparing in the luxuries for his old friend! But the Captain had never been one to begrudge his fellows any luxury he could partake in regardless of the circumstances. This is the sort of thing that had endeared him to his men during his time in the Army of the Revolution, and it was the same trait that had stood him in such good stead at his home amidst his neighbors.

I had always understood this innate leadership in my friend since it was in accord with my own view on how a Man of standing should act towards all. And of course we both were distinct men of standing. Otherwise, we would have no business being here in the first place.

I took a deep sip of the wine, basking in the warmth and subtle nuances of the elixir. A glass of wine was something I had not had the opportunity of imbibing for almost a year now and though perhaps I would have preferred something a bit stronger I was certainly not about to complain and I enjoyed it immensely, lingering on its subtleties and waiting for my host to begin the conversation.

We stared at each other for a long moment until I felt almost compelled to speak, but I held my tongue because I knew that my old friend could not resist hearing where I had been and what I had seen. He was always most attentive when I weaved my tales of the lands to the West and I knew it was only a matter of time before his curiosity would overwhelm him.

Getting him to move was the very reason I was here and knowing my friend as I did I understood it was only if I could spark his curiosity would I be able to convince to move upon the path I sought.

I settled back in the comfortable chair and stared into my wine with a forced patience, biding my time until ole' Abe could stand it no longer.

Sure enough, The Captain broke the prolonged silence after but a moment.

"My old friend. Please, I know the hour is late but, you must tell me something of your travels. You know how I revel in hearing your tales of the great wilderness beyond!"

"Well, well my dear friend," I responded with a laugh and a grin, "it is indeed on this very point in which I have come here this evening. My very wanderings of recent months have seemed to have been for just one reason and one reason only, which is why I am here."

Captain Lincoln now was perplexed, and frowned a bit in confusion. "What is it dear Daniel? Is there some need or want that brings you to my humble abode this late in the evening? You know all you need do is ask and what I have is yours. Our families are so entwined that you are and will always remain a brother to me, if not in blood, then surely in spirit."

I looked at my childhood friend earnestly, trying to read in his face the answer I sought for my next question. The Captain stared back, oblivious to the fate which me, his dear friend was drawing him near, only in abject innocence or ignorance to hear me relate my most recent adventure.

"Well," I began slowly weighing my words carefully. "I am loath to bring this up my dear friend, knowing how much you adore your place here within this fine community. Here you are the 'Captain' and hold a title of eminence amongst your peers."

With that Abraham gave out a hearty laugh and interjected, "Indeed Brother Daniel! It seems the people here do hold me dearly and I can't help but admit I do enjoy their company and the title of Captain amidst the community. But I have begun to feel the itch for something more. I have even begun to ponder reenlisting again, even as a private to cure this longing. And I do have a secret dear fellow. Do you know why it is that I am always the first to desire to hear your tales of the great frontier and your bold undertakings?"

"Well, I guessed it was much like everyone else, to hear tales of lands you would never see with your own eyes," I answered somewhat sheepishly, a little unsure as to where this conversation I hoped to initiate was heading.

Lincoln quickly answered his own question, cutting off my musings. I was willing to let him continue for my thoughts had been scattered a bit by his sudden earnestness and wanted time to regather them. "There is certainly some of that common awe and curiosity I will admit, but that is but a small part. I have come to find there is a restlessness in myself that I have been dwelling much upon recently. I have thought long upon this feeling within and it seemed tied at first to a longing for the sense of responsibility, risk and glory from my days leading my fellow countrymen."

"My long musings have not quelled this longing but they have only increased it. I have come to consider it is not from my days as a leader of men that I have missed but something much more. You know as well as I that my family first came to America from the homeland and settled in Massachusetts, where some of my kin still dwell. My ancestors had moved across that fair state before settling for a short time in New Jersey and thence in Pennsylvania. It was there that both you and I were born, less than a decade apart. In my youth my father brought me here, and it is here that my family has dwelt for over a decade."

I had heard all of this before but always enjoyed to listen to The Captain's tales, his voice was truly enchanting and I was certainly not immune to its charms. While I had recovered from my initial confusion, I began to have an inkling on where my old friend's thoughts were leading and a twinkle came to my eye, and a relief to my belly, as I thought my task may be far easier than I had at first surmised.

"But that restlessness from the wanderlust that brought us across the great ocean and through much of my adopted country has not abated. No indeed. It has grown within me and now stretches as vast as the sea my forefathers had once crossed. I have been thinking hard about returning to the lands I had once traveled years ago, but with an *eye to scratching out something of my own from the wilderness."*

"This land here is beautiful and full of wonder and rich in resources. But I know there is more for I have seen it with my own eyes, if only for a short while, and I long to stretch my legs once again upon the unsettled land across trails seldom traveled by my countrymen where only the buffalo and untamed Indians dwell. I wish to start something new and fresh, but I am at a loss as to how to proceed, or even if I should. Things are good here and perhaps now is not the time to begin what will likely be a hard, treacherous journey into the unknown. By the same token the land here is beginning to fill up and I get the sense there is little room for my expanding family to grow. The place is beginning to seem cramped, but I don't know if Bathsheba is even willing to migrate our whole family."

I could see now that The Captain was itching to go and just needed a little nudge to set him on his way. This settled my thoughts in a moment and gave me an opening to give him the push he so ardently desired.

"Well, Bathsheba is a fine, strong woman," I mused. "And she is loyal to her dear husband. I feel she would be proud to accompany you to wherever you lead. She knows you well, and likely knows your heart better than you. I think if you press this question upon here she will be a willing companion in this new phase of your life. Now is better to start then later. The lands to the West are vast and as yet unfilled, but in time even they will seem as crowded as Virginia seems to you now. You are strong and are in the prime of life, but it will not be that way forever. Your boys would do well to learn the ways of the world in the untamed frontier. It makes one strong in mind, body and soul and a self-sufficient pioneer is more than a match for any city boy or rural farmer."

Abraham refilled my goblet and then his own while reflecting, "You are quite right about that, she is a good woman. And my boys are good, strong boys, Mary is much like her mother and little Nancy, my newborn, is healthy and god willing she will remain so. I think you are right. The time is ripe for a new beginning. I will settle my affairs and look upon setting forth next year to begin anew out West!"

The two of us sat up late that night, I telling him of my most recent exploits and describing choice locales to settle, while The Captain discussed how he would break the news to his father and strategies on how to convince his wife, should she prove unwilling. The latter proved to be the easiest part, as I suspected. Bathsheba was a fine wife and readily agreed to Abraham's idea. His father was not as agreeable to the idea, but he had little say in the matter.

So it was that Abraham sold his house and land and set his bond on some 400 acres of land in Virginia's vast northern county of Kentucky. The last I had seen of him was in 1781 prior to his setting off with his family. They seemed to relish the opportunity their father was providing. I had since heard nothing but good tidings until news of his untimely death at the hands of natives. But that is the story for another time from the mouth of another."

Willie was looking wide eyed at his father and was most reluctant to go to bed. It was late, true enough, but the President was ever loath to abstain from telling another tale and his son's big pleading eyes were irresistible to his warm-hearted father.

"You wish to hear more, my dear boy?" Lincoln asked with a grin.

Willie nodded enthusiastically as he made himself more comfortable in his father's lap, "Tell me more about great grandfather, Pa."

"Well then, I think I know just the tale to end the evening."

Lincoln's aide John Nicolay entered the room just as the President was beginning. He quietly seated himself down on a nearby chair, always willing to listen to a mesmerizing story from the tall, lanky man from Illinois whom everyone found so captivating.

THE CAPTAIN & THE INDIANS

"Well my dear boy, you wish to hear more about your great grandfather? So you shall!"

Abraham Lincoln shifted slightly in his seat while his young son sat upon his lap gazing up towards him. His personal secretary, John Nicolay, remained seated in one corner waiting quietly for the President to finish entertaining young Willie. It wasn't often that Lincoln had the time to spend with his children and he always grabbed these occasions with both hands, so to speak. John didn't mind since he always enjoyed his boss' stories. After a moment Honest Abe continued with his tale, jumping forward in the story of his family history and turning it from the musings of Daniel Boone to a narrative.

"It was five years since Abraham "The Captain" Lincoln had brought his family across the Kentucky district to settle in an untamed forest near the fort known as Hughe's Station. The land was thickly forested with a large amount of undergrowth with but tiny clearings like small islands amidst a vast sea of trees. But it was fresh and pristine, just bristling with potential. This potential The Captain felt his family was ideally suited to master with hard work and dedication. His five years here had proven the promise of the land was well founded, as was the merits of his family. He thought back upon the meager beginnings and his thoughts surrounding his first months in his new home.

Upon their arrival, Abraham had wrestled with the vast wilderness around him for weeks. He, with his two eldest sons had soon cut a large clearing out of the dense foliage and completed construction of a small hut which the Lincoln clan lived in for a few months while Abraham and his enterprising boys finished the rudimentary cottage that was to be their home. It was a far cry from what Abe, his wife and children were used to but The Captain was quite proud of his progress so far. He had staked a claim a few miles from the nearest fort and had begun to carve, literally, a new life for his family out of this unblemished wild land. It was everything that Danny said it would be.

Things were hard, how could they not be, but the freedom and the potential that lay before them was invigorating. Every small success brought a sense of great accomplishment. He was now a true pioneer, out at the very edge of civilization and making a foundation he could truly call his own. Everything was there for the taking for those who had the will and means to grasp it. This is what Old Dan had been preaching and now that he was here, Abe felt the same sense of wonderment and awe that only those few that had done this before him could fathom. It was indescribable, the sensation of being the first to do something, and the knowledge that others would soon follow and would settle in and amongst the community he was creating was a great incentive to Abraham.

But it was a hard task before him. This land of Kentucky was rich and bountiful but the acreages he had claimed were untouched by the hand of Man and the wild vegetation around him grudgingly clung to their holdings with a voraciousness that would have put a score of men to the test. The Captain had but his three sons to aid him, his two young daughters, and of course the ministrations of his dear wife, without whom he was sure he would have succumbed within his first week. She was surely the unsung hero, or should be said heroine, of this venture. Abraham was a hardy soul and had been through many trials in his life, but the first few months here had been like nothing he had been through before and it was from his wife that he drew the strength and inspiration to continue on his chosen path instead of conceding defeat and trekking back towards the Shenandoah valley in humiliation and despair.

He looked upon his wonderful wife, Bathsheba, sitting contentedly on a rudimentary chair he himself had made for her. It was a far *cry from the luxury they both had been accustomed to in far off Virginia in their old home in the Shenandoah Valley, but here they were making a stake for themselves and their family that would last generations. Their descendants would be the undisputed leaders of the community and would always have the prestige that comes from those who founded the land upon which others laid their stake. That sort of opportunity does not come often, and it is not something that others who came afterwards would take lightly. Yes, the Captain smiled, looking on his wife who sat out front of their somewhat primitive wooden cabin and was now sewing a new pair of breeches for himself while his daughters were spreading the linen for their mother. They were making a game of it between them trying to see who could complete their task first.*

There were few opportunities for youngsters to find leisure time for games so they would invariably find a way to make a game of any chore their parents lay before them. From shucking corn to gathering eggs, the girls would find a way to make it fun. The boys were the same. Be it carrying wood to the pile, to milking the cow or lugging wool to be carded, or corn to be ground at the local mill a good 10 miles away, if there was a way to make the chore more agreeable or a friendly competition, the children would find it.

He had been in lands like this before, and not too many years earlier. He had even been a leader amongst the men he traveled with to these parts. Then he had been but one Captain among many and certainly not the head of the expedition. He was but a head of a company under the leadership of a General and conducted with the task to build a fort with no intention of being amongst the men who were to garrison and defend it.

This time it was different. Again, he was the leader of a company, but now it was but one company that was on this expedition, and this company was composed of three young boys aged 8 to 15, two small girls, a middle-aged wife and himself. Certainly not the stuff of which he had been accustomed to the first go around and even that last foray hadn't been a picture of success.

Michael John Joseph Del Toro

The Captain was determined this one would be anything like that last one. He had already placed his stake on his claim and with his sons, steadfast wife and daughters, would make his mark upon the land. Of that he was certain. He had always been a determined and resourceful man. It was a hallmark of the Lincoln breed and his standing in Shenandoah Valley was a testament to his breeding and his accomplishments. His boys were showing themselves to be fine young men and his wife was an ideal woman. The girls were a bit too young to have proved much merit yet, but both were bright and were sure to be a great boon to the family and make good wives to worthy fellows. They would do well. Abraham continued chopping away at the wood pile before him.

Harking back to his old home where he was living in comfort and wealth in the not too distant past, the Captain's mind dwelt on an old painting he had fancied but sold with most of his possessions when he made the great move to Kentucky. It was a landscape of a farmer and his family at work on their farm. It was an iconic setting and Abraham wistfully thought this autumn day would be an ideal one for their own painting of the rich and multifaceted life of an American Pioneer, with himself, the star.

Today the family was all just outside the cabin. The Captain himself was splitting a newly cut chord of cleared logs.

A pure pioneer, the Lincolns were at the edge of the Wilderness. There were no cutting parties, where all the neighbors and relatives for miles around would gather to lend a hand in ensuring the new neighbors would have enough rails for fencing and firewood to last the winter, even though they were new neighbors or not. That was beside the point since there were no neighbors on hand for help other than the fort a few miles yonder.

Adding a fierce red skinned Indian with a sharp axe in hand lurking in the woods bordering the painting would add a slightly ominous tone, but Abraham was a grim realist and with a determined grin Lincoln brought the axe down splitting the wood before him. The elder boys scrambled before him to pick up the pieces to place neatly on a row of firewood, while their father grabbed another log to chop and young Tom gathered up small shards to add to an ever-growing pile of kindling wood. That would certainly round out the painting and add to the sense of danger that all who pondered it would appreciate. The storyteller within him liked to add a bit of flavor to even his most idle musings.

The thought of Indians gave him pause and a sudden premonition came to his mind. Abraham looked up for a moment
– CRACK! –

The gunshot rang clear and shrill through the still air, while the bullet caught The Captain in the chest. He dropped like a stone and moved no more. The sound of the murderous shot was so incongruous in the Kentucky setting that everyone froze for a moment uncomprehending. The stillness lasted just a moment, for an Indian appeared along the edge of the forest, musket in hand, and rushed upon the three boys still near their stricken father.

Mordecai immediately sprang towards the house calling for his youngest brother, Tom, to follow and for Josiah to get help at the fort. He knew he had only seconds to get to the safety of the house. His mother was already rushing the girls into the cabin. His other younger brother, Josiah, obeyed him in an instant and dashed away in the direction of the nearby fort.

Hughe's Station was some miles away and It would be two hours at best before help could arrive from that direction. The Lincolns were alone, and this battle would be fought by them alone. While the eldest son had run towards the cabin, Thomas, the youngest, had stood rooted to the spot in fear and shock. The Indian who had killed his father approached quickly, bounding across the rough ground with an agility and familiarity that came from living in such an environ his entire life. The young lad had seen only eight summers, and he watched in horror as the Indian quickly scalped his father then give a cry of victory before reaching down to grasp the terror-stricken child.

Mordecai had now reached the cabin and rushed inside, returning a few seconds later with a gun. In a moment, the fifteen-year old boy coolly assessed the situation and took fast aim striking down the Indian threatening his brother. He had practiced with his father's Revolutionary War musket, which Abraham had never shot in anger, and was an excellent marksman. Mordecai then dashed out to his youngest brother and picked up poor little Thomas along with the Indian's gun, bringing him back to the relative safety of the cabin. Bathsheba and the girls had quickly begun boarding up all the windows.

Mordecai took a position right behind the thick wooden door. He took his father's gun from his sister who was holding it for him and bid her to keep loading the guns. She nodded and quickly started loading the Indian's musket. It was fortune alone it was the same type of his father's.

As it was his father had only about a hundred rounds of ammunition for the musket and the young lad hadn't the presence of mind or even the time to search the Indian for any. The Lincolns had maybe a couple of hours before they would be forced to flee to the fort. That would almost surely mean certain death or capture, and the Mordecai had heard stories during their journey to Kentucky describing the tortures Indians would do to white men they had at their mercy. The boy squatted and took aim through a crack in the door that had been enlarged for just this sort of situation. He peered out through the door just after a few Indians had come from the same area of the forest as the original assailant and scampered along the identical route towards the remains of The Captain and the Indian.

These three moved more cautiously and kept closer to the ground. Two of them were armed with muskets, which had a much shorter range than the bow the third carried. All were useless against the boy hidden behind the well-built cabin, which was constructed like a miniature fort itself. By the look of the reaction they had when Mor-

decai took them under fire proved they knew it too. They didn't even try to shoot but quickly retreated back to the forest and the protection of the trees. At first the boy thought they had fled but this forlorn hope lasted but a moment as he noticed a shadow flit from one tree to another. They were just regathering for another attempt.

This stalemate held for a few minutes before the Indians began to move against the cabin. They were methodical because they knew they had plenty of time before any help could possibly make it here, or perhaps they had caught young Lincoln's other brother before he could reach the fort. Mordecai and his family sure didn't know."

The President glanced down at young Willie to see if he had fallen asleep, but the boy was silently looking up at his father in awe, enraptured by this tale of his family' heritage. He was a little taken aback that the story had taken such a turn. It wasn't like the other story at all. Abe Lincoln's young secretary had heard the tale before but never in such detail and was amazed as the young boy. The President continued.

"Regardless, Mordecai was determined to hold out as long as he could. He came from stern stuff and this day the young Lincoln showed his mettle. For almost three hours Mordecai held his lonely vigil and held off all attacks his Indian enemies could muster. But the Indians had tightened the semi-circle around the cabin and now it was only a matter of minutes before they would be in a position to rush the door and windows.

They could not fully surround the cabin because the rear was nestled up against a small forest that had no small game trails and was composed of that same lush undergrowth so common in the area and was nigh impossible to traverse, even for an Indian, at least not very quickly. It would take hours just to go through the forest. It didn't matter now. It would only be a few minutes before they could rush the cabin from three sides. Escape was no longer an option. Once near the cabin the boy wouldn't be able to get them all before they could get inside.

Michael John Joseph Del Toro

The Lincolns were in dire straits. Grabbing the Indian's gun gave them double the rate of fire, but as he didn't pick up any ammunition, they were now down to their last seven rounds. Mordecai figured these were the only three Indians left but they were all adults and he was just one boy, however brave. He knew he would be no match once they got close enough unless he could somehow get to them first at a distance. His fear was mounting but the young boy kept himself under control. He took a shot at an Indian peeking his head up causing him to quickly drop and scramble for the nearby cover of the slaughterhouse shed. Now down to six shots.

The Indian on the opposite side of the cabin used the distraction to sprint about 15 yards and jump to safety behind a jumble of logs. Now whoever was shooting couldn't see him from the door. The Indian sat up quickly and began to move stealthily towards the cabin. He smiled grimly knowing their prey was now within his grasp.

A sudden shot rang out overhead and made him drop to the ground, but it was the second shot really startled him. The Indian jumped back up and oblivious to the threat of the cabin he looked away from the cabin towards where young Josiah had run off earlier.

Sure enough, there were several figures silhouetted by the afternoon sun along a small rise running towards them. They were still several minutes away but as far as the trio of Indians were concerned, the jig was up. They skedaddled immediately and high tailed it out of there helped along by two last parting shots from the young bold Mordecai Lincoln.

Mordecai saved his family that day but nothing he could do could stem the horror brought on by the loss of their father, a terrible memory that would stay with each of them forever. Mordecai eventually wound up with the family farm and became notorious as an Indian hunter, his hatred for the natives never abated by time. His mother, brothers' and sisters' fate would lead to all becoming separated. They were all shunted off to various relatives to lessen the burden of care for them.

Poor little Tom had it the worst. He never really got over the emotional shock of his father's death. But it was the bouncing around from family to family, the boyhood years of working all sorts of odd jobs to get by, and no schooling left in the wake of his father's untimely death that had the greatest impact on the unfortunate youth.

At first the hapless lad and his mother were taken in by her parents off to the east, but soon afterwards the boy was shunted off to his late father's immediate relatives. He spent a few years first with one family then with another, none of which really gave him the opportunity to either learn a trade or gain any education. It was not that there were few opportunities to gain any real education where he was, he just never had any opportunity to even gain any rudimentary scholarly knowledge since even as a youth he had to work at any job he was able to just to make ends meet.

There were blab schools where he was living. There were a few teachers or tutors here or there that could have provided some education for the lad. That is true. But the time and money needed were not there. Tom and his mother had gone from an affluent situation to a pioneering one, and from there to one of having to bounce from one relative to another, grateful for a roof over their head. Anything more was at the time virtually unthinkable.

Eventually one of his uncles gave him the chance to be apprenticed and learn carpentry, and Thomas having a quick mind was able to pick it up rather quickly. He always remembered this trade and it managed to come in quite handy when he came to adulthood. He was often able to supplement whatever money he could get from other jobs from his skill as a carpenter and this gave him a leg up on his peers when choice farming opportunities became scarce, as it often did for a youth in the West. Carpentry was a great boon to him and his future family and gave him the skills needed to add certain amenities to his home that were not common in other farming households."

Lincoln looked down at his son again. By this time, Willie's eyes were fluttering as he struggled to stay awake. President Lincoln lifted him up easily and brought the young boy into his bedroom to sleep, returning in a few moments to speak with his secretary on the ever-present military matters and current political situation that took up so much of his time these days, and nights. It would likely be several hours before he himself would be off to bed to catch a few hours of shut eye then start a new day in his almost insurmountable quest to heal the wounds of the nation.

THE COURTSHIP OF ABRAHAM & MARY

Mary Todd Lincoln was reaching for the door before the carriage even drew up to the Methodist Episcopal Church on 20th Street. With her today, as on most of her semi-secret forays, were two young black girls. They were part of the White House staff and they traveled with Mrs. Lincoln to assist her when she went outside the White House on her excursions.

To most of the people who read the newspapers in any of the major cities, and even most of the small towns that dotted the landscape between them, the only time Mary Lincoln left the White House would be for a much-publicized shopping spree or to a ball or private party where she lavished her wealth and position most ostentatiously. She would be sure to have the most luxurious gown and be adorned with the finest jewels, in order to outshine any would be rival for the claim of the Belle of Washington.

There was definitely some truth to this. Mary Todd was a Kentucky Belle after all, and fully understood how she was looked down upon by the Eastern Elites, and this prompted her to try and outdo them on occasions in order to show she was the foremost Lady of Washington. She also did have in her a temper, as the local newspapers would always comment, that could be tempestuous to put it mildly, and was insecure of her position and standing in the community to an extent that did not bring dignity to the position of First Lady.

But the tabloids and even more respectable newspapers took this sort of behavior, including her tirades, to an extreme that approached libel. It was most certainly true she did all of these things and it was also true that she could be outlandish in her spending habits, and was quite a viper when it came to what she felt was an affront to her honor or place, or most especially any attack on her husband.

But this was not the norm and it was the drive to sell papers that drew the reporters to remark on this far more frequently than anything more mundane or becoming, and what could be more scandalous than a First Lady who was a harpy and spent taxpayer money on dresses and jewels while poor soldiers fought and died in battle. This didn't happen as often as those who wrote these stories vividly portraying the First Lady as a spendthrift while the nation was at war would have led the people to believe.

What few citizens of the United States realized since only a handful of those who understood Mary Lincoln well even knew, was her daily trips to the many hospitals that had sprung up in and around the bustling capital. The nation was at war. Nowhere else was it more evident than in Washington DC, where soldiers were seen marching to and from forts dotted along the landscape on the periphery of the city, and there seemed to be a hospital on every street. Many of these makeshift hospitals were in private homes, schools and children's wards, but most were converted from churches and chapels. It was here that the Lord's work was found most clearly in the care of the wounded and dying in this Great War for Freedom.

Today she brought with her in the carriage, along with her usual attendants, five baskets arrayed with an assortment of gifts for her wounded charges. There was a basket full of strawberries freshly picked by the two young girls from a small garden outside the White House. Another was full of various flowers filling the carriage with their assorted fragrances making one of the black girls sneeze incessantly, much to the amusement of the other. Two were full of lemons and oranges, gifts from a local vendor, while the last was packed with bread, sweetmeats and even some candies and cookies baked from the White House chefs themselves.

It was early mid-morning when she arrived, well before the city began to bustle. She was brought through a side entrance holding the basket of strawberries, while her two aides walked behind her, side by side with a basket under each arm. Mary began her rounds visiting each of the many wounded in turn. With some who were very wounded and not conscious she would softly speak a prayer and leave a flower or two on their bedside. She felt this was a way to brighten up their day even if they could not awaken, and also a way to keep the almost pervasive stench of death, disinfectant and decay from them.

To others who were awake she would give them a gift of strawberries, some delicacy, or lemons and oranges, though most of the latter would be given to the hospital staff as well to help combat the ever-present risk of scurvy. Then she would either chat lightly with them about simple matters to help take their minds off their cares, listen to their tales or wants and needs and often she would regal them with a tale of her own. These last would frequently revolve around her husband, especially when the wounded soldier recognized her as they often, though not always, did.

Today she spent a long while with a severely injured young private who longed for home. He had told her how he missed his young wife and would dearly like to hear a heartening tale of Mrs. Lincoln's meeting of the President, if she was willing. She was only too willing for while these tales brought its own sense of relief to herself and her own misery in losing her young son, she realized how much these stories could lighten the burden of those grievously injured, if but for a little while.

Mary was at her most lively during these times and one could catch glimpses of the vivacious young belle that her husband must have found so enchanting in her now aging visage. Today she was at her most energetic reminiscing about her love of the great Man now fretting day in and out of the many cares besieging him.

"What a boy he was! Such a boy in a Man's body. He was such a torment to my soul, this Abraham Lincoln. All who knew him, including myself, saw he was a Man's man. He was so tall, I think he was well over 6 feet when we met, and as strong as an ox. He seemed a giant to me!"

"His strength and bearing alone would have made him a leader of men but that was only a small part of the quality of my Abraham. More was certainly needed if I may say so myself to court one such as I, the Belle of Lexington, and the most eligible bachelorette in Springfield in the summer of 1838. I had many suitors vying for my attentions that first summer, but it wasn't until I returned to Springfield the next year that I met Abraham."

"Lincoln had the physical qualities that made him stand head and shoulders above many a man, but it was his intellectual qualities that really made him unique and the most formidable man in the community. I was smitten with him quite early on though certainly not in the first encounter, and he was most definitely not the only distinguished man to court me in Springfield. I had many suitors and I dare say I could choose between the most eminent of men, the likes of the great Stephen Douglas for example, but it was the tall, lanky Abraham Lincoln that stole my heart."

"I think in the end it was his humor and that mischievous bent that gave him a twinkle in his eye that finally won me over and made him the only one for me. It was that way with his father Thomas who won Nancy Hanks' hand, so the family legend goes. She was far his intellectual superior in education and bearing. Thomas came from the most humble beginnings, shifting from household to household in his youth after the death of his father, and a drifting laborer bouncing from job to job as a young adult."

Mrs. Lincoln had a way of brightening up when given free rein to talk at length. Mary's eyes drew wistfully away for a moment, as if taking in some long off memory then returned to her story.

"Now I never happened to meet Tom Lincoln, and certainly not the President's dear old mother, she passed when Abe was only 9 years old. But Abe would often speak of her in the most glowing terms and during our courtship he at times compared our different backgrounds with those of his mother and father's. His mother Nancy came from a family of means who lived about a hundred miles west of here when she was born, though Nancy never lived in Virginia herself. She left with her grandparents when she was just a month old and grew up in Kentucky, a few days ride from Lexington where I am from, and even closer to where the President himself was born. Her grandfather died before her tenth year and she then wound up moving to her aunt's home on her mother's side nearby where she spent her early childhood, and there she grew up. It was when she began to live and work as a seamstress for the Berry family over in Beechland that she first met Thomas."

Mary became more animated as she spoke and bounced around from subject to subject at a bewildering pace, often leaving her audience a bit befuddled. The First Lady had now become lost in herself with her tale and virtually ignored the young wounded soldier as she wove her story. To him she looked more and more like his own mother and a smile crept slowly across his lips adding a bit of color to his pale face.

"Coming from a wealthy family, Nancy was well educated for a frontier girl, much the intellectual superior to her husband as I said. She had an intelligent mind, friendly disposition though she would move towards melancholy at times, much like my dear husband if I do say so myself, and was very compassionate. All these traits our beloved President has and I'm sure they were what attracted Thomas to Nancy."

"To many it was a mystery of what attracted the more cultured Nancy to Thomas. I think it was their closeness, for Thomas was often at the home where Nancy worked as a seamstress before their marriage. But I also think Thomas must have struck her as quite a pioneer and ambitious in his own way. He had been in the militia, a constable, a county guard, and a jury member. An upstanding god-fearing young man who was well liked in the community, he was also a bit of an adventurer, once taking a ferry all the way down to New Orleans and was quite a carpenter and farmer to boot. By the time he had met Nancy he had purchased some nice farmland so his prospects must have looked very good to the young girl and her guardian. And I dare say he must have had some of the charm of Abraham for he was said to be as great at weaving a tale as any man of his time. I can well see how such a man would attract a young girl."

"At that time, much like it is today out West, young couples would meet and court each other within the homes of their parents and guardians. This was the way it was with Abraham and myself. As I said, I had been visiting my sister and living all the way in Springfield, Illinois for a summer when I first met my Abraham."

"I had returned to Springfield in the summer of 1839 and stayed into the winter, and it was in December that year that I first met the President. Our first meeting had its moments of incidental comedy. As I said, I was the most eligible young woman in Springfield at the time, for I had come from a well-to-do family from Lexington, if I do say so myself, which made me an ideal woman for any Kentucky man, which our dear President is. I had quite an upbringing and was educated in the finest schools at the state capital, Je peux meme parler Français, and was accustomed to all the luxuries such a woman could expect. Abraham was altogether different. He was a man's man, that is for sure, but he came from a most decidedly different social circle which became readily apparent in our first meeting. We were having a dance at the Edwards' home when Abraham came a plodding over to me slouching a bit, with not one bit of the social self-awareness that comes from the type of upbringing I was used to, and he was wearing a rather well-worn white shirt and ill-fitting tan pantaloons of carded wool. Now something in his bearing drew me to him for I would not normally have given him a second look with such an abrupt manner and homely appearance. He extended his hand in a most awkward fashion and said in that backwoods drawl of his, "I would like to dance with you in the worst way." And he most certainly did!" she ended with a chuckle before continuing again. "This began a long courtship that first winter and as I said I had many suitors, but each of them dropped off one by one until it was only Abraham who was granted admittance into the home to sit with me."

"At that time, we could only meet at the home, though we often would take walks or rides on the estate and it wasn't until December of the next year before Abraham proposed to me, and a little to my own surprise I accepted."

Several of the other wounded soldiers who were awake and within earshot were listening intently now, as Mary's tale both alleviated their boredom and distracted them from their myriad pains both physical and psychological. Mary's two young servants had returned by now, their baskets empty and the fragrance of freshly picked flowers and fruit filled the air of the makeshift hospital ward. The basket of strawberries, now half full, was in Mary's lap as she continued her story.

"We were set to be married on New Years Day in 1841 and I was happy as could be. However, the engagement was not consummated. Abraham broke it off and I was distraught. I didn't know what to do at the time, or why he had decided not to go through with it. I was miserable for a long spell and was quite put out by his abrupt breakup with me. I felt he was not a man of his word and I became a bit stubborn when he finally came around to desiring to see me again. It was quite a while before we met again, but the circumstances surrounding our reengagement taught me more about the man than I ever had before and led me to believe more than ever deep in my heart I had made the right choice after all."

She now leaned forward a bit and her voice lowered in a conspiratorial sort of way, as if she was speaking in strict confidence to the young private. The others nearby had to strain their ears to catch this part of the tale.

"It was at a party in the summer of 1842 that we met again, and we were drawn together in a sort of conspiracy that a lady of my upbringing should have never been a party to. I dare say it was quite the scandal at the time. A couple of friends of mine were in the midst of writing a letter meant to slander the prominent politician James Shields, who was of a political leaning we were solidly against, all of us being true Whigs. And I can see by the look in your eyes you know of the illustrious General. He is the very same one who was a General in our War with Mexico, a brilliant Senator and recently a General in our army, and the only one to defeat the dreaded Stonewall Jackson!"

Several of the other soldiers nodded their heads in agreement and one of them stated that he was there with Shields during the engagement at Kernstown. This seemed to be the first time Mary was aware others had been privy to the conversation. The First Lady blushed for a moment but nevertheless after standing up to bow to her audience she sat back beside the young private and continued her tale.

"Now Shields was a bit of a rival to Abraham, during his time in Illinois, which is probably why Abraham took part himself. Now normally Abe was too forthright to do something like this, but he had been hankering to renew his courtship with me, and as I had mentioned, I had been a bit stubborn. He learned of our little idea and decided it would be best if such upstanding ladies like ourselves were perceived to take no part, so he took it upon himself to oversee the drawing of the letter, which made it much more poignant since with his wit he has a way with words that could bite a man to the core."

"This letter certainly did. And in the weeks that followed we sent off a number of others that were just as sharp. We heard that Shields was in a wrathful mood and while he was a diminutive man, he was also known as a skilled one with the pistol and said to have no fear. My Abraham was a gentle soul and never once shot a weapon in anger at anyone or thing. So when it came about that Shields found out who was behind all this mischief the first thing he did was level an insult to my dear Abraham and challenge him to a duel. Of all the gall and wormwood, my little hijinks was now about to take away the dear man from me! Abraham of course showed himself a man of honor and accepted the duel, but being a smart man he drew in the fangs of the enraged Shields by declaring the weapons would not be pistols, but swords."

"This didn't stop Shields one second! He is certainly a brave man. Abraham stands a head taller than him, but James was not deterred and the two met, each with their posse at the agreed upon place, the aptly named Bloody Island. Now dueling wasn't legal in the state of Illinois, but the island sat betwixt that state and Missouri where the dreadful practice was still allowed and that determined the locale. But it was there that after long talks between their respective seconds, and oaths sworn back and forth betwixt the two would be duelists, that finally cooler heads prevailed, and both men walked away with their honor intact. It was this that showed me the lengths that my Abraham would go to protect me and soon afterwards I accepted his proposal and we were wed."

Mary fully beamed with the memory and the men around her

were silent, learning a bit about Lincoln they never knew before, and which in time would add to the myth and mystique surrounding this most unique man in American history. But the First Lady was not yet done with her story.

"But that is not how Tom and Nancy came to be wed. Theirs is a much more mundane tale. The two were wed in the very house they courted and Nancy settled down for what she believed would be a long time living in the beautiful farmland Thomas had purchased at Mill Creek, and where their first child, Abraham's beautiful older sister Sarah was born. But that was not to be for Thomas had a bit of the wanderlust, as all the Lincoln's do, or the ambition to find more opportunities, and it was always to the West where our Men would look to find a place where they could bask in the Sun and stand out amongst their peers."

"Thomas had an eye for good land, and it was during his time trapping bears and clearing land for roads and helping build log cabins that he spied a pristine spot for a farm right next to a bubbling spring that emanated from an underground cave near Nolin Creek. This new land was great for hunting, as all the animals would perchance go to the spring for an easy drink so it didn't take much for Thomas to bring home some fresh game to help ease the pallet and add some strong meat to what they could grow and raise on the farm. It was here that my Abraham was born."

"The land near Nolin Creek was bountiful in game but it wasn't the most fertile land and wasn't situated close to any well-trodden roads, both of which a budding farmer needed to make any sort of inroads on the way to wealth. Thomas perceived this after a while, and it was why within two years after Abraham's birth he moved his family to a new, more fertile plot of land called Knob Creek. Thomas finally found a spot that could have made him a wealthy man. In a few years he was one of the wealthiest in the area, and it was here that Abraham spent his early childhood. It was here his brother was born. It was here that he first went to school. At one of the blab schools I heard about. I never went to one, like I said I was from one of the wealthiest families in all of Lexington, so I was able to go to the best schools and learn from the best teachers. My Abe was not so lucky, and neither was his father. It was here that his luck began to turn. Thomas started to lose his wealth from laws made in Frankfort, and the land that was rightly his was taken away and he had to move from place to place, bringing his family with him, and finally settling for a time in Indiana...."

Mary looked up again and found that most of her audience had drifted off to sleep. This happened much of the time when she spoke to her young wards. She didn't have the gift of gab like her husband that so many men, young or old found entertaining, but hers was of a more gossipy type, more fit for the parlors and environs of the ladies. The First Lady didn't mind. She knew her stories helped distract these brave young men from their daily torments and it also gave her the same sort of distraction.

And so she got up from her seat, left the young private one of the largest and plumpest strawberries then went about her daily ministrations bringing warmth, comfort and a sense of home to all the young men who fought so bravely to ensure the Union would persevere in its greatest moment of trial.

ABRAHAM'S BATTLE AGAINST A RIVER

Abraham had been the postman of New Salem for only a few months but was already coming to know his adopted town quite well. This new job had been taken to give him some means to gain his daily bread. He had made many friends during his short time in the burgeoning town and they were quite willing to let him board with them, provided he repaid them by some manual labor like fencing in their property, tilling the land or shucking corn, but young Lincoln needed more than the sustenance bartering could give him. Coin was always rare on the frontier but far more common in towns, and once Lincoln had a taste of the economic freedom currency gave him it was always in his mind to want more.

He had had a string of bad luck after first coming to New Salem. Things had started well enough for him. After returning from his first boat ride down to New Orleans, he had been a clerk at Denton Offut's general store for some time and he did well at the work, which also gave him ample time during the slow seasons to devour most of the few books pioneers brought with them on their journey west, as well as a few periodicals sold at the store. The store itself wasn't doing well but Lincoln felt it was due to mismanagement from Offut who overspent as much as he over talked. He felt if given an opportunity he could fare better as a clerk and merchant. Many of the residents of New Salem found him a most congenial clerk and spent quite a bit of time in the store during their hours of leisure. Abe was not only big and strong enabling him to pick up the heaviest of loads, doing the work of two men, and reaching the highest, most inaccessible items with minimal effort, but he was a genial man and it seemed the entire town would often stop what they were doing just to listen to one of his entertaining stories from the seemingly endless tales stored in his mercurial mind. Offut quickly noted Lincoln's exceptional mental abilities and added to his physical duties the bookkeeping responsibilities of managing the day to day activities of the store and even running Offut's mill nearby.

This insight and experience gave the young man the confidence that when the opportunity presented itself to Abe, he was able to take over the store, and it's debts, when Offut skedaddled from New Salem to avoid having to pay his many creditors. Abe went into a partnership with his friend, fellow clerk, and a corporal in the Militia company Lincoln captained, William Berry. The two had a handful competitors within the small but prosperous village and they went about eliminating this competition by buying them out one by one through absorbing their debts unto themselves.

Eventually this left them as competitors to only James Gentry and Samuel Hill himself, who owned the leading store in New Salem. However, their stores were well established already and the compounded debts the two young men inherited, or more importantly the interest these debts incurred, quickly overwhelmed them when their creditors began trying to collect. Added to this it must be said that Lincoln was not a business minded individual, was a rather disintereested shopkeeper who was more inclined to reading and telling stories and while honesty was a desired trait in many occupations, as a shopkeeper it often went at odds with profit making ventures. Suggesting to prospective customers they didn't really need a product they were interested in procuring or the item wasn't of high quality were not beneficial to the trade.

This led to the rapid decline of their store, and after his partner disappeared one day, it was young Abe who was left with the balance of the debt and had to close his store. His days as a merchant were seemingly over.

But Abraham didn't run, like so many others who accumulated debts in the rough and tumble West. He stood pat and took the responsibilities of the debt, which helped give him a moniker of honesty he kept his whole life and stood him in great stead during his political run in the 1840s. This nickname aided in his famous but failed 1858 Senate campaign which catapulted him into Presidential contention and eventually into the White House itself. But that is a story for another time and place.

He was still very young and full of beans and had the utmost confidence in himself and his abilities that his disenchantment faded quickly. He found numerous opportunities to find work, even within the fiercely competitive environment of many other young men who were rivals for these limited chances for employment. This work consisted almost entirely of a physical nature, for there were very few jobs that required skills outside the sphere of manual labor.

This stood Lincoln in good stead because he was of a stature in height and physical bearing that made these sort of jobs come naturally. But this was not the type of work that young Abraham feted. It was actually quite the opposite. This was the work he had done since his youth and he abhorred it. It reminded him of his days under his father's care and charge, and it was this that caused him to leave the family in the first place.

This was where his many friends came in to help. Lincoln may have had many peers and competitors when it came to physical labor, but few were his equal in storytelling or as a jokester and none were in his league in charisma and the mental faculties that created avenues of employment that his rivals could never match.

Through these friends and connections, young Abe won from President Jackson the opportunity for himself to get a real cash

Legends of Lincoln

paying job as the duly appointed postman of New Salem. This job came as a bit of a godsend for Lincoln. Not only did it allow him to get out from under the rut of being a farm laborer in an area with few long-term prospects with real financial rewards, as his ambition convinced him manual labor would lock him into and he was determined to avoid, but it also gave him a chance to see the land and people around New Salem and more importantly he was paid in real coin for his efforts. This was one of his first opportunities to have actual money in his pocket though it never amounted to much because he had a huge debt hanging over his head. But as was said, Lincoln was unlike many fellows of his time in that he was determined to repay the debt and not succumb to the lure of fleeing to the west to avoid the financial burden this debt presented to any chance of acquiring real wealth and standing in the community.

This endeared him to his creditors, most of them anyway, and many of these same creditors gave him the opportunity to pay them back in his own time, and even helped earn Lincoln the nickname "Honest". Another instance of solidifying the name of "Honest Abe" was when, a few years later, the Postmaster office was closed in 1836. Abe was still the postman at the time and he had in his keeping $17 of federal money. Rather than use any of it to help him in his financial straits Lincoln never touched it and, according to all accounts, that when he presented the money to the collecting agent who came to square the books some time later, the agent was a bit perplexed and asked if Abe didn't make use of the money in the short term and get paid back later for it. Lincoln stated, "No, sir, I never make use of money that does not belong to me."

If you square that with the accounts that when he was a storekeeper and happened to accidentally overcharge a customer 6 pennies, he walked three miles to give the customer back the correct change, you can see he was a most honest man with peoples' money. Another account states that he once charged a woman 4 ounces more tea than she had actually purchased at the time. When he discovered his error, he promptly closed the store and delivered the tea personally to the rather surprised woman, who would have been none the wiser had he not appeared suddenly at her door late one evening with the package of tea under his hat.

Honest Abe he became and as was said, used this name later to help launch his political career. And in politics, a moniker like "Honest" was invaluable in a land dominated by small farmers always at the mercy of unscrupulous creditors, merchants, lawyers, government officials and peddlers, all seeking to take advantage of the unwary or uneducated.

This all came later. For now, Lincoln basked in his newfound freedom from the dull days when he was cooped up in his store stressing over how he could make ends meet. He had money in his pocket, little though it was, an open road beneath his feet, and the opportunity to meet new people and visit new places.

However, one of the biggest benefits of his new occupation for the young man with a voracious appetite to learn about everything was the chance to read. Among the many letters he needed to deliver, often keeping them in his hat to allow his hands to be free, were included newspapers and periodicals, and even some books. He would frequently be seen by residents aimlessly walking to someone's home to deliver a letter while reading someone else's newspaper or magazine, fully absorbed in whatever it was he was perusing.

So it was with Abraham today, and this led to a bit of a mishap. His errand took him outside the cozy confines of New Salem to one of the outlying farms about 10 miles away. He was tasked to deliver a small paper bundle to the farm and a periodical known as The New York Mirror to a closer farm he had already passed. He had decided to hold onto the magazine until his return back to the town to provide him the time needed to read it. The New

York Mirror was a periodical he particularly enjoyed for the variety of articles within it, and for the rarity in which he was provided a chance to read it. This particular newspaper was the late May 1831 edition, which contained a poem from the legendary American poet Edgar Allen Poe. It was sent by a relative of one of the nearby farmers. The relative was a resident of the bustling cosmopolitan city of New York and had been sending this magazine on to his brother for quite some time. Lincoln was quite pleased that this relative was dedicated to sending these periodicals to his brother since Abe was a big fan of Poe's poetry and had read both "Tamerlane" and "Al Aaraaf".

The magazine was quite old, over two years really, but this was often the case with this type of mail. It was likely the brother in New York had read the paper himself and only sent it off after he had finished it. The mail being what it was in this time in America, there were no railroads yet in Illinois and wouldn't be for another five years or so, it was likely to take six months to reach this frontier town. Not caring for any of these insignificant facts, Abraham engulfed himself into this latest work of Poe's and became enmeshed in the poetry of the great artist, reciting the words again and again as he walked, to commit it to memory.

He tucked the package under his arm, for it was much too large to possibly fit under his hat, as he trudged along the small road towards the farm. The road leading into New Salem was not of the best quality and its condition quickly deteriorated to little more than a dirt track as one ventured farther from the center of town. There were many pitfalls for the unwary and as Lincoln absentmindedly read from the old edition of The New York Mirror he certainly could be described as unwary.

He had quickly learned as all young frontier boys and girls did, to always be on the lookout for danger when he was traveling or working the fields, especially in areas far from population centers. The hazards were not so much from the roads themselves, though these at times did offer some peril, but more from unseen dangers along the fringes of woods that often lined the sides of the roads. Illinois was heavily forested at the time and within these forests dwelt all sorts of predators. These ranged from packs of ravenous wolves or lone coyotes, both the bane of farmers and their cattle. Cougars who were rarely spotted and if they were it would most often be too late, and the occasional bear seeking the easy prey of a domesticated animal or lone unwary traveler. These were amongst the animals whom most often waylaid both traveler and farmer alike in their killing grasp or bite.

Lincoln still remembered vividly the time as a young lad of but ten years having been sent by his father to a watermill about a dozen miles away to have some grain recently harvested ground into flour. He had traveled alone riding atop the family horse with the grain bags hitched to each side of the saddle. The journey to the mill was uneventful as these journeys most often go, though the young boy found the sights and sounds a wonder, this being his first time taking the family grain to mill by himself. He enjoyed his time away from his family feeling like an adult with the responsibility of such an important task, besides the welcome fact it was time spent outside the drudgery of manual labor which he detested from even this early age. He spent the night at the miller's for he reached their abode too late for the return journey.

The next morning he started early, after a hearty breakfast, and was still munching on an apple as he swayed back and forth on the saddle when he spied a lone, large black bear about ten yards off the side of the road digging at something on the ground. As he got closer the hair on the back of his head rose in fear. He had never been this close to a live bear before. He had seen many a dead bear, killed by hunters for their pelt or by farmers to keep them away from their livestock, but a live one was an entirely different story indeed!

The road twisted around a bend as it wound past where the bear was, never getting any close than 30 or so feet from the bear, which suited the young boy just fine. The bear seemed engrossed in his digging and it was only as Abe neared that he discovered what held its interest so much. It had gotten hold of a bee hive from somewhere nearby and was busy digging out the honey. The boy was close enough now to see a few bees still hovering nearby vainly trying to drive the furry monstrosity away from their home. The bear completely ignored the buzzing insects and boy alike as it munched contentedly on its prized delicacy.

The distraction and danger was passed in a few moments though young Abraham dwelt on it for much time as he thought of ways to embellish his encounter when he returned home to recount the tale to his family. He relished the opportunity to alleviate their boredom after dinner with a bold story of the chance meeting, chuckling to himself as he pictured his sister Sarah and stepbrothers John and Dennis staring at him with wide eyes, his stepmother filled with concern, and his father with amusement and pride.

Things didn't turn out that way exactly as both his father and brothers were away in town when Abraham returned, but he did enjoy the expected responses from his sister and mother and the opportunity to tell the tale a second time with a few additional details he thought about the next day as he chopped firewood. John tried to outdo him that evening with a story of a brawl he and Abe's father had witnessed in town but young Abe's tale still was the highlight of the evening and though his father sat expressionless throughout the telling, Abe saw a glint in his eye that indicated he enjoyed the story.

Abraham's reminiscing was cut abruptly short. He had not been watching too closely as he was daydreaming and wandered near the edge of the road, which dropped precipitously off into a small ditch as it neared a riverbed. He stumbled for a moment, dropping the magazine onto the road and the package into the ditch with him as he sought to free his hands to catch himself from tumbling headlong into the small ravine. He managed to keep himself from falling face first into the ditch but his shin had caught on a jagged rock, cutting through his jeans and leaving a long gash along his leg.

The wound did not bleed too much and Lincoln quickly bound up his leg by ripping off the rest of his ruined pantleg and using the cleaner interior side to bind it. However, the pain was excruciating and the young man decided to rest a few moments to gather his strength and rub his leg a bit. First of course he had to gather up the package which had fallen to the bottom of the ditch. When he scrambled down to it he discovered the paper bundle had been torn and most of its contents dumped along the slope and bottom of the ditch.

Lincoln gathered up the items, silently berating himself for his foolishness when he spied that one of the items was a small book and another was a letter. He picked them all up and climbed back up to the road to rest along its edge. The chance to read the book and letter proved too much for young Abe, as it often did on his deliveries (one of the other perks of his job), so as he sat along the edge of the road he decided to read them.

The other contents were some clothes, a necklace of some type of metal, a pair of small well-worn shoes, a bible and a pair of eyeglasses. Having read the Bible countless times and committing many passages to memory, Abe was drawn back to the other book and letter. He decided to check out the book first.

It was a small book well used with a cover that was partially torn and it had numerous smudges and other discolorations from food, dirt and use. The writing was at first a bit jumbled, the penmanship very poor and the writing quality not much better, while the content was a little boring. However, both the writing quality and penmanship sharply improved, but unfortunately the content of the book itself remained a little bland.

It turned out it was a young boy's journal. The boy, named Joshua, seemed to be in his early teens and had been born in Indiana since one of the earliest entries remarked on his longing for his first home there and his family now living in Illinois. He was now living in St. Louis with his uncle's family and was an apprenticed to him as a cobbler.

Most of the entries spoke about the daily chores of a cobbler's apprentice, which proved rather dull to Lincoln who already knew a bit of what such work required and wasn't really interested in it to begin with, while the few remarks about the city of St. Louis drew a bit more interest. However, the boy's perspective was rather limited and the sparse entries relating to the bustling city didn't do too much to add to Lincoln's personal experience and memory of that city. Abraham had traveled through St. Louis twice on flatboat trips to New Orleans, though he never stayed there more than a day or so and didn't venture too far from the flatboat that was his charge.

It seems that the boy's family was originally from the South as a couple of entries that brought up the topic of slaves certainly struck young Abe as coming from the perspective of one accustomed to the Southern affliction. Abraham certainly was not, as was his family on his father's side though they did spend a generation or two in both Virginia and Kentucky (Lincoln being born in Kentucky), but this boy was no doubt perfectly at home with the idea of human servitude. Abraham was also familiar with Southerners since many of those that came from the south lived on the southern side of the Sangamon river and this river cut New Salem neatly in two. One of the entries did catch the eye of young Lincoln for the boy compared his apprenticeship to slavery, as Abraham had often done with his own ordeal of time in forced labor under his father during his days as a young boy.

Abraham himself felt so strongly against this version of indentured servitude that as soon as he felt able after his twenty second birthday he had left the home of his father only to return only rarely afterwards. This time also left Lincoln with a marked disdain against the policy of apprenticeship and the institution of slavery itself. These views Abraham Lincoln would hold for the rest of his life and while at first they were passive, its abhorrence to him would evolve over time and circumstance to leave their indelible mark on both the history of America and the world.

Abraham next took up the letter and carefully unfolded it so he wouldn't bend or otherwise damage it. He had a sort of reverential view to letters and the written word. It was something to him that was not to be violated but rather respected. Words delved into a person's soul and that to Lincoln was something to be honored and held dear. A letter was a personal transference of one's thoughts and feelings that was not lightly trodden upon, and while Abraham would do so because of his innate curiosity and insatiable desire to learn, he always tried to respect the medium that a letter represented.

The letter itself was quite short and as depressing as it was curt. It was written by the uncle and was addressed to the father of the boy, who was the husband of the uncle's sister. The letter told of the news of the young boy's untimely death from drowning in the Mississippi river. Evidently on one of the boy's few days away from his uncle's shop he took it upon himself to accompany a few of his classmates to the river for a swim. It was a cloudy spring day and the boys were frolicking in the river and had swum out quite far, according to the testimony of one of the boy's companions. Joshua had drifted a bit from the others, and not being a very strong swimmer, he was caught in the deceptively fast current. The river had become swollen from the spring rains and while the other boys vainly tried to swim after their screaming friend, Joshua began to swallow water. He had choked on the water momentarily before slipping under and disappearing altogether.

Joshua's body had been picked up a few days later several miles down the river. His uncle Robert had shipped Joshua's remains back to Illinois with his regrets and it should be arriving in New Salem within the month. Lincoln seriously regretted having slipped and fallen, since otherwise he would not have read the unwelcome news and expected to get a few cold stares from the farmer and his family for having inadvertently opened the package.

He was struck by the unfortunate boy's cause of death since it brought back a memory he had all but forgotten of his own clash with a river in his youth. It had occurred not long before his ninth birthday and a few months before the death of his mother. On this occasion, he had gone with a friend to play in the woods surrounding a creek near his boyhood home in Indiana.

Abraham had been a most adventurous child when he was very young. This sense of daring stood with him up until just before he turned a teenager and it was this near-death experience that first began to quell his sense of always seeking the limits of his ability and luck. It was not as if his sense of adventure had disappeared entirely, but it turned itself inwards, into a greater search of his himself and his soul. It was these events that really began to open himself up to the power of the mind, and the gift that books and literature could bring to bear.

As a boy and up through adulthood, Abraham had always been the biggest and strongest of all the children, or men for that matter, anywhere he went. It was said he could do the work of a man as a youth and when he was in his early teens people would remark upon finding Lincoln in the woods cutting down trees that from the sound of it, they had thought as if it was three full grown men at work, not one teenage boy. Even at the age of seven, young Abe was the best athlete among his peers and was always the first picked in any games that required teamwork or an able body.

This physical superiority over his fellows gave the young Lincoln a remarkable boldness that was only tempered by a series of mishaps that quickly taught him his limitations and quieted the stirring in him to always push beyond what others deemed possible. This dampening didn't quell his adventurous spirit entirely but more accurately diverted it from the physical sphere to honing and expanding his intellectual capacity and eventually his political ambition.

As stated earlier young Abraham had gone off to a creek after he had been working at the far edge of the neighbor Gollaher's farm with the farmer's son, his friend Austin. The duo were supposed to still be working on laying fence rails to mark the boundary of an extension of newly cleared farmland. However, they had grown bored with the work and had decided to steal a few moments to run off and play in the woods nearby.

The two were engrossed in a game of tag, one chasing the other through the game trails. This play brought them near a large fast running creek that marked the furthest edge of both families' farms, and which yesterday's rain had swollen to overflowing. It was just across the creek where the two had noticed a covey of partridges while they were taking a rest during yesterday's labor. Austin's coaxed young Abe into joining him in trying to catch some if they happened upon them.

They decided to "coon" their way over a log that was lying across the stream where the fast current and recent rains had created a cut along the shore several feet deep. The log was a few feet over the river, quite soggy and slippery to the touch. Austin, being the elder by three years ventured across first while Lincoln waited for his friend to pass over before beginning to cross himself. When he was about halfway across his nerve suddenly failed him and he stopped still precariously balanced atop the log. Austin was calling him over when his feet suddenly gave way, dropping the boy heavily into the water. As Abe fell he clipped his head on a large branch of a tree at the water's edge, momentarily stunning him. Austin watched in stunned horror as Abe fell and he came up to the edge of the creek just as he saw his friend dip under the water.

Abe struggled mightily against the river, but neither boy had ever learned to swim. His great muscles availed to naught as the strong current began to drag him under the water. His strength began to ebb and Abraham came only once more to the surface before he sunk for the last time.

Thankfully, the other boy was as quick witted as young Abraham and darted forward about ten yards ahead of Abe floundering in the creek barely keeping his head above the water. Austin got to the water's edge just as Abraham was passing by and Abe's head slipped under water. Without a moment's thought or hesitation Austin grabbed a large stick lying atop the muddy riverside nearby, which turned out to be a water sprout and pulling it up with a strength drawn form an adrenaline surge, he stuck it into the water near where Lincoln had dipped under and young Abe somehow managed to get a flailing hand onto it. Being a rather strong boy himself, after a herculean effort Austin was able to wrestle Lincoln to the surface and drag him to the edge of the creek several dozen yards from where he had fallen into it.

Austin shook his young friend to try to revive him but to no avail. Then in a moment of inspiration he turned the lad onto his side and Abe belched up a tremendous amount of water and began coughing. The two lay on the water's edge for several minutes panting to catch their breath and regain their composure. It wasn't long before they boyish spirits lifted and the two returned to where they had been working about an hour earlier.

When they got back they stripped down to allow their clothes to dry before returning to work for the rest of the day, Abraham much chastened by the ordeal and with a bloody head to remind him of the event. It was a warm sunny summer day so it only took a few hours for the clothes to dry, but the boys were unable to do much more work. The two were young and strong and had done quite a bit earlier so it didn't seem like they had been idle when Abe's father Thomas came to fetch him that evening.

Abe did need to do a bit of explaining about his head injury, but the younger Lincoln's storytelling ability stood him in good stead, though his father gave the two boys a long hard doubtful look as Abraham fed him his tale. The story of slipping and cutting his head on one of the split logs didn't really ring true to ole' Thomas, but his son did have a way with words so he let it slide for now, but kept a mental note to be a little bit more strict with his son in the future. Thomas knew full well where a rebellious spirit combined with ample physical attributes could lead so it didn't take much imagination on his part to reflect the story was probably not what really had happened.

It is needless to say that it took quite a long time before Abraham Lincoln allowed his desire to frolic to interfere with his work. However, it wasn't to say that Abe, when given the chance to play, ever shied from doing so. He just was a bit more circumspect when he did and certainly continued to thoroughly enjoy himself as the next boy or girl, if not more.

AMERICA'S PIONEERING SPIRIT

Dennis was sitting near the fire smoking absentmindedly on a pipe as he pondered how he would relate the tale he wanted to tell of his friend and cousin, the late great Abraham Lincoln, and Abe's father Thomas Lincoln. Of late a number of stories had been circulating about Thomas and both his wives, his first (and Dennis' Aunt) Nancy Hanks who died when Abe was nine, and his second Sarah Bush Johnston Lincoln, who was old and feeble but still alive, and some of Lincoln's wife Mary. Now these stories did not reflect too kindly on any of them, especially Mary, but Dennis felt it was time to set the record straight at least with regards to Thomas, whom he knew intimately.

Now Dennis Friend Hanks was no storyteller like his illustrious cousin or surrogate father, but he could make due when the fancy took him, as It often did. He decided to get right out to it. Theophilus, who was seated nearby staring thoughtfully into the flames, was almost twenty now so it would be best to be as frank as possible Dennis thought.

"Now look here, boy. I know you been hearing some tales by folks got no right talking about the Lincolns. They aren't our kin so they shouldn't be making up any stories, especially since they don't know us, and they certainly didn't know your grandfather Tom and Aunt Nancy. And I know they don't know your grandmother, bless her heart."

"I know your sister has been relating some tales about Uncle Abe's wife Mary, and they aren't too kindly I gather. Now Harriet spent a good deal of time with the Lincolns in Springfield when she was going to school. I know she told you about her doing all the housework for Mary and how Mrs. Lincoln was a bit of a banshee. I don't know how much of that is true, but since I never met Mary Lincoln and dear Harriet is a good honest woman, I reckon much of it may be. I don't know the particulars of their relationship and I don't care much to know at this point. I don't reckon we will be seeing any of Mrs. Lincoln now that Uncle Abe has passed."

"I want to speak to you about your grandfather and I was to set the record straight with you about who he was. These tales you been hearing got it all wrong about him, so I want you to hear it from one who knew him better than most. I dare say I reckon I knew him better than anyone 'cept his wives."

"Abe and I were good friends. I was the older brother he never had before. I lived with his father for years after Abe left to find his fortune. As you know I am the one who is there to take care of his mother, his real mother, Sarah Bush Johnston Lincoln."

"I was there when Abe's father Thomas died. I was there for his funeral and burial. I was there when Abe wasn't. I saw the things in his father, Uncle Tom, that Abe never could see. It wasn't that poor Abe didn't take the time. He was too young when he left to see his father for what he was, and later Abe's demons kept him from trying to see his father in anything other than the way he would like, that would justify why Abe stood away so long and wasn't there at the end. Abe's ambition couldn't allow him to see his father as the great man he was. If his father wasn't then Abe would never have been as great as he was. I don't want to slight Abe for what he did, but the story needs to be told."

"I did see Ole' Tom. I saw him in ways no other one of his family did, though many of his friends and acquaintances saw Tom the way I did. I was 10 years older than Abe, born in the year before the 18th turned into the 19th century. I was older than Honest Abe and I saw him grow from a tall gangly youth to full manhood."

"Abe and I spent many a day out in the fields, joined with our step brother John Johnston and later on my cousin John Hanks.

We toiled all day and late into the night. It wasn't just Abe who did this. We all did it and it was what all families did across the West. But Abe didn't like it. He didn't like it one bit. He always thought that he should be getting something for his labor. He never did think about how the family depended on him. The family depended on all of us. Abe was always thinking and complaining about how he was abused, how we all were abused but mostly him. He was a big strong lad as I said so he took it like he was privileged and something special. He did more work than most so he thought he should be getting something extra for himself."

"Now it wasn't as if Abe was some sort of Lazy Lawrence, far from it. Even when he was a young lad, he could do the work of two men, some said three, but he sure never loved it and that's a fact. Any time he found he could get away with taking a break that was all he needed. Now Ole' Tom didn't like that, didn't like it one bit, especially when he had lent Lincoln out for labor. Tom was always a fearing that if the one he been lending him out to saw Abe laxing off from the chores he been paying him for then the farmer would want some money back. Now Ole' Tom never did have much and never enough to go around and was always full of worry that if word got out that Abe was being lazy then he wouldn't be able to get a good price for his son's work. Now as I said Abe was no Lazy Lawrence, and everyone knew it, but Ole' Tom came from pretty poor beginnings and was always scared he might get back to that place, and he had the responsibility of a family, so he did worry some about it."

"Ole' Tom, now he always thought the grass was greener on the other side of the horizon. And for Tom that horizon always pointed West. Many a time these moves of his family brought us into a worse condition but more times than naught they brought us prosperity in our own right. Some didn't see it that way. To them it was money that was all, but that's the new way of looking at things. In the West of my youth through my elder years the families who lived in the West, money wasn't what drove them day to day. For most of them, even now there wasn't much money to go around. We were still a trading one good for another good and the only price for the goods were what they were worth to the persons doing the trading."

"Now Tom never could settle down until his legs and arms just weren't like they used to be. It was then he had to depend even more on his kin but by then he had more kin than most. To most of the settlers dwelling hereabouts that was what made a Man rich. It wasn't what jingled in their pockets, for most didn't have anything to jingle and a good many more didn't have pockets, at least ones that didn't have holes small enough that any coin wouldn't fall through, if they ever got the chance to get any."

"Now Ole' Tom's youth he been a wandering one. First he was bounced from family to family, him and his mom, and then on his own. It wasn't until he was apprenticed out to a carpenter that he spent any time in one place for more than a season or two. I think that is what set in him the wanderlust, though I been told more than once by Abe's real mom, Mother Johnston, and then many a time by Tom himself, that his family was always wandering. Their eyes were always looking towards the setting sun, like it was leading them to a promised land just over the horizon. That's what set Ole' Tom and his family on their many wanderings, and all but one time did they head west, the last being short distance east to the land where he spent the last decades of his life and built his family and fortune, such as it was, and where your grandmother is now."

"As I been saying. Tom was an old pioneer in the truest sense. He didn't like to till soil that had been touched by man before. He had a mind to make his way by treading where none been before. "

"This made things hard for us in the family, but we didn't read none into it. We followed Tom because he saw things others couldn't. He could picture a beautiful farm in the midst of trees. Now we were old school southern planters. We were all from Virginia stock. The way we started a farm was to clear out some forest and build it from there. We never thought anything about using the prairie. To us the soil there was good for one thing, grass and grazing. We learned later how good prairie land was for farming, but while Tom was moving about that was the way we thought. "

"We liked to use a term to describe the land we cleared. Knobby. Now both Knob Creek and Pigeon Creek were knobby. Knobby as a piece of land could get they were. Full of deep hollows, ravines, cedar trees covering the parts and knolls. Like I said as knobby as you would see on an old gnarled tree. "

"I got to Pigeon Creek when it had already been cleared, mostly by Tom but also by his sprig of a son who appeared five or six years older than he was. Tall and gangly, just like he would be when he grew older, young Abraham was like a stalk of corn. He remained this way until the end of his days but I say to you he was never weak, in mind or body. I think even when I first arrived at Pigeon Creek Abe was using the axe of a man and he made use of it better than most men I knew even, at that young age. "

"Nancy Hanks was a superior woman. I knew that from before I began to live with them. She was a good housewife, could do all the chores but she had that lofty spirit that one has from being a little educated. She always wanted Abe to go to school but there wasn't much of a school roundabout Pigeon Creek, so Abe didn't get much a chance of learning when he was there. Mother Johnston was like minded and when schools did open up, she got Abe to go as much as she could get a chance for him. Life wasn't easy over there and the schools weren't much. I never did take a liking to them anyhows."

"Now Tom never had a chance at an education, so he didn't really begrudge Abe his, and never did place much importance in it. He just felt that there was so little time for that in the hard scrabble life pioneers led. Tom was practical minded, and he could do everything a person needed to be able to do to live all alone or support a family with everything they needed. "

"Perhaps he couldn't give them everything they wanted but he always made sure they had everything they needed. If he had to walk one thousand miles to do it, he would. He once or twice tried to make some extra money by loading up a flatboat with all the hogs he could spare and made his way all the way down to New Orleans with them. After he sold them he trekked the whole way back, on foot mind you. You don't do that if you don't want to try and make a better life for your family. I did it myself once or twice and I can tell you there is no romance in trudging back hundreds of miles all alone, or even with a companion. "

"That didn't make him barely enough that it cost him so after doing that a couple of times he felt that it wasn't worth the effort and he didn't do that anymore. But it was the practical mind and strength and all the knowledge of farming and making a living with nothing and most important his speaking that Abe got from Ole' Tom. "

"Tom didn't move for a while after settling in Pigeon Creek. I think he finally meant to stay there his whole life if it wasn't for one of his daughters. I use this term lightly for Tom had one daughter by blood, the angelic Sarah. She was a blessed soul. I think so much so that God determined he needed to have her by his side. She died while giving birth and unfortunately her child died too. God, I miss her. "

"It was soon after his beloved daughter's death that Tom got the whole clan up and moving. Now it wasn't really Tom's doing. My cousin John, who was about Abe's age had moved into the New Salem area, in Illinois, and said the land was right plump for the pickings. The Sparrows has already moved there and John with them. He was married into the family, his wife was one of Mother Sarah's daughters. John came back to us in Indiana, and he was really begging to have us move there. Tom wasn't really inclined to go but his wife didn't want to part from her beloved daughter so up Ole' Tom went and we was off to our new home.

Tom would do anything for the family. I think that was because when he was young he never had a real one of his own."

"Now Ole' Tom was a pioneer in every sense of the word. He would go out first to lay out his claim by the traditional pioneer method of burning off the corners within the forest. Then he went back to get his family. They would load up all their belongings onto a wagon, or if they were close to a creek or river they would build a flatboat off of the available wood, always plenty of wood around, and then they moved them down to the closest place to disembark. "

"Most often there would be no road to the claim. The claim would be in the midst of a forest, or later on it would be on the edge of the forest with a little prairie for other uses like grazing. Either way the only road that would go to their claim would have to be made by the farmer. And this meant that these roads were pockmarked, as full of stumps and rocks as any smooth parts of pounded dirt. They looked like an old tree. Then if it happened to rain more than a day or two then this road became a little muddy slog where these stumps and rocks could be fatal to the unwary. That was our lot in life, and we took it proudly."

"He had been apprenticed as a carpenter when he was young. He had spent some time as a militiaman and was even a constable. Tom had shuffled about a bit when he became a man and was able to set off on his own in Kentucky, but never too far. He bought a small farm a little ways from Elizabethtown, Kentucky, and soon after met Nancy Hanks, my aunt. She was a seamstress at a home, and Tom was friends with the family. The two courted for a short time before getting married and moving to a home in town after Tom sold his farm."

"This didn't suit Ole' Tom none. He soon got itching to leave and they moved off to a farm a little to the south. He was settling in nicely. He would farm during the summer then during the winter he would get on as a carpenter. He specialized in being a wheelwright. Sometimes he'd make the big wheels you see on wagons but most often he would be making smaller wheels since he could get more for them. There was a little sprig of water running from the creek and was called Sinking spring. That was where they drew their water. It was here that Abe and his elder sister Sarah were born."

"Tom had stayed there a few years, but he got a hankering for something new and the rich speculators had begun to eye his holdings, which he still couldn't pay off completely. This is when he moved a bit north and found a perfect spot to raise a family on a clean spit of land right off the Old Cumberland Trail. This was old Knob Creek and the family stayed there for about 6 years. They probably would have stayed longer since it suited Ole' Tom well. He was right off the main trail where pioneers were setting off out west by the hundreds each year. He could sell his wares and would be fixing travelers wheels and each night he could spend hours telling wayfarers who roomed in their spacious cabin tales."

"Some say it was slavery that drove Tom to move his family north out of Kentucky and settle in the wild region of Indiana. True it is that Ole' Tom hated the institution. He hated it with all his heart as most Lincoln's did but that ain't why he moved. "

"The reason was the damn government. Kentucky was selling claims left and right and speculators were making a fortune selling land to two or more people or overlapping claims and Tom didn't know nothing about the law and such, so he barely managed to get his plot tilled and harvested before someone came up with a claim to the land as theirs. Every time Tom would lose his fair share, see land that was rightfully his dwindle away to others and soon enough they would be up and off to a new place. "

"About this time the land of Indiana territory north of the Ohio river was opened to settlement. The US government controlled the territory and with the federal government if you had a claim it would stick. That's all Ole' Tom needed to hear. There was already speculators looking to get their greedy hands on his plot of land at Knob Creek. That spit of land was in a perfect situation off the old Cumberland Trail and offered good opportunities to sell goods to any and all. "

"Tom knew he would be facing another lawsuit and he didn't have the mustard to deal with more frustrating lawyers. He was off lickety split with the family and all they could load up onto a wagon and made their way over the Ohio River with a claim from the US government itself. I think Abe was about seven this time. "

"Tom's new farm was about fifteen miles north of the river and was big for land was cheap then. He was living large. He managed to heap up two nice feather beds and he had a couple of horses and soon after arriving had bought a good milk cow from a neighbor. He was now a proud pioneer in an up and coming territory."

"Ole' Tom, used to make his claim on the land the old fashion way but he had to do things more legal like when we got to Pigeon Creek. Nowadays you have a surveyor go and create plots of land and someone goes and buys one at a claim office sight unseen. Then he goes out and finds the spot. That is the first time he would see the land that would be his. "

"Now Tom did it in the old way where he went and found some land. He then burned off marking points to let others know the land had been claimed. He had to do things a little bit different when he went to Indiana. He still marked his claim in the same way, but this time stayed, or squatted, there for a season or two then made his way to a US land office to make his claim there."

"When he did this for the Pigeon Creek farm, he and a couple of others with neighboring plots had to trek some three score miles to the land office and make a payment in hard cash for about a quarter or so of the total of the claim. He did that for Knob Creek and his other farms but didn't have to pay so soon and like I said these were not recognized by later claimants so he moved. The federal government did things right and proper so now his claim stuck and none could say they made an earlier one than him."

"Now all this was what Ole' Tom told me plenty of times because I didn't settle in with the family at Pigeon Creek until a year or so later, just after Tom made his first payment on the land but we lived there for ten more years before we moved on. We spent most of the first year hunting and carving out the land. Civilizing it from the primitive Indian lands it had once been. We carved out about 20 acres of land and set about planting mostly corn but we had some plots of wheat and a little of oats for our livestock and some meadow for grazing. "

"The rest remained untamed forest and that was where we hunted most times. That way we kept out of the hair of our neighbors though sometimes we would catch a glimpse at them yonder when we was off hunting, and maybe have a bit of a talk if the mood took us. We mostly kept to ourselves except if we ever decided to venture off to town but that was rare usually just to buy some things we couldn't get ourselves and mostly to sell anything extra we grew or some hogs but we usually didn't have much more than we could spare for ourselves. "

"Now them Indians had given the land up only about 10 years earlier, but we never seen one of them in all our time there. They had done up and packed long before then since us white men had been trekking around these parts for many a decade before. Up around the time of Daniel Boone himself I reckon. "

"After a whiles some more of our families settled with us. Some Sparrows, Hanks, Johnstons, when Tom remarried, and one of my cousins, John, had a mind to move west and settle in the land around the new state of Illinois to the west. He got a hankering for the land and set in some of us a mind to move there ourselves. John and I went to find a spot and I wanted to see what the fuss was about. "

"He did pick a nice spot and it was everything he said it was. This got some of us wanting to go since the land around Pigeon Creek was starting to fill up. Now Tom was starting to get on in years. He was still strong as an ox and stubborn as one too so he wasn't hankering to move but when mother Johnston's own daughter set her mind to go Sarah couldn't bear to part with her so the whole family up and moved on to Illinois. "

"Now we settled there for but one season before the Winter of The Deep Snow set in. I tell you it takes some getting used to those Illinois winters and many never wanted to get used to a cold like that so many would just up and leave and never come back."

"That winter was the worst there was and it set in Tom's mind that he had enough of the cold and decided to move the whole family back to Indiana. Tom was a hale man, but those winters be harsh and the fevers and chills had to be seen to be believed. Now the whole family was agreed, and we started on back but we didn't get too far before Tom was convinced by some friends who settled in around Decatur to try his hand for another season. "

"Tom was reluctant, but he was never no quitter and so he said ok and most the whole family, been living around Decatur ever since. All that is except John Johnston who, like Abe, was thinking there were greener pastures away from the family but things didn't work out so well for him as they did Abe. Tom since passed, bless his heart, but I'm still here with mother Johnston and before he died he had one of the biggest families in the Decatur area, a fine reputation and could boast about being one of the wealthiest men of the land. "

Dennis sat back and reflected a moment. His son was riveted on his every word, his every reaction. "He did good, Tom did and I was right proud of him and to call him my father."

"Now Abe. He stood with us even past when he was twenty one. We all knew he wanted to make his own way, but he was a good lad when push come to shove, and stuck it out with us that first year. It was a godsend that he did because I don't think we would have lasted that first winter if he didn't. But come spring and as soon as the roads became passable Abe let it be known, he would be going on to make his own way. While the rest of us were setting to head east, Abe set off west to his destiny."

"Now he would come back once in a while, but soon it became once in a long while then he didn't come back again except but once. That was when you were still quite young. The only thing that ever drew him back was his love of his mother, Sarah Lincoln. Abe loved her dearly and while many say she is what made Abe the man he was, there was certainly truth to it. Abe was very attached to his mother, but he got a lot from Tom even if Abe didn't admit it."

"The last time Abe came back it was a long time since he had been back to see his family now only came back because we all feared that old Tom would pass. Abe to his credit came back to us to see his father but when his father became well Abe seemed to take it as if his father just said he was ill to get Abe to come back. And he never did return. "

"When Tom finally got the illness that ended his life Abe didn't seem to think it worthy of him to come back. He figured Tom would recover and said so in his letter. He didn't think to believe it when Tom finally did pass, and he never did come to the funeral. I thought it harsh that his son didn't attend Tom's funeral, but I don't know the mind of Abe and he did resent his father some. "

"Now when our dear old mother Sarah Lincoln got ill Abe sent us some money to help us care for her. He had sent money to Ole'

Tom once or twice to help the farm, and Abe did come and see her right before he left to become President. And he did go and see Ole' Tom's grave but after that he never did make it back to Illinois himself except in a pine box. "

"I wasn't all that pleased with Abe for the way he treated Tom after Abe set off to find his way in the world. He seemed embarrassed by him. I think he was embarrassed by our whole family. I do know that when he was President, your Uncle John was looking to get a helping hand from him since he leped Abe in his campaign. I thought if Abe should give him a job that would be great for the family. "

"Now Abe had been handing out jobs to most everyone who came looking, if these people could help him in politics or for past favors. But he didn't seem to think it proper to give any to his family. Now we had been through many a hard time together and Abe knew this. He seemed to think that the family didn't try to better ourselves. We kept at living the old way and Abe seemed to think there was something wrong with that. "

"I think Abe thought the family weren't progressing enough for him. I don't know nothing about that but I do know John could have progressed a bit quicker if he had given him that job but he didn't. He claimed it wouldn't be right to give out jobs to family members and his enemies and critics would say he was favoring his family and use it against him. "

"I don't know. I think they could say the same for all the others he gave jobs to but that didn't set right with Abe. He never did give your Uncle John the job. He did come to helping some of the folk in our town who were wronged, and as President Abe helped set it right but he didn't do the family no personal favors. I managed to turn out all right for me own end and made a pretty penny or two if I do say so myself. "

"Now Abe could have been able to do all the things he wanted, and did do, without having to move a hundred miles from home. He could have visited more often and been more of a son in his later years to his father and mother like he was as a youth but that is neither here nor there. Abe did the best he could is all, and I don't hold a grudge none since we all turned out to be successful in our own ways."

"I did go and see him after he was basely murdered and went to his funeral. It was shameful the way his life ended, but I think Abe did great as President, he did great as a lawyer, and if we didn't make him proud maybe, he sure made the family proud. And I am sure his father would think the same. Tom would be proud of what your Uncle Abraham had become and what he is to everyone now. The Great Liberator."

Dennis sighed for a moment and looked his son over. He didn't know how much of that would sink in or how much would stay with the boy. Dennis foresaw the tales of Ole' Tom being an unambitious failure would stick far longer in people's memory than the truth. That is often the case if someone hears something enough times, a person tends to believe it no matter how much they know it isn't true.

"Well boy. I hope you remember this, and keep it to heart, for Ole' Tom is as much a relative of yours as he is mine, and we come from fine stock."

Theophilus looked at Dennis with a firm expression, "I will Father. Don't you worry. I will."

*The Lincoln clan, which consisted of the Lincoln's, remnants of the Johnstons who intermarried with the Hanks and Halls, moved into Coles Country. This was near Decatur and Charleston. Dennis' family were "urbanized" and became City Folk in Charleston. He became a prominent citizen there and owned a gristmill, a tavern and worked for a time as a shoe cobbler. Abraham Lincoln would visit the Hanks once or twice a year while on circuit, and would sometimes visit his mother and father. The last time Dennis Hanks saw Abe alive was when he went to Washington to plead for the release of several men in prison for their part in the Charleston Riots. This was also when he reputedly requested a job, which Lincoln refused. Dennis would die after being struck by a carriage when he was 93 years old.

*Dennis Hanks became a successful businessman and didn't live with Tom Lincoln and his extended family after Tom moved to a farm near Decatur. He was still living close by in a town called Charleston (about 10 miles from Tom's farm) and was able to visit often, which he did up until his surrogate mother's death.

PA BRINGS US A MOMMA

It took me a long time to write about Ma. I didn't feel it right to write about Ma so soon after she passed and it makes me hurt some when I think about her. Then I felt all awkward like thinkin' about Ma and momma and it makes me confused is all. But now I think it is right to tell you about my Ma.

It had been weeks since Pa had left us but this wasn't the first time since Ma died that he had to leave us. Pa was a proud man. He wanted to care for us but he knew he couldn't by himself. Little Abe was a big boy for his age, a giant. But Little Abe was not old enough to do the things needed to take care of the family.

Pa needed help and he believed he could find a way. When Pa believed hard enough, he always found a way. God helped him find a way. Sometimes we couldn't see it right way, but God always helped us. When times were worst it was hard to believe but then a thing would happen that would show us our faith in the Lord Our Savior was not misplaced.

Like the time Pa went to bring whiskey from Kentucky. He had saved lots of money and went down to see his old friends in Kentucky. He borrowed lots too to get a whole boat full of whiskey. It must have been 30 barrels. He had the flat boat loaded up and was bringing up the whiskey up the Ohio but one day he hit some rough weather and the boat flipped!

Most others would just given up and went home but not Pa. He spent days there bringing up the whiskey and loading it back onto the boat all by himself and he saved most of it he did. He said he made enough to pay back the money he borrowed but I knewd he didn't. But Pa didn't give up and next year God brought us our good cousins the Sparrows and with them came dear Dennis Hanks and they came and lived with us.

They was livin' in the old half-faced camp Pa built when we came that first spring. We had a little better cabin by this time. It had four sturdy walls and a roof, but not much else. But we were comfortable enough and the Sparrows never complained one bit about havin' to live in our old hut. They were just happy to have somethin' to settle in when they first come. Never made no fuss about anythin'. Everythin' was lookin' fine and dandy and we were all one big happy family.

Then the worst thing in the world happened. It was after Ma and I had milked ole' Lassie after she'd gone astray a bit. Lassie wandered outside the land cleared by Pa, Dennis and Abe. They hadn't been able to fence it all in yet and Lassie went out and was a grazin in some weeds. Abe and Dennis picked out ole' Lassie and brought her back. Next day Ma and I milked Lassie.

None of us thought 'bout things like that then but a few days later it was that Ma and me got sick. It was the worst feeling I ever had. Ma and me couldn't get out of bed. I prayed so hard to get better. I knew Pa and Abe did too. After two days I began to feel a bit better but my Ma didn't. I prayed so much and stood by her side day and night but nothing helped. We didn't have no doctor to come and look after us. We just had to try and do what we could to see our sick through. I got lucky but none the others that caught the sickness did. After a few more days Ma closed her eyes and never opened them again. The Sparrows now they had dun gotten sick too. And none of them got any better. They all died one by one even before Ma and me got sick, and left just Pa, Dennis, lil' Abe and me.

Now Ma died right in our cabin on the bed. She wuz laid there all day and night and the next day. Pa had gone outside and cut up some wood with Dennis. Abe and me we stayed inside and cried on Ma. Pa and Dennis returned that night with a bunch of wood and we ate in silence with Ma still lying there not moving.

Pa spent the whole of the next day pounding together a coffin for Ma. Pa did this the same for the Sparrows when they died a little earlier. Abe and me cried a lot both when Ma died and when the Sparrows died. Dennis cried too. Pa didn't cry but we all knew he wuz sad. Pa always liked to talk but he didn't talk none for those days.

Now when Pa finished the coffin he set about having a funeral for Ma. Only us wuz there and the Sparrows were already buried. We done had a funeral too for them when they passed and joined Our Lord.

Pa he would go out every day with Abe and Dennis, he was our cousin and lived with us and didn't get sick like Ma and me and the Sparrows, and they would plant the crops for the year. They spend all day on the farm. They would get home at night. I would cook them their dinner and have it ready every night when they come home.

Once Pa and the boys got the crops all planted he told us during dinner that he would be setting out next morning. We were all nervous and had a bundle of questions but Pa shut us up with one look only he could give.

He said he couldn't do everything for us. We needed a momma. He said he knew where he could find one and he wuz going to go and fetch her right quick. He said he be gone a long while but would come back as soon as he wuz able and he would bring us a new momma.

He said I was a good woman already and I could do all the chores around the cabin. I would be the momma until Pa come back. I would cook and clean and make sure everything is dun proper. I told Pa I'd make a good momma until he found us a real momma.

He then looked over at little Abe. Abe was still young. He was only just nine years old but he was big. He could already use big axe like the men use. Abe also knew everything about taking care of the crops. Pa knew he could trust little Abe to take care of the farm. So he told Abe just that. Abe make sure the crops grow good and strong and he make sure he come home each day before dusk and help me with any chores.

Pa told our cousin Dennis that he will be the hunter and Abe would be the farmer. Dennis would have to go and catch us some deer or turkeys and maybe some possum, muskrats, rabbits, ducks or geese if he can finds any.

Pa made us promise to be good and say our prayers each night before bed and every morning and Pa would come home soon. Dennis would sleep up in the loft with Abe and I would sleep in Pa and Ma's bed. We told Pa we would do everything he asked and would pray he come home soon with a momma.

And next morning off he went. Now we were a mighty scared, even Dennis and he was already man tall but a little skinny and his eighteenth birthday had passed. Dennis likes to hunt and he was a very good hunter. Every day he would set out when the sun rose and he would come back when the sun was setting. He was good at finding where the different animals would hide during the day and sleep. He knew where there was a salt lick nearby and he come back almost every day with something. So we almost always had good fresh meat. Only one time I remember he couldn't find anything for some days.

And Abe was turning into a good farmer. And I was good at cooking the meat. Abe and Dennis would clean it and salt it and I would cook what Dennis caught the day before. And we had some vegetables that I would find around the farm each morning. I would clean all day and mend the boys clothes.

We all were so tired each night that after all the work and eating dinner we would fall right asleep. We slept so good we would never wake up until morning come and we would do the same thing again and again and again.

Michael John Joseph Del Toro

But Pa still didn't come home. We were very tired and worried and scared. Dennis said it was a long ways back to Kentucky where Pa said he was going. I knew Dennis was right but I was still very scared. Pa would always tell us things are very wild and we could see bears at night even from our cabin. We could hear wolves and coyotes howlin' and sometimes one of the mountain lions would scream.

Without our Pa I sometimes would be cryin' at night because I worried so much. I think I cried many more times than I remember. I know Abe would cry too. I could hear him but he tried to hide it in his pillow.

Sometimes a neighbor would come and check to see if we were ok. They didn't come by much and they didn't stay long. They were very busy too and their farms were a long way off and the road wasn't very good. It was nice to see them but we still felt all alone in the world. Nobody could help us. We was just an eighteen year old boy, an eleven year old girl and a nine year old boy all alone in the world.

It was many many months but one afternoon I was outside mendin' Dennis shirt that got caught in some thorns when he wuz out hunting. It was a fine afternoon as the sun was shining bright and no clouds in the sky. Dennis and Abe were nearby making fence posts. The crops had been planted weeks before so Abe had less to do and Dennis was waiting for me to mend his shirt.

Then I saw a wagon coming up the road. It was moving around the road like the driver knew all the bumps and holes. I could see it was a man drivin' the wagon and there was a lady next to him and three children walking alongside. The wagon was full of all sorts of things piled way high on top of each other.

I knew right then it was Pa and our new momma. I called out to Pa and he was far but he waved. Abe and Dennis came boundin' over to me and the three of us waited by the farm.

I was very nervous about seeing our new momma and we didn't know what she would think of us. I was holding Abe's hand with one hand and I could tell by how hard Abe held my hand he was nervous too. Even Dennis was nervous.

But when I saw my angel mommas face I was very happy. She was so pretty to me and I started to cry. Our new momma took one look at us and said, "My what a bunch of urchins you are! Is there any part of you that doesn't have dirt on its dirt?"

She then ordered us to take baths. We plum forgot to take baths and we was as dirty as if we never saw any water our whole lives. She had us shipped off to the bath right quick so she said she could see what we looked like. It took some time to clean us up but when we did she took one look and told us that now we looked human. Our new momma is always sayin funny things like that.

Now momma she got to fixin' things right quick she did. She made Pa fix up the cabin nice and tidy. I had tried my best but there was so much to do and I right say I might have been a bit neglectful about some chores. Momma never said one word about it. She knew I did the best I could and she said she was right proud of me being such a grown woman already. Momma always knew how to make us happy and she always smilin' for us.

But she had Pa fix up the cabin. Made him patch things up so there wuz no more wind comin' inside. She made him add another window so there was more light. It sure did brighten things up some. Momma said the cabin was nice and all but she wanted to add some things to remind her a bit of her home when she was a little girl.

Momma had three children from her old husband who died three years before. There was Johnnie. He was one year older than Abe and the two became good friends, like brothers. They all slept in the same bed in the loft above Pa and momma's bed.

Elizabeth and Matilda was a little older than me and they became my big sisters. Elizabeth and Dennis fell in love and soon got married. But before that we all slept in the new bed that Pa built for us. It was nice to have new brothers and sisters. Abe and me had little Tom but he died when he was only three days old so we never had any brothers or sisters except each other.

Dennis and Elizabeth lived next to us in a new cabin built by Pa, Dennis and the boys. Matilda soon married our cousin Squire Hall who come to live with us and they had a cabin for themselves. So I got the new bed all for myself and felt like a princess.

Momma she loved reading and Abe loved her very much and they would read together most nights. Momma thought it proper that we get set to educatin' ourselves so she had us go to a school that was four miles away. We would walk there whenever we could.

Now Pa didn't see much good to work on educatin' as there was so much work to do. If he didn't have Abe and John out in the fields with him or choppin' wood or hired them out to neighbors when the crops were ripening or after harvest they would go to school. But that didn't happen much. I got more schoolin' than the boys but I didn't like to read that much.

I do like to write. I write poems and momma reads them at night to us. I like when she does that. Sometimes Abe will laugh and poke fun at them and make the boys and my sisters laugh. Momma would only smile and then tell Abe it wasn't proper to poke fun at his kin and then Abe would apologize.

Momma was always good at settin' things straight and Abe loved her so much he always did exactly what momma said. Johnnie wasn't always listenin' and Abe often mimics momma to settin' Johnie right. Momma always says Abe was a perfect little boy. Abe is mighty proud of momma.

Momma didn't tell stories much like Pa and Abe do but my favorite story wuz how Pa and momma decided to get married. Before her husband Daniel Johnston died he was the jailor of the town. They all lived in the prison and momma would feed the prisoners. After he died momma moved into a cabin with Johnnie, Elizabeth and Matilda.

Now Ma and momma had been good friends when they all lived in Hardin County and Pa new Daniel. Suddenly after three years a widow Pa showed up at her cabin. Momma says she was outside washing some clothes and up pops Pa and he calls out to her. She looked up and Pa was leaning against the fence looking her over.

Pa said he had heard about Daniel and then told momma about Ma passing. Momma and Ma knew each other from before they wuz married and wuz good friends. That's how Pa knew momma. Then Pa straight and away asks momma what he would need to do to marry her. I guess Pa was worried about us and in an awful hurry to get back. Momma says she told Pa "I owe too much."

Pa asked her how much she owed. She said about two dollars and a half. "Well," Pa said. "I think I can handle that." Then Pa got to braggin' about all the things he had. He was right proud of the bed and described in this and that a way so momma come to think it was some wonderful bed. Tom kept going on and on in the way he has a talkin'. Now momma knew Tom from way back so she knew how to get him to stop jabbering.

Momma then said, "Well you had me when you said you would pay the two dollar and a half. I'll marry you."

So Pa paid momma's debt and then he got a wagon and momma packed it up with all their belongings and off they went lickety split.

Michael John Joseph Del Toro

Momma brought us so many things when she first come to us. We now had a new table and a set of chairs. We had a booru and new forks, knives, spoons, bowls, dishes, sponges, brooms and all sorts of things to make cleaning easier. Momma remembered how Tom was talkin' up the bed so much so she thought it was some wonderful bed. Then when she sees it all she could say was she thought it was some fine bed, and it was only a hickory one he had made himself. He said well yes indeed he did but it's still a nice bed. They got a chuckle out of that.

Momma likes to keep things clean. She always says cleanliness is next to godliness. That is why she had us get cleaned up when she first saw us all dirty. Momma says she wanted us to look more human. She always laughs when she says that. I laugh too.

Momma loves a good joke. Abe always likes to tell jokes because he loves to hear momma laugh. And he tries to get Pa to laugh. Pa pretends he doesn't like to laugh but we all know he likes a good joke with the rest of us so we often laugh together.

I am very happy Pa brought us a new momma. I love Ma very much and miss her so much but I love momma too. Nobody could ever replace Ma but Pa was right that we needed a new momma and I think momma is a perfect mother for us now.

I thank God for bringing our families together and I know that Ma is looking down and smiling that Pa and her good friend are taking care of us all as one big happy family.

ABE & THE RULE OF THREE

It was upon the battlefield of Chickamauga where I first had the desire to set my feet towards the lush fields of the north. Particularly the fields of Indiana, but it wasn't for reasons of glory or plunder. It wasn't to extend the life of the Confederacy, though I was a simple soldier in Bragg's army and basking in the flush glow of victory I believed at that delusional moment anything was possible. Now I didn't start off that way, Hell's no! I was a proud member of Longstreet's Corps. The old First Corps that looked the Army of the Potomac in the eye and made them run like a bunch of scared rabbits.

I saw plenty of battles before I ever got to Chickamauga but that one was the first one to prick up the hairs on the back of my neck. After that we spent some time gawking at Rosecran's boys fiddling around in Chattanooga. All bottled up like fish in a barrel. We liked to think they were our prisoners and we had them feeding themselves down there. Then Bragg and Longstreet got to quarreling about this and that. Bragg wasn't much of a General but he was sure good at picking a fight with just about everyone. None the Generals below him took a liking to him and Bragg never did anything to make us lowly privates take a shine to him.

After Bragg and Longstreet had their spat we found ourselves marching off to lay siege to Knoxville but that didn't go too well for us. It was a weird sight to be laying siege to a place with about as many of the enemy in it than we had outside it. Nothing good going to come of that even if it was the luckless Burnside who was leading the Federals.

When Grant got to Chattanooga he got to fixing things pretty quick and the next thing we knew we were hightailing out from our intrenchments outside Knoxville and heading for the hills back to ole' Virginia. Not to say I was disappointed. I had been itching to get back there from the moment we first set off on the trains to reinforce Bragg but we didn't like that it had to come about after a defeat, though we didn't take it that way. We didn't lose anything. We just failed to win is all.

Anyways, it was when I was first at Chickamauga after that fight that I first had any inkling to head off and see the North. Never cared one whit about it before then. The thing that got my mind a twitching that way was when I was scavenging for some Yankee boots I spied after we put the scare on the Yanks. They had run off as fast as their feet could carry them, least ways those that had any strength left to run. Me and the boys were rummaging around the battlefield on detail to pick out any wounded when I took a fancy to some nice shiny new boots one of the Yankees was a wearing. Now seeing as he didn't need them any more on account of him being dead and seeing I had only one good shoe left and no socks, I didn't mind relieving him of his boots and socks.

I was going to go for his overcoat too, since the overcoat was one of the most prized possessions of a Yankee for a Confederate, but his was all torn up in the back so as to make it almost useless. He did have one valuable item in his jacket and that was a photograph of Abraham Lincoln. Now I heard tell that these photographs were pretty common up North but down south it was as rare as some clean britches it was. I was figuring I could fetch a fair price for it from one of my fellows and shoved it into my breast pocket then clean forgot about it from all the excitement when we began to march north to Chattanooga.

It wasn't until the winter that I remembered it when I was fidgeting through my pockets one day while in camp and set my eyes to it some. I kind of took a liking to it and decided to keep it after all. Maybe one day after we won the war I would go up north and take a gander at the prim and proper farms they had sprinkled about the countryside.

We didn't own any slaves. We barely had enough to eat for ourselves so to have to feed an extra mouth would have been a hardship indeed. But our family was of the sort that was all too uncommon in Kentucky. We were pro confederacy from the beginning even though we didn't own any slaves and didn't care much for the high falooting planters and politicians who did. Me and my two brothers had joined the confederate army soon after Sumter. There were a number of Kentucky boys who joined up early but not as many as come over when our state was invaded, first by the south and then by the yankees.

Many a family from Kentucky was as divided as the country. Some families had brothers fighting brothers and father fighting son. Our family might not have had slaves, but we didn't want to see the Negro put on the same level as us good Christian white folk. That was plain wrong and I still believe it so. It don't matter none now because even though we lost the war and got drubbed pretty good we got our laws in place where no negroes can vote and most can't even leave the land they are bound to so all is well in the end. You could even say though we lost we still won.

But up until I met Lincoln all of that was still in doubt. Things weren't looking as good in the south as it had the spring before when we were getting set to invading Pennsylvania and Grant was busy digging holes in the mud around Vicksburg but we still had a fighting chance and morale was high in Lee's army.

It was during the first few days' fighting in the accursed tangle of brush and briar called the Wilderness that I was injured and captured. I felt damn lucky about that since many of my comrades that got wounded in that infernal forest were burned to a crisp all within earshot if their comrades. The hot lead and burned cartridges and exploding shell had started hundreds of little fires and with all the dried brush and undergrowth it was no time at all before a dozen different isolated blazes had burst forth around the battlefield.

No one could come to help the wounded for fear of being shot. Even at night the slightest movement would be all that was needed for a dozen or more shots to ring out from both sides of the lines. Anyone stuck between the lines were in their own no man's land and it wasn't likely we could get to them come morning. They would just burn and die being unable to move through fear, fatigue or loss of blood or limb. That was one of the evils of this most evil war.

I had gotten a nasty leg wound when my division had stormed the intrenchments the fabled II Corps had holed themselves up in after we had flanked them out of their first position. Some of my regiment had gotten close enough to the abatements in our last charge, filled with vengeance against those who had caused our General, Old Peter, to be shot, though his wounding was by our own men. Same as Stonewall Jackson, and we hoped the same fate was not in store for Longstreet.

My mind was not on anyone else but myself after my injury. I greatly feared I would be yet one more one-legged ex soldier, if I managed to survive my amputation, but the doctors said I would heal and they didn't need to take the leg off. That was rare those days, but I wasn't complaining you can be sure about that! It was the best news I ever heard far as I was concerned.

They sent me up to Washington with other prisoners and some northern boys who got the worst of it too. We were all kept together, North and South. I was bedded next to a young white boy from Wisconsin, part of them damn black hatters but he was a nice enough fella.

It was while I was recovering in this church turned into a hospital ward that none other than President Lincoln arrived one day, God rest his soul. I never had any ill feelings toward Lincoln. I didn't know him so how could I? I just knew he had wanted to prop up the Negro. I had heard many rumors about him from others, some good and some bad, but I liked to judge a man by what I saw and not what I heard.

Now I never expected to even speak with a President and certainly not this one but here he was walking up and down the rows of beds stopping and talking to each fella as if they were old friends. It was as unexpected as a slab of beef in our daily rations. But there he was right in front of me asking me how I was doing.

"How are you doing my son?" Lincoln asked. "I hope the doctors are treating you well."

"Yes sir they are indeed. Better than expected. It's the first good meal I had in a year." I blurted out a little stunned to be speaking with our arch enemy.

"Well that's mighty fine to hear. Now from your accent I say you must be a Kentucky boy like myself. Is that be the case?"

Lincoln had dropped into a Kentucky accent like my own as easy as can be and that made me pluck up right quick. "Yes sir! I'm from right around your parts and lived there my whole life."

"Well I'll be," the President replied, and he started a banter with me right quick. "It's been a long while since I was around those parts, but I always remember fondly my time in Kentucky. It was there I first began my education and learned the Rule of Three which I will not soon forget. Have you done much schooling there? I know schooling was hard to come by in my day. I was always hankering to learn whatever I could so it always perks me up a bit to hear how things fare around the rest of the nation. Has it changed since then?"

To have the President inquire me about such a topic took me off my guard but he had a way of speaking which made one as comfortable as talking with your favorite uncle. I think they call it charisma. But whatever it was Abraham Lincoln had it in spades.

"Yes sir! I did a little schoolin' when I had some free time away from my chores but not so much as you I think. I done barely a year before the war."

Michael John Joseph Del Toro

"Well I dare say that's about the same with me my young friend!" Lincoln replied with a hearty laugh that made all around smile. "When I went we had the same sort of school. My father never took a liking to them. I think one reason was they required a subscription and it wasn't very often our family had the means to pay for either my sister or myself, much less both of us. Do tell now my boy, do they still have those blab schools that were all the rage then?"

"Yes sir. Indeed they do. I went to them my whole time a schoolin'. I dare say I wasn't the best of students. I spent more time just flapping my gums than learning my lessons. "

"Flapping your gums indeed! Well maybe you just don't have the bellows for that sort of work. I well remember the hard work my lungs had shouting the lessons again and again. My teacher plum thought I was the next Solomon by the din I would make. Flapping gums indeed! You are a funny bloke! I might not have been able to find the time to go to those Blab Schools as often as I liked but I do remember walking by it often enough on some errands or with my father. Even approaching the schoolhouse you could tell if there was class by the shouting you would hear every so often with an interval of the teacher reciting their lessons. It reminds me of a story of the day we had a new teacher for a day. "

Lincoln then began a tale that transfixed us as if under some sort of spell. He had a way with words that he weaved like some spider spinning a web so when he was done with his yarn it was like a perfect spider web.

"This day was just after a wet spell and since there was a lull in harvest season each day my sister and I would trudge the three miles to the schoolhouse for our lessons. I do believe the was the shortest distance I ever had to travel for school. "

"I had to travel five to get to school when I gone," I added happy to be a part of the conversation. "I once had to travel seven miles for school!" Another ward chimes in just as happy to be a part.

He turned out to be a union loyal boy from Tennessee.

"I dare say getting to and from a school was often as challenging for us as learning anything there!" This remark from Lincoln brought laughter and knowing nodding back and forth from all around as the great storyteller continued, "I don't think I ever had to walk as far as seven miles to get to any school. That must have taken some doing. I believe the most I ever had to walk was a bit over four, that was when I had a fine kindly gentleman named Swany as my teacher, but even that distance took a couple of hours just to get there. And I know you all know as well as I just how difficult it could be to get from one place to another. The roads were nothing to write home about and you could still see wild game off the sides of those roads along the edge of the forest or some distance on the prairie. Even wolves or a bear now and then. That would certainly make you quicken your step a bit!" This brought a lot of nods and even more laughs.

"Now for my short tale. This was when I was living in Knob Creek right on the old Cumberland Trail. On this day it turned out we were to have a treat. It seemed the day before our teacher had come down with some ailment which kept him from being able to open the school. But much to our surprise, and I might say chagrin, the day before a carriage had arrived in our little village. In it was a great scholar from none other than Philadelphia itself! He was on his way to Chicago to found a university for higher learning there, the first of its kind in that area. He was passing through on the way to catch a boat in Louisville to bring him down the Ohio river and thence up to Chicago. At least that's what he told us during his long introduction. "

"I tell you I thought I had some bellows on me but this scholar had a pair that could put mine to rest in no time at all!" Chuckles all around. "He continued on for a bit until he noticed the dull faces looking back on him. None of us had any idea what he was talking about. For all we knew he was speaking Greek or Latin. He then went on to ask what was the extent of our learning."

Michael John Joseph Del Toro

"I think not one of us was past ten years old and none of us had much schooling to speak of so we didn't know what to say until one blurted our she had learned to the rule of three. Well that opened up a spout from our new teacher that seemed never ending. He went on and on about how that type of teaching had fallen out of favor long ago out East and this was why he was intent on opening a university in the West to illuminate our fertile, yet virgin minds to what true learning was all about. I can only say most of that fell on deaf ears. Most of us didn't even know why were at school and I don't know how many of us at that early age had any intention of attaining or even an inkling what "higher learning" was. He could have been talking to a wall for all the good it did."

"He seemed to not mind or even notice but began to set up a chalk board and show us what he meant by higher learning by "teaching" us the fundamentals. He seemed quite excited. I think he had been itching for an opportunity like this all his life and we suddenly became part of some grand experiment. He then went on this long explanation of things like square routes, hypotenuse, the curve of a circle being pi and much more that to us sitting there, now with our jaws agape, seemed like some sort of magical formula. "

"Eventually he became aware of the completely blank stares greeting him when he finally looked up after what seemed an eternity. He vigorously erased his scribbling, all of which I had tried to duplicate myself on my own slate but had fallen hopelessly behind and had no idea what I was writing anyway. "

"He lamely ended the class by stating he had been invited to Chicago by several prominent families and was sure his teachings would take there and be a great boon to the burgeoning town and predicted it would soon be a metropolis second to none in the west. "

"I think he was a bit disappointed his teaching didn't take well to us, but it didn't seem to do anything to dampen his ambition.

I do believe he was quite right in his predictions about Chicago. It is certainly one of the rising cities of the West now but unfortunately that bright man never lived to see his dream of founding a great university fulfilled. "

"Why not?!" several of us asked in unison completely entranced by the unique story.

"Well it seems he had become friendly with the elderly lady with whom he boarded during the few days he was in our neighborhood resupplying. They wrote a few letters back and forth up until he reached the confluence of the Ohio and Wabash rivers. There was some sort of mishap and the boat he was on sunk. As the scholar was not so fit and couldn't swim he wound up drowning like several others of his fellow passengers. It was a most untimely end to what seemed to be a promising career. But he will forever remain a wizard in my mind's eye, even if his sorcery didn't extend to walking on water, but we all know that is the exclusive domain of our Lord Above. "

That brought a few more chuckles as well as several prayers to our Lord Jesus. The great man then said his goodbyes to our small group he went amongst the rest of the wounded. He must have spent over an hour with us all and I am sure the memory of that extraordinary event still sits with all of us. It gave me a new appreciation of the man and set me to vow to visit the land where he grew to adulthood to try and understand more about him, should I survive the war.

I did survive and here I am now to fulfill the vow I made that day. What I hope to learn from my visit here I don't rightly know, but that one talk with Lincoln already taught me much. It provided me the inspiration to not only make this trek but take in some schooling in Washington DC during my long convalescence. It was enough schooling to give me a leg up in the world and now I have taken up the study of law and hope to find my fortune, if not in Indiana or Illinois then off to the Far West, to California if that's what it takes.

Michael John Joseph Del Toro

I guess Abraham Lincoln spurred me to much more than I ever dreamed when I first came upon that little photo that far off day in Tennessee, a photo which I still hold proudly in my breast pocket, and have ever since that fateful day.

TO KILL A TURKEY

All my other friends had done it and I was beginning to become something of a pariah (I think that's the word). My reluctance to do it being deemed the hallmark of a coward. I am not sure where my reluctance stemmed but it was never in my blood I think. I was a gentle soul at heart.

Butchering an animal I could do but even then I wouldn't jump at the chance and most often left that task for my step brothers or my father. They soon understood it wasn't something I really liked doing and since I was usually the one who did the lion's share of the work around the farm nobody in the family ever pressed me about it. I was always willing to give a hand at the skinning, either grabbing a leg or the skinning itself and I wasn't squeamish of blood, well not that much at any rate. I felt a sort of empathy for the poor animal, they had become akin to me as my pets, like a dog or a cat or the family cow.

Others were not so keen to pass up an opportunity to tease and heckle a boy's perceived weakness, boys being boys, and I was never one to shirk a challenge since that was what it had come to. So one day I took it upon myself to try my hand at bagging some local game with my father's gun.

All farmers had a musket or shotgun and my father was no different. Some of them got their gun for hunting and others had them from their time in the militia. I don't rightly know how my father came about acquiring it, but he had it for as long as I could remember, and one of the first tasks any child learned on a farm was how to clean a musket. I don't know what type of shotgun it was, but I did know how to fire it and I came to be a pretty good shot while practicing near the cabin.

My father never did take a liking to us practicing on anything other than real game. He called it a lark and nothing more than a waste of powder. Seeing as powder was a commodity that was dear and quite expensive for a farmer, I could see his point. Sometimes we would go off and shoot a bit if he had gone to town or on a long trip, but the only real practice we had was to take a shot or two before we set out on a hunt to make sure the gun was working and get the hang of it again.

My cousin Dennis would often let John Hanks, John Johnston and me go with him on a hunt, during the short time he was staying with us, that is before he got married and moved off a ways and then only came to visit a couple of times a month. After that it was just John and I. Even after John knew I wouldn't do any of the shooting he would still take me along. I could always help by scaring up some of the birds, like those who had a dog to do it, or I would always be handy to help him bring back any game we managed to catch.

My brothers never had any qualms about hunting for game when they got the chance and every so often they would go off and, being pretty decent shots themselves, after a while would come back with a hare, pheasant, turkey or some other small game always found nearby. I do say I never shirked from the task of eating some and did my fair share of that you can be sure.

John Hanks was a dead shot, better than me or John Johnston, so he was the one who was usually getting to do the shooting. John Johnston liked to shoot but he wasn't so good, and once father learned this he told us to let John Hanks do the shooting since he wasn't so wasteful. Father was always a practical sort and not one to be wasting.

I don't know how often John Hanks would let Johnnie do any shooting, but he only let me do it a couple of times. Now as I said I was pretty good at handling the gun. I could hit a target we marked when we practice. That was none too hard for me. I think he caught on pretty quick I didn't like to do the shooting and since he liked to do it aplenty there was no harm to each of us in our special arrangement.

Now eventually it got around to some of the other boys that I wasn't too keen to be shooting anything, and that I never actually did shoot anything other than a tree. It was one day when we were in town and was able to spend some time with some of the neighboring boys, while waiting for Father to finish buying the goods momma wanted. He was haggling away with the merchant so we boys had some time on our hands. We came to throwing stones at a fence post and I was doing pretty good at it. I was hitting the post more often than not and one of the boys remarked that I must be a dead shot at hunting.

John Hanks was with us and he replied, "Ah no. Abe might be good with throwing but I'm the one who's always doing the hunting. He can't hit the broad side of a cabin when it comes to shooting deer and such."

That brought hearty laughs from the boys and I got right plum embarrassed by the laughter at my expense. I was quite used to getting folks, kids or adults, laughing anytime I wanted so I wasn't very used to getting laughed at myself. It sure takes some getting used to and it took me a whiles before I could just join in with no fuss.

This time around I got as red as an apple and couldn't say anything. Now I thinks those boys would have got to needling me some if they had half a chance but Father just so happened to have finished his bartering and came a calling to us to stop messing about and get to the wagon. Not too often am I happy to get scolded for any reason and certainly not for having to stop socializing but I was right happy then and there. I scooted my way back as happy as a cat with a mouse.

But it did get me to thinking. I didn't like the sound of laughter at my expense and I was sure the next time we got to talking one of the boys would bring it back up and I would have to go through the embarrassment again. If they didn't do it next time it was bound to happen again sometime. Either way thought it would be right easy to nip that sort of talk and jesting in the bud right quick by just going out and bagging some game on my own.

Once I get a notion in my head, it's tough to get it out of there so the next time my Father brought up one of us had to go hunting I volunteered. Now Father didn't exactly take to me wanting to go since I did more than my fair share of the chores for the most part and since today we were supposed to be clearing some forest I would be sorely missed. I was much better at that than my brothers, and if I do say so myself I was better at it than most adults twice my age or more. But I pleaded with my Father and said I could do the hunting alone so with both my brothers helping him Father could get as much done as if I was there.

That did it and my father reluctantly agreed after getting me to promise not to come home until I caught something. He knew well enough I hadn't shot anything myself since that was common knowledge in the family. I assured him I would and soon enough I was on my way with my father's gun and a pouch full of paper cartridges and a large knife in case I caught large game and need to dispatch it quickly to put it out of its misery. I didn't want to really think about that but rather just to kill it in one shot.

I was happy and surprised Father trusted me with the paper cartridges of shot instead of insisting I make due with makeshift shot we had made ourselves. These were of metal shavings, wood shards or anything else we could fit down the barrel and thought would be lethal to small game. I didn't have solid shot and ole' Bessie (that's what Father called the gun) wasn't really made for hitting anything past 50 yards so I would have to get pretty close or wait for some unwary prey to come to me.

I decided to do what John would do and just trek down the animal trails and try my luck on happening upon some game up to just past noon and if that didn't work I would find a likely spot near a watering hole or some other spot we know the animals like to visit and see if something comes my way. Slinging ole' Bessie over my shoulder I headed off into the forest with high hopes and a lot of trepidation.

I decided that since it had been a while since I had taken any target practice, once I was a little ways from the cabin where my mother and sisters couldn't hear and I knew my father and brothers were off on the other end of the farm I unslung my shotgun and took a few shots at a couple of trees then checked on my skill. It only took three or four shots before I had enough confidence that I could hit any game I happened to come upon on my hunt.

I had myself all loaded up and ready to go now. I think I may have been a bit too overconfident or a bit too nervous since the first game I came upon was a deer and I blundered into it so that it scampered off before I could get a clean shot but I took one anyone and missed wildly. The next game I happened upon was about an hour later. It was a rabbit. Hardly enough to really shoot at but I determined to anyway. When I did nothing happened. In my anger I had reloaded improperly and ruined my shot.

I took out the ammo and reloaded silently berating myself on my foolishness. It took another two hours before I was able to find more prey. This was another deer, or perhaps it was the same one I had come upon earlier. Whatever the case I took quick aim and let go another round. This one was closer to the mark but still no luck and the deer perked its head up and ran off towards a clearing that was about a half a mile away.

I followed off in the same direction hoping beyond hope I would get another chance at it. That was not to be for I saw something a bit more to my liking. Turkey! One of my favorites!

Now I saw the turkey just outside a large bramble in a small natural clearing I had often been through on previous hunts with my brother John. There were probably more in the bush itself. It was my perfect opportunity! I could have taken the shot at the turkey pecking around at the ground but I wasn't all that close and was a little nervous that if I missed any other turkeys in the brush would take flight before I would ever have a chance to reload.

I knelt down and picked up a large stone and placed it next to me while unslinging my gun. I then quickly loaded the shotgun and rested it upon my knees while crouching. I picked up the stone and lobbed it high in the air then quickly brought the gun up taking aim at the bush.

By the time I brought the shotgun up to my ear the stone had landed within the bushes. Sure enough a flock of them took flight filling the sky. I took quick but careful aim this time and with one shot I managed to knock one out of the sky. It didn't take me long to get to it and by the time I got there it was dead. Looking down at it I was filled with remorse. I knew in my heart this was something I didn't ever want to do again. But I had done the deed and I wouldn't be poked at again by anyone.

I never did figure why it is I don't like to do any killing. Maybe it is the blood spurting about, though I see enough of that when I'm skinning or butchering. Maybe it's the look in their eyes when they breathe their last and knowing I was the one that did it. I think though it has to do with the time I had to kill a sow.

It was right after my Ma died, my real mom. She died of the milk sickness. It was a sad time for my sister and me. We were all alone, except for Dennis, but Dennis was away a lot so my sister and me were usually by ourselves and since I was doing a lot of farming and things outside we both had a lot of time to ourselves. That was a very sad time for us and we would cry a lot.

After a while, Dennis had a hard time finding any game when he would go out hunting so we run out of meat. Dennis had fallen sick and couldn't even get out of bed for a few days. We were scared stiff. We thought we might be left all to ourselves and we didn't know if Father would ever come back. This was the saddest and scariest time in my life.

We needed to get some meat, and we had a few hogs running about so we decided to kill one of the sows. Now Dennis couldn't do it on account he was so ill, so it was left to me, the man of the house so to speak. We went out to the fence with the gun. My sister crouched next to me as I peered through the fence at one of the sows and shot. Bang! It was a good shot, right in the head and the pig keeled right over.

We ran over to it, but it still hadn't died. It breathed a little bit and then I saw its eye glaze over, roll back into its head, and then get all glassy. It reminded me too much of the death of my poor mother and I started to cry. My sister cried with me and we sat there a bit next to the sow and cried our hearts out. Then we had to drag it a ways to get it close to the house so we could butcher it. I hadn't thought of that before, and it was a hard chore for us being we weren't too big.

I think that had really taken something out of me that I could never get back. I still haven't gotten the look of the hog out of my mind and I think I might never get it out. Its not something I like to think about and I'm hoping by writing about it now it will help keep it from festering in my head. I hope it does.

Now while I had finally done the deed and should have rightly been proud of myself it turned out I was a bit ashamed. I was quiet all that night and my kin knew something was wrong since the only time I kept my thoughts to myself was when I was reading. I was just staring off absentminded or looking thoughtfully into the fire. My Father asked me what was wrong and I replied, perhaps too quickly, that I didn't like doing any killing.

I was surprised but my Father didn't seem to mind that answer at all. He just said well I wasted enough powder doing it once so that should be enough for me. Besides I could still do a better job clearing forest and most of the other chores than my brothers combined. Momma, she said she was proud I didn't want to kill anything and if I didn't mind doing any skinning or helping with cleaning the meat then it was fine by her. That ended that with my family and it was like a big load off my shoulders.

It didn't end it with the boys in town. They came around to hearing how I wouldn't do any more killing. I don't know how they came to hearing about it but eventually they did. I think its like any town where everyone knows everyone. You can't poop without everyone knowing what color it was and so it was with me being shy for killing.

Anyways, the boys got to heckling me about it, but I managed to end that right quick indeed. Now I was bigger, quicker and much stronger than anyone my age and most much older. So when those boys got to rousing and heckling me I just stood up straight and walloped the one closest me. He went a flying and was laid out sprawling on the ground. It was quite a comical sight, but I was all riled up and ready to tussle with any and all of them.

I then looked them all in the eye and asked if anyone else wanted to poke at me. Now my two brothers were nearby, and when they saw the fighting start they of course ran up behind me and stood with me against them. Now not one of the boys would like to tangle with me, and all of them didn't want to have any sort of fighting with the three of us. We were all pretty tough since we did our fair share of wrestling with each other, and since we were brothers we always stuck together when it came to fighting others. That's what brothers do.

Then I just looked them over real hard and said I don't want to hear any more fuss being made about me not wanting to kill anything or they'll be sorry they opened their mouth and have a black eye to show for trying to be smart with me. That shut them up right quick and I never did hear a peep from any of them after that.

But we all made up quick like afterwards since it was a small town and its not right to be mad at anyone for long. We would need help from someone soon so it was better just to forget about it and move on with more important things. That's what we all did and things turned out all right.

*Other sources state Abraham Lincoln would hunt just as much as other kids and adults but I chose to stick with him being most reluctant to kill another animal. Not for any other reason than I think that at the time others were stating he was fond of hunting was at a time when it was fashionable to be a hunter and deemed a manly pursuit. While it still is today, the stigma attached to one who doesn't like to hunt, for whatever reason, is not in vogue today as it was during and for quite some time after Lincoln's time. He wouldn't shirk from helping to clean the game once killed since he did like to eat meat.

*Lincoln didn't mind being teased later in life, and it helped disarm those teasing him and endear himself but I tend to believe it was a trait he learned and like most other folk didn't take kindly to it at first.

THE EYES OF DESPERATION

An excerpt from Allen Gentry's Diary:

Dang it! What those dang darkies would have done to me I know not but what having Lincoln with me to hold them off. I do say I gotten used to this swearing now but I hope it is because of my situation. This journey is wearing on me and I hope never to have to do it again. Next time it goes to the help, like Lincoln. I want no part of it!

Lincoln is sure some wonder. He is a mystery to me though I've known him for quite some time. I still remember when I first laid eyes on him I thought was just like any other cracker. We Gentrys come from means so I guess I looked down on Abe on account of his looks and he being a Lincoln he was of a poorer sort. That was before I knew much of him and after I spent some time with him I knew he was not some regular cracker but he had some means to him, if not in wealth but in bearing and in the head.

But I never did see someone fight before like he did last night! He took four of them down himself and done saved me from the other two after I took out the first. We didn' kill none but I guess they run off to find some easier pickins. I don't know what or where those darkies were after or from but without dear Lincoln I would be a dead man for sure. Those darkies were determined but Lincoln sure did make them fly!

Let me catch my breath some before I tell this one.

"Their eyes! Their eyes!", Lincoln says to me. The first thing he says after we managed to pull ourselves offshore from those dang darkies. I didn't know what he meant and said so to him.

"Didn't you see? How could you not see those globes of white amidst their obsidian skin?!?"

I replied I was too busy warding them off with the oar to look into their eyes. And who cares about the bandits' eyes when our lives were at stake.

"No!", Young Abe stated with an earnestness that drew me to him and etched his words forever into my soul. "It was their eyes that told the truth and their story. It was their eyes that showed me the torment in their soul. It was almost like a mirror of my own eyes."

I'm no poet with words like Lincoln was. I don't have the gift of gab that he does. I can only give you a few feeble words about what he said last night. I might not remember the words but what he told me is beginning to change the way I thought of them darkies.

He told me of a time, after a long day's work at our neighbor's farm about 11 miles yonder from his home. He said he spent the day shucking corn and he was as tired as a man could be. After the work he had done he was expected to get a look see at the neighbor's book of Thomas Jefferson's biography or some such thing, I don't rightly remember, but his father had come earlier in the day and demanded his own price set rather than the price young Abe had agreed upon.

Abe said he was haunted by that day. It was he that had done the labor, it should be he who could and would demand a price, whatever it be. He said he remembered himself vividly he said as he was washing himself off when he looked upon his face in the water like a mirror by the riverside as day ended when he had finished his work. He remembered one thing, and one thing only. It was his own eyes. And he said this evening that his own eyes were reflected in the darkies that attacked us.

He felt nothing but compassion for them though it was Abe who did the most to keep that little band of beating us off and probably killing us. I don't rightly understand my companion. I've never spent so much time with him before but I am gaining more respect for him daily as much as he is becoming more mysterious by the day.

I don't know what tomorrow will bring but I know with Abe by my side I stand more a chance of being successful than without. My father made one smart decision by picking Abe as my companion on this trip down to New Orleans.

****

Joshua Speed leaned back taking a sip of some fine bourbon as he pondered the question. He was reclining at his fine home, as was his wont, and trying to marshal his thoughts. Joshua dipped the pen into the inkwell and began to compose his letter to his brother, currently serving in Frankfort, Kentucky as a member of the Upper House of the Legislature. It was November 2nd and for the past month his brother James had been fulminating in a series of speeches against the recently issued Emancipation Proclamation of Abraham Lincoln. He railed not against the issuance of the act, but in declaring the Act did not go far enough in denouncing slavery and in granting freedom to those currently within the portions of the South controlled by the Union forces. These thoughts were echoed across the land in many newspapers and even scorned in the Old Country across the ocean. While a few praised the Proclamation as a worthy document, far more heaped scorn upon it, while in the South it had already become the most notorious of documents ever issued by the hand of Man and denounced as a writ meant to create insurrection and rebellion by the very property the Southern man was hoping to preserve for all time by their own separation from their mother country.

Joshua's Farmington plantation was a mere fifty miles from the capital but both brothers were busy men. James Speed was a prominent politician, Joshua a distinguished wealthy planter and real estate investor. Joshua owned slaves and while he understood that immorality of slavery, he was still a willing participant. This is what he felt would carry added weight to his letter.

James knew much of his brother's past in Springfield. He knew of Joshua's intimate relationship with Abraham and he hoped by reflecting on this with his brother he could temper the heated rhetoric his brother could bring forth in his speeches on the Kentucky Senate floor. Kentucky was in the midst of two wars. One was between North and South, the other like its sister border state of Missouri, was the far more vicious war, a war within itself. Many brothers and fathers were fighting on different sides of the conflict. Kentucky was surely a House Divided. While Joshua may not have seen eye to eye with Lincoln, or his own brother, he was still intensely loyal to the Union and would support the cause no matter what.

This led Joshua to write to his brother and brought him to reminisce to himself upon first meeting Abe and the special bond the two held with each other as he sought to order his thoughts.

My Dearest Brother,

I am writing in earnest about a cause which touches us dearly though in different ways. I have been noting in your recent speeches, which are reported in our local papers, that you have mercilessly attacked our mutual friend and President, Abraham Lincoln, about his lack of forthright action regarding the irrepressible question of slavery that is behind the current insurrection of our Southern brothers.

I think I can best address your concerns on Lincoln and his views on Slavery. I know you understand full well my views and how I think if the North would just leave the South alone there would be no contention between North and South. I know you and Abe had lengthy discussions during his long stay here decades earlier, but you two never explored the slavery question to its fullest extent. You dealt more on the legal matters you shared and were instrumental in assisting him in his law studies.

You are aware of the intimate relationship Abe and I enjoyed during our time together in Springfield, but let me elaborate on that so you may well understand what it is I will relate to you. Please bear with me dear brother if I happen to repeat stories you have heard. You know my memory fails me at times.

I missed the days running my old grocery store in Springfield and the days filled with throngs of men who came to talk about the current events and politics, which were one in the same in America, and hopefully buy something too.

Good ole' Abe Lincoln…..MY God! I think he did more to make me money when he stood with me than I ever made any other time running my store. He drew people to my store in Springfield by his gift of gab, and perforce they would buy something here and there and that in itself was more than enough to compensate for him sharing my bed during those years.

I remember well, as if it happened yesterday, my momentous meeting with Abe Lincoln, whom I would one day count as my dearest friend. I was keeping shop in the general store below the room where I was residing in Springfield when one fine day this tall lanky man strolled in lugging a bag over one shoulder and after introducing himself inquired if we had any household goods for sale."

I was going over the books when he ambled in and without looking up I returned the introduction and claimed we did indeed. He then asked, "How much would it cost for the furniture for a single bed, the mattress, blankets, sheets, coverlids and pillow?"

Still without glancing I went over the items quickly in my head and estimated the cost at about seventeen dollars. To this Abe replied in a glum drawl that that was "perhaps cheap enough" but confessed he did not have the necessary monies to complete the transaction. He then asked if I could credit the funds until Christmas, about six months time and as he remarked "if my venture in the law pans out I can pay you in full but I must confess that if it doesn't I might never be able to pay you back."

That drew my curiosity enough to finally glance up and give the young lad a look over. I never saw a sadder looking face as his at that moment in time. I recalled him instantly for I had heard him make a stump speech about a year earlier. He had impressed me then and impressed me now. I replied,

"You seem to be so much pained at contracting so small a debt, I think I can suggest a plan by which you can avoid the debt and at the same time attain your end. You see I have a large room with a double bed upstairs, which you are welcome to share with me."

With a look of surprise Lincoln bounded up the stairs and came back down without the bag, and with a face utterly transformed from one of misery to one of extreme delight, "Well Speed, I am moved!" And knowing Abe as I know him now the pun was certainly intended!

We came from as different family backgrounds as could be possible, yet we are kindred spirits, Lincoln and I. You know I was educated at some of the finest schools in my region, while Abe was what you would call self-educated. I could have remained at home basking in a life of luxury and ease while Abe was forced by the circumstances of his family to remain there in poverty or seek greater prospects to the west.

But we both had the ambition to improve ourselves and our circumstances through our own efforts. We both had similar likes and dislikes and had an interest in poetry, reading and politics. We became fast friends and later soulmates. We discussed our desires and fears each night as we lay down in search of sleep. We always discussed prospective ladies and measured our chances with our respective conquests and helped each other devise ways to win their hands.

When it came to women we advised each other as intimately as in every other aspect of our lives. I, if I may be so bold, was a great inspiration to Abraham in giving him the confidence to pursue Mary Todd. She was clearly the most eligible and most desirable woman in Springfield. She had a dozen suitors and in many cases their credentials were immaculate.

Abraham didn't have those credentials but he did have some things in his favor that the others didn't. Now Abe was a large man and could be physically imposing but he didn't present himself in that manner. He certainly didn't dress in a way that would bring distinction and he lacked many of the social graces the others had.

Abe did have the confidence and respect of virtually every male, and for that matter female, resident of Springfield. He was often at the tip of their lips when discussing the town events. They always had gone to my store, more often just to chat or more often listen to Lincoln than to buy anything.

When he was postmaster he was well acquainted with every family in New Salem and the surrounding area. As a surveyor he showed that he was honest and hardworking. He was elected Captain during his short stint in the militia during the Black Hawk War and he had represented his district well in the state legislature. Many of these people had settled in Springfield when New Salem relapsed into obscurity.

Michael John Joseph Del Toro

When it came to my love life, Abe was of primary importance in helping me over my romantic difficulties with Fanny prior to our betrothel. When I went to Kentucky after Fanny and I had broken things off it was Lincoln's letter that helped sway me to pursue her. Lincoln's advice to me on love: be more realistic. Love is only idealized in novels and history. In life it is like anything else. More practical and in line with day to day living. This helped Lincoln in his own troubled courtship and by advising me he brought himself to realize he did love Mary and should marry her. It is wisdome that we all should cherish, in love and in life.

We slept together for four years up until our subsequent marriages and throughout that time I learned everything about him and he of me. He became a successful lawyer while I made my fortune as an investor in real estate and through my ownership of the general store. We were both men of our times and sought our future in the west as many of our generation did.

My ambition was sated by the station I gained as a leading citizen of Springfield , until my return to our home here,but Lincoln's always strived for more. His was of a mind to seek to be the best wherever he journeyed, and that ambition eventually took him to the White House.

Abe had seen many a slave while a young boy living at Knobs Creek as they passed along the Cumberland Trail but only at a distance. His first interaction with the Negro race he would one day free from bondage was in a decidedly different manner and one not altogether at odds with the role he would play as a liberator.

But after he moved off into Indiana he didn't catch sight of a slave in many a year. It was known to him that there were slaves, but they were as far removed from his station in life and location as if they were in far off Africa.

But there were two occasions that I want to bring to light to you that may palliate your anger and resentment for what you feel is a betrayal to the trust placed in Abe by his party and it's platform. The first of these was in a letter he had written me some years back and brought back to my mind a time we had spent traveling down the Ohio and Mississippi rivers. On this one boat we chanced upon seeing a slaver board the vessel with a number of slaves in tow.

One of those unfortunates happened to be a bit slow in the eyes of his master in shuffling along with the others and in order to hasten him, he cuffed the young slave across the mouth knocking him and all the rest off their feet. This brought a curse from the slave trader and his charges were quick to get up on their feet and move along in a disjointed fashion towards the cargo hold where they would remain for their portion of the journey.

Abe brought this to mind in his letter and remarked that this event still stands clear in his mind, though I must admit I had long forgotten it, and he said it was a seminal moment that forever ingrained in himself the wish for him to strike a blow to that dreaded institution if ever afforded an opportunity.

This gave me cause to remember another incident he had spoke of, this time while the two of us lay next to each other in bed, neither able to summon the sleep we both desperately needed. This instance had happened even years earlier, on that self same river.

This time he was well on his first journey with a load of cargo towards shipment to New Orleans. He had with him but one companion. They had to stop for the evening in an uninhabited part of the river. They found a suitable landing spot and planned to camp out for the night along the riverbank before starting off again in the mornting.

Late that evening they were accosted by a number of runaway slaves, I forget the number or the details, though I am sure Abe still remembers it all as vividly as if it happened only moments earlier. Whatever the case, he and his fellow companion were able to keep the band of desperadoes at bay long enough for them to lose heart and flee, leaving the two alone with their thoughts and with their cargo intact.

The two had left the riverbank in haste fearing they may return and yet in greater numbers. Lincoln told me the most impactful and fateful memory of that encounter was not the fight but it was the eyes of his attackers. He remembered the desperation he spied in each of them, and how well he reflected upon it. He said that was the first time he ever felt akin to them as Men and he had vowed that night to himself that he would find a way one day to do whatever it took to ensure that the evil institution of slavery would be forever eradicated from the soil of the Union and never sully the land of freedom again.

So I understand your trepidation. I understand that you may believe that Abe doesn't hold the same feelings in regard to ending slavery within our beloved country. I just wish to ensure you that you are mistaken in this belief. Nothing could be further from the truth. Give him some time. I am sure he has put as much thought into how he may achieve the end both of you desire and this Proclamtion is but one small, but important part to play in the end game you both seek. He has a wisdom far beyond us both, and knows the temper and mind of the people better than anyone.

Have faith in him and in the Lord Above and we shall see our Union preserved in the way you most desire.

Your Most Beloved and Humble Servant,

Joshua Fry Speed

NO WAY TO MAKE AN ENTRANCE

"Gosh darn it! I'm not one for swearing but this day it brought it out on me. I guess I had it coming but I wouldn't have thought so if you asked me a week before, dang (there I done did it again), I wouldn't have thought it yesterday."

John was the type that liked to go out a bit sometimes, let off a bit of steam. In the past he took advantage of the celebrity afforded by being the cousin of the late, great rail splitter, Abraham Lincoln. This helped ease the cost of the fun but on some occasions he just wanted to have a quiet drink or two.

Tonight was one such evening. He had a long week, had just gotten to town, and wanted to top it off with a couple of night caps from a local watering hole. But it was the risk a celebrity like himself, who had basked in the limelight of the most amazing time in living memory in America, that he was bound to be recognized and sure enough he was there barely five minutes before someone came over asking if he was the rail splitters friend. John figured he might as well make it worth his while so, after confirming his identity and quaffing down the rest of his whisky, he had offered to spin a yarn about the legendary President in return for a drink. This was quickly accepted. A story about The Great Liberator was always welcome. And so John had begun his tale of Abe's (and his own) unintended introduction to the New Salem community.

"There was this bloke," John continued. "a real talker he was. I guess you could say he was a windbag. We didn't rightly know this at the time. I just knew he had a store in town and heard he was looking a boatman. I had some experience in running flatboats along the Ohio river so I figured I would see what the man was looking for. Turns out he wanted to float a boat full of his goods down to New Orleans. I had done quite a bit of boating but had never made that trip. I wasn't about to let Offutt know that so I brought up my cousin Abe."

"Now since Abe had all the experience in going down to New Orleans I figured it would be best to get him in on the job. He had done the trip once before for James Gentry and once Offutt heard this he thought he could use someone with Abe's skill to give his grocery store some cash and get the jump on the competition, especially Gentry who's store was already firmly established in those parts.

"Offutt thought he was quite keen and using his rival's help would be a way of getting one over on him. Offutt was a big talker and spoke about the trip to us as if he had the biggest boat to haul the most groceries down to New Orleans and make the most money. This made us awful excited about joining such a big and profitable venture and we believed him. Plus he was offering a nice bit of money for us."

"I went back to fetch Abe, got his step brother John Johnston to join and the three of us rowed ourselves to Springfield to meet Offutt. That's when we learned that Offutt didn't have a boat. That was the first inkling we had that this gent was a bit of a windbag. We didn't learn the whole of it and being youg and full of beans looking for adventure we were still raring to go."

"So when Offutt told us he didn't have a boat for us there was nothing to it but to build a flatboat ourselves. Now we never had built a flatboat before and Abe had the most experience in the river trade. He had worked on a flatboat before when he operated a ferry boat a couple of years earlier on the Ohio River. He had also been on a flatboat another time a year or so earlier and had got all the way to New Orleans. We were there because we would help with the hauling of the goods onto and off the boat and to listen to Abe. Abe was the "captain" of the ship and he said last time around he had a bit of trouble so could use the extra hands. Plus Offutt always wanted to outdo anyone and since Gentry did it with two hands, Offutt would do it with three."

"We built one according to Abe's instructions. He took over the whole project. We all helped but he built the ship and if I may be honest he was the one who hewed all the wood. Never did I see ever anyone who could chop wood like he did. We did most of the hauling and piling the planks to dry them up a bit."

"Now we didn't have all that much time to get this work done before we were due to meet Offutt in New Salem so we could haul the goods from his grocery store and get going down to New Orleans. We were floating along nicely. We were approaching New Salem. This was where we would pick up our main cargo to go down and bring to New Orleans. "

"John Johnston had never been out on his own like this before, and I never been down to New Orleans, so we were both looking forward to see the Elephant, to experience a new town off on our own. Three boys on a lark. Now you know at that time seeing a flatboat on the Sangamon river wasn't a common sight, I tell you that. Abe told us that when we got there it would be like a carnival. The whole town would want to come and take a gander at the three of us and we would be right famous for a day or two. So all three of us wanted to make a showing of bringing the flatboat in all professional like and have the local townsfolk agape at our skill and swagger."

"It didn't turn out like that at all, now that I can tell you!"

One of the other patrons had been listening intently to the tale and now chimed in, "You sure are right about that! I can recall it just like it was yesterday. I was living in New Salem in those days and was working at the mill, which had a dam across the river. I was the first to catch sight of the boat coming down the Sangamon. I see'd these fellas steering their way down and now the river was getting a bit low so when they came upon the dam the boat careened over it and lo and behold got stuck plum in the middle of the river on it!"

"Now it would have been a pitiable sight if it wasn't so downright comical. You had this flatboat the looked like it was cobbled together with some green wood stuck up atop the dam like. The bow is clear out of the water while the stern is barely touching the river which was flowing at a snails pace. For the life of me I couldn't figure what they were thinking trying to get it over the dam in the first place."

"Then you got these three lads going from one side to the other scratching their heads in disbelief and confounded as to what to do next. And one of these boys is all tall and gangly like he was all arms and legs and wearing some of the worst ill-fitting clothes you ever had the misfortune to see."

"As I said, I was one of the first to spy the boat in its predicament but in a sleepy town like New Salem it doesn't take long for word to get around and faster than you can skin a hare you had half the town out along the shore shouting, jeering, placing bets and watching wide eyed."

"I admit we were in some pickle," John replied and then continued his story, a bit peeved at having his own well practiced monologue of the incident anticipated and ruined, and not wanting the newcomer to lord it over him. "Now Lincoln was springing about, darting here and there like a hare hunted by a pack of dogs. He'd scamper from fore to aft and seemed everywhere at once. He had the two of us running about as well. We must have seemed like three spring chickens with our ears cut off!"

"The townsfolk had gathered about the soreline, like he says. They must have been laughing something awful seeing us in such a predicament. Must have been the whole town gathered about to take in the fun. It was turning out to be a holiday for them."

"It wasn't anything like that for us. I wouldn't even look towards the shore. If I did I would get red faced watching the people cavorting here and there. I knew they were talking about us and none of it good from where I was standing. That's for sure!"

"Oh we were having quite a time thanks to you boys." The man chimed in again with a grin remembering the festivities and the unforeseen holiday. "It didn't take much to get people roused up in those days. It's not like we had much in the way of entertainment in those parts. Not like today. And it being unexpected made it all the more novel. I must admit we were enjoying ourselves something fierce at your expense." He laughed heartily at the memory almost falling out of his chair and spilling his drink.

John laughed too, deciding to let the fellow have his fun and add to the story, then said, "I can laugh too now but I was not laughing then, you can be sure about that! I was falling apart, going all to pieces I dare say while you all were having your very own holiday bee on the shore, but not ole' Abe. Lincoln had us a running here and there and at first I couldn't figure what it was he was doing. All I could think was things were going from bad to worse and as far as I could tell it was only going to keep going downhill. I just wanted an end to my misery but I did as Abe asked."

"He first took off some of the cargo onto a skiff that floated over to us from the dam, to make our sturdy little boat a bit lighter. The owner said he could haul off all the cargo for a fee but Abe wouldn't hear none of it. He was a man with a plan! He then picked up an auger from somewhere and bore a hole in the boat's bow to drain most of the water it had taken on as quickly as he could. First I didn't understand why he did that since we had pumps to use but he had another job in mind for those. I'll relate more on that in a moment."

"I was the more experienced boatman, and the one who got us the job, but Lincoln had more brains than John and me put together and then some!

"As bad as I felt I had confidence that if there was any way for us out of this not looking a fool or three then Abe could do the figuring of making it happen. And sure enough after a while I began to see what it was he was planning and things started to shape up."

"I don't know how it was he done his figuring and I'm still not sure how it was he did it, even though I was one of the ones doing the doing. All I do know is things were starting to look up in more ways than one."

"I might not remember things like I used to but a few things still stick out to me. This is what I can still recall. The top and bottom of the buoyant bags were made of stiff planks, the cloth bags were nailed onto the planks and we had to keep pumping them because they leaked something fierce even though we had slapped on some pitch made from resin we had handy for plugging leaks around the edges of the bags to try and seal them. He had us making these things lickety split and faster than you could say "The United States of America" we had these contraptions built and were fastening to the sides of the boat fore and aft. We used the pumps we had made for using when we needed to drain water to keep the air up and I must say they worked reasonably well enough that the boat started getting higher on the stern side where the boat still rested a bit in the water."

"We had to work at this for a while and it was back breaking labor. All the while the gents on the shore were hooting and jeering at us. We paid no mind to it since we knew if this didn't work we'd be the laughing stock of the region for some time to tell. I reckon not to many folk even remember this now but sure as there's a tic on a dog you can bet they still be talking about to this day if we couldn't get that dang boat off the dam. It'd probably still be there now! I do say I began to see the light and began to work in more earnest as the ship began to shift a bit from its unwieldy perch atop the dam."

"But we did it after what seemed an eternity, and suddenly the boat slowly began to tilt to the fore. When enough of it touched the water the current pullled the rest sliding and scraping off the dam until the boat was all clear, and that turned the jeers to cheers. The whole community that was laughing at us one minute were cheering themselves hoarse the next. We gave them a good little holiday but soon the crowd got back to their daily business and we met ole' Offutt at the shore and began to pick up the stock we would be hauling off to New Orleans."

"Yes indeed. You boys finally did get the boat off the dam and ended our lark. But it was fun while it lasted. And for that I thank you enough to repay you with a drink on me."

John was happy to hear that, and gave the man a toast when the new drink was brought to him.

"Now that wasn't the end of it, though I'm sure it was the end of it for you. Lincoln not only got a bit of a reputation for having a head screwed on right, he got even more out of our ride on the dam."

"Now at that time everyone wanted to be seeing improvements along our rivers. I think you can agree with me on that." Both men nodded looking at each other then back at Hanks, and John kept with the story. "Many of them wouldn't allow a small raft to float down them in the summer and autumn with all the shoals and obstructions. Lincoln was just like the rest of us in wanting to make the towns more accessible. It make it easier for all to be prosperous if we could get our goods to market easier. "

"Now like I been saying, Lincoln didn't think like the rest of us. We were all looking for ways to make the rivers themselves improved. Now Lincoln thought that way too. I mean if you look at all his speeches in state and federal campaigns you see he talked about that more than anything else combined."

"But Lincoln also tried different ways to make the boats themselves able to just skip right over them shoals or deadwood just lying in the water. Instead of clearing out the obstructions why not hop over them all crablike? That's the way he thought about it and this is how he come to that idea I reckon."

"He thought so highly of his idea he even sent a plan of it to the US Patent Office, and don't you know they gave Lincoln a patent for it! Now I don't rightly know how often someone got to using that idea of his. While I seen it work with my own eyes it seemed more trouble than it was worth and all."

"Either way it just shows how Lincoln and his mind were always thinking on another level than us normal folk. I guess that's what made him so popular and right successful it did. He used his wits all during the war. We had some poor Generals serving him during the first years of the war. They did so bad for us Abe had to do the generaling himself."

"He could see a winner. He saw Grant as a winner long before anyone else did but it took him a while to bring over to face ole' Bobby Lee. When he did that it didn't take long before Lee was whupped and we won. I often wondered why he took so long to bring over Grant but I guess it was good he did. Otherwise we might still be sitting outside Vicksburg and fighting the South all the way up to the Ohio!"

Like I said, he had more brains than me and then some. I reckon he had a sight more brains than most of the Generals and politicians in Washington. We could certainly use him right about now."

To that all agreed wholeheartedly and after polishing off his last drink John bid the gentlemen a good evening, and left to get some sleep get an early start in the morning for another long day.

*seeking some financial benefit, and at least some positive effect of his two years in Washington it was after his congressional term and almost two decades after the event that he successfully applied for the patent for "floating boats over shoals".

With this in mind the above reconstruction of the actual event is an interpretation of the original, not the patented device, which Abraham Lincoln had ample time to refine into a viable product that would all but eliminate any of the kinks or imperfections of the first working model created that fateful day. However, it was never used except on that one fateful occasion.

*as with many of the stories concerning Lincoln's youth and young adulthood, there are often multiple versions of the same event, and these just as often differ in the particulars. For this one and the next story I took this version from John Hanks being the one originally offered the job to float a boatful of cargo to New Orleans from Offutt. He convinced Offutt to hire Lincoln and his step brother John Johnston, and that all three of them made the entire trip down to New Orleans.

THE CHAINS OF BONDAGE

I had heard him tell a few times of the ordeal he had with several fugitive slaves on his first trip down to New Orleans, the first time being when I accompanied him on his second trip there in the spring of 1831. We took a flatboat down the Ohio River after bringing the boat in from the Sangamon. Going by boat down the Sangamon was a most perilous undertaking, that river had never been navigable through its length. It took us some doing to make it into the Ohio but from there it was far easier getting to the great Mississippi River and the thriving city of St. Louis.

Here it was that I had my first taste of a big city. Abraham had been here before but for John and I, it was our first experience of the grandeur of such a place. We had never expected so many people to be gathered in one area and it was a very moving experience.

John was a bit older than either Abe or me and he already had a family to look after back in Illinois. We had expected to have set off from New Salem about a month earlier than we did and John was becoming more worried about the welfare of his family he had left behind. It was while we were at St. Louis that his worries overcame his sense of adventure and thought of money.

I think it was the sight of the many families in St. Louis that brought the sense of responsibilities of family life home to John. He decided then and there that it would be best for him to not continue with us and he turned back to head home.

The Old Man was a wide river and slow moving. I think that's why they called the river "Old Man". I don't know where the name came from but it sure stuck, as much as the water would to the sides of your stomach if you had to drink it. It was so muddy people would say if you drank a gallon you would have a sand bar a mile long in your gut. I had a draught or two of it and I dare say they may be right. I felt heavy as lead afterwards and it took some doing to get me on my feet again.

The trip took a ways and there wasn't much work to be done

going down. The weather was mostly fine and Abe was as good a boatman as could be. He did most of the steering, while my task was to keep a good sight ahead in case there were some obstructions. We learned about that up on the Sangamon so we were always wary for something sticking out of the river. But the river was wide and deep so we had no hitches.

My other job was to help shore us up at the few harbors we came upon. Most often we spent our time anchored a little off one of the river banks, Abe having had a scare the last time down these parts and he was itching to have none of that again. I dare say I didn't mind it one bit. We always stood out as poor farm boys whenever we did happen upon a town and while some people would like to hear a story or two, some of the towns were downright hostile to folk like us as the following would show.

The slow pace gave us plenty of time to take in the countryside and ample time to relax. Each night we would tie up on the shore so no mishaps would occur by navigating blindly down the river in the dark. We were all too aware of what happened the last time Abe had come down this way and the two of us would take watch in turns, but nothing happened.

Our disheveled appearance did cause quite a stir when we passed by one town, Beardstown, in Illinois. We were floating along the near bank of the town preparing to dock. It had been a while since we had a chance for getting cleaned up, and we were feeling dirty and itching to have a roof over our heads. We were just docking and were greeted by cold stares and it seemed like the entire town came out to laugh and jeer at our appearance. This made so we just cut off right then and there and left in a hurry. After this our desire to stop off at towns was less than the risk of any danger of staying ashore for the night in the wild, so we often bypassed towns entirely and took the risk, but we were always wary.

I didn't mind none. I was having the time of my life. It was good to have the fresh breeze blowing on you and I had more fish to eat than I had ever had in my life, before or after. I surely did like to spend my time fishing. Just throwing a line over the side and waiting for something to bite. It was a sight better than hauling or chopping wood or day or clearing a plot of land for planting. That's the type of work I never minded to miss!

Michael John Joseph Del Toro

Finally the day came where we reached the famous city of New Orleans. And what a sight it was! I thought St. Louis was a big city, even though we didn't' get to see much of it, but New Orleans was bigger in every way! There were buildings upon buildings and so many people clustered around the harbor during the day you could barely get enough room to stand.

You were always jostled here and there and everyone was busy! You never did see so many people going here and there and shouting this and that. We been to plenty of markets but this was like ten of the biggest put together. Everyone shouting about how they had the best stuff you could buy, while others tried to out shout them how theirs were better. And people haggling over prices and this and that. It was enough to make your head spin!

It was in New Orleans that Abe had his first real experience with that part of the undesirable institution that afflicted our grand nation from its birth until the Great War Between the States, the slave trade. We had went to the market and there happened up a slave auction taking place, as it so often did in the South's greatest city.

The bonds holding the poor dregs of humanity and their haunted looks and eyes weighed heavily on young Abraham. We saw some physically beat upon, whipped and even scourged. This was painful to watch for us both, but having been beaten a time or two, Abe too, we didn't pour our souls out to them. Maybe that was what pained us in the first place, having had a similar experience ourselves.

We saw one of them, who was chained up with some of his fellow slaves being brought onto the block scourged something fierce, the soles of his feet struck again and again. All that for being slow. I didn't figure how scourging was going to help him walk any quicker, but I wasn't about to make a fuss about it.

We figured maybe they had deserved it in some way, but what struck Abe most was the treatment of a young Mulatto girl. It must have struck Abe as a most unfortunate event at the time but for the nation it proved to be the most fortunate incident in Lincoln's young life.

It was there that the desire to free our country from its humiliating affliction was forever burned into his soul. He watched as the young girl, who would have been considered white where we were from, was treated in the most humiliating fashion.

She was bound, as were all the others, in chains around her wrists. She was being looked over by a number of prospective buyers, all of whom were busy pinching, feeling and otherwise examining her as she was handed over to each bidder for inspection. The owner assured all gathered that she was certainly still sound and would make an ideal house slave.

She was maybe 10 years old. She seemed tall for her age and a bit gangly, all arms and legs. Just like Abe was at that age. She was of a lighter complexion.

The girl could have easily passed as a daughter of many of the families we knew back home in Indiana. I think maybe that is what touched home to Abe. She was like him in appearance and if not for a slightly darker skin there was no telling she was a slave.

Slavery was a strange curse. Lincoln couldn't fathom how the color of ones skin made one less a person. Circumstance might or predilection, but not the color of their body. We both saw plenty of friends and neighbors who were darker than the poor girl.

At this point she was still on the block, still in chains. Now there were prospective buyers pawing at her. She was then stripped naked in order to make sure she had no blemishes or marks that indicated poor discipline and prior beatings.

They were squeezing her arms and legs to check for muscle tone, had her open her mouth to inspect her teeth and gums, then peered into her eyes, ears and nose. They looked over her hands and fingers to check to see how calloused they were, then her feet and toes, for what reason we knew not. They then bent her over and peered here and there I dare not say where.

All the while they were pestering the slave trader with numerous questions. We were much too far away to hear what they were saying but by the gestures the buyers used they weren't friendly and if I'm sure they were downright demeaning. A few times they seemed to ask the girl a question and were even more marked in their obvious disdain.

New Orleans was a buyers' market. The demand was high, but

the pickings were numerous. Some of the buyers were traders themselves. These would take the most promising slaves and travel to more isolated areas where the prices favored the seller and they could make a tidy profit.

There were a large number of slaves who were so dark they seemed like the blackest night. These knew absolutely no English or French and it seemed pretty clear they came from either the islands littering the Caribbean Sea or from the dark continent itself. Importing slaves had been illegal for some years now but it was one thing to say you couldn't do something and another thing to keep them from doing it anyways.

It was that way with bringing slaves to America. Not many do it and most who did bring them in would unload them at a smaller port and then bring them into New Orleans or maybe Mobile, Alabama by land. That way it would look like the slaves were domestic property. It didn't matter much since federal agents usually looked the other way or took a little money to ignore it. The agents were mostly southern born anyway so they didn't mind the trade, especially if it lined their pockets a bit.

I was looking around and taking in the sights but Lincoln had his eyes set on that little girl the entire time. I saw his hands clench and unclench several times and I could tell he was working some things out in his brain. He finally looked over at me.

"The sooner we get our business done the better. I'd like to put some miles between us and this accursed town as soon possible. If I had to walk from here to the fabled holy land I wouldn't mind if I never had to see the sights I saw today ever again."

I myself found the whole incident disgusting but it didn't affect me the way it did him. We didn't speak about it again during our time in New Orleans and we stood there only a short time before we began the long walk back home.

Much of those first miles were quiet. I was cheerful enough, but Abe was unlike himself. He was deep in thought most of the time and even when we were eating he was mostly silent, which was odd indeed.

Finally about noon on the second day he opened up a bit. Right as we squatted down to eat some food we had in our handkerchief we each had dangling from a stick. Without even looking at me he just spoke with a most somber and serious voice.

"If I ever am given a chance to strike a blow at that infernal institution, I will strike it hard. I swear it." He swore.

After his vow he opened up a bit and the rest of the trip turned out to be uneventful but always entertaining with Abe's never ending gift of gab. I was thankful for it since I didn't want to trek 1000 miles without speaking!

*this is an alternative version of the previous tale of Lincoln's second trip to New Orleans and in this version John Hanks is said to have turned back towards home in St. Louis. Whether true or not is anyone's guess at this point in time.

*this story is often cited as the driving force behind Abraham Lincoln's desire to keep slavery from spreading to the territories. He did not believe the President or Congress had the right to address slavery in the states. That was a question for the states themselves or through a Constitutional Amendment (according to Lincoln's many statements (on & off the record) on the subject).

THIRST FOR KNOWLEDGE

Stephen Douglas sat as if he was a king presiding over his court, in this case a court of sycophantic supporters and reporters. The Little Giant was in his element. Among those seated about him were some of the most prominent newsmen of the day from Illinois and the surrounding states, and even a handful from large cities along the east coast. They were there to report about the Illinois Senator running for reelection and a possible future run in the next Presidential Election of 1860. He was big news as always, but maybe never bigger before than he was now during what eventually became known as the Great Senate Race of 1858.

That was how Douglas felt about it. He knew he faced a formidable opponent. He probably knew more about his rival than most and had tussled with him before whether behind the bar or in more personal matters like wooing the same girl. Douglas had lost that particular fight, but he had won many of the others and felt this election was a foregone conclusion and a fitting stepping stone to the Presidency. And this was one stone he was determined not to stumble over on his quest to achieve his lifelong goal.

All were hanging on his every word, recording his every gesture, and the Little Giant did not fail to disappoint in giving them a show. He was quite the showman, as many of the most successful politicians of his day, and certainly afterwards had to be. But Douglas was the best, or at least the most famous. Oratory was a politician's bread and butter these days. If you couldn't hold a crowd with your oratory skill you were all but doomed to fail.

The topic of the evening, as these great wordsmiths sipped wine, brandy, whiskey, or whatever their preferred poison and smoked their cigars (virtually all smoked cigars or pipes, as cigarettes were rare and the smoke filling the room made the scene a bit hazy), was Douglas's surprising debate opponent. Abraham Lincoln was relatively unknown compared to the nationally prominent Douglas, except to the state officials in the room who knew all too well about the tall, lanky, former Illinois state representative and representative to the national House of Representatives.

Abraham Lincoln had dropped into obscurity after his one and only term in Congress almost a decade ago, and that term turned out to be undistinguished at that. His only claim to fame, or more like infamy, was his assertion the Mexican War was illegal and his demand for then President Polk to point out the spot where Americans were said to be attacked to start the Mexican War. It was never a wise policy to resist a war in American politics and even though Lincoln subsequently voted for every war appropriation bill during his term, he was remembered for his ill-chosen words on the ill-fated bill he had sponsored during his time representing his state in Congress.

Most northern politicians had long forgotten one other bill Lincoln tried to have passed just before his term expired, but no self respecting Southern politician did. That was Lincoln's effort to have slavery banned in the capital. This was remembered with a burning intensity by the Southern man and was the font from which their hatred of Lincoln forever brewed.

What brought him back into the political trenches and as a founder of the Republican party in Illinois and nationally, was the heated slavery issue surrounding the Kansas Nebraska Act, sponsored by none other than Douglas himself. This lit the veritable fire in Lincoln's belly that was never extinguished. It became his calling card, his rallying cry and as one of the founders of the Republican party in Illinois it reignited his career from the ash heap of political failures.

The New York reporter, unaccustomed to western politics

chimed in "These are some spacious accommodations for a train ride Senator!"

Douglas took the bait as he so often did and ran with it but in a way the easterner could not have predicted, "Yes indeed. George McClellan treats his patrons very well."

"Do you think your opponent Lincoln has such comfortable surroundings?"

"To each his own stature my friend." This was accompanied by a string of laughter by Douglas' numerous sycophants. But the illustrious politician continued, "Lincoln is a man who needs not the creature comforts to feel at home. It is not to say he is a lesser man. It is to say the accouterments we might find pleasing may be alien to him. It's not to say they wouldn't be most welcome. They just may be wasted upon a man who needs them not."

This didn't do much to quell the New Yorker's curiosity but rather played into it. "What sort of man might not find these comforts acceptable? I mean, what sort of man is Lincoln? Are you facing a cave man, like the one found recently in the mountains of Germany?"

This referred to a discovery just published illuminating the educated masses about a completely different sort of Man that had no schooling in faith and was thus of the most uncivilized and uncouth a man as could be. To tie Lincoln to this breed would hold much weight in the east indeed.

Douglas would not fall for the bait handed to him. He was far too polished a campaigner, and he had known Lincoln far too long to ever believe he could be anything other than the most cultivated of men, no matter what his lineage or upbringing and he made sure to make his feelings known here and now, be damned to any who would besmirch his worthy opponent.

"Lincoln is no more a cave man than I am," Douglas proclaimed. "And you can see right clearly I have not the height nor prominent chin or brow to proclaim my birthright as kin to that unworthy race!"

Much laughter ensued as Douglas wished. But he desired the listeners to know more about his worthy opponent, a man he had known for twenty years and always respected, as much as Lincoln respected him. They should know this man By God, because Stephen Douglas knew he was the most formidable adversary he had ever faced even though this is the first time they opposed each other in the political arena.

"Abraham Lincoln rides in this very train with us, though in much reduced circumstances." He began. "But this does not mean he should be slighted in any way, shape or form. As he has proven in this first debate, he has every reason to not only be taking the platform to speak against my views, but he has every reason to believe he may win."

"No! No!" His entourage chimed in unison.

"Yes, yes indeed." Douglas answered. "Lincoln is a most worthy adversary. I posit he is the most worthy of all the opponents the Whigs, or shall I say "Republicans" to coin the term they now wish to apply themselves, could ever prop up against me."

"How can this be?" Asked the New York reporter incredulously but ever eager for a story to send back to his newspaper. "I have never met him, but I heard he is a most uncouth individual if I ever did espy one!"

"Well he is that," answered Douglas after a quaff of his glass of bourbon and a quick smoke. "He certainly isn't much to look at and quite queer to the eye he is. But that's not what he is about. Lincoln is not a man whom you judge by looks. You don't judge a book by its cover and for Lincoln that expression is more apt than to most."

"Now you have to understand the man before you judge him, and I know Lincoln more than most anyone. We have been both friends and foes for nigh twenty years now and he has been a thorn in my side more than once."

Now all those gathered leaned in a bit and started puffing away at their pipes and cigars or taking a quick swig or two of their glass knowing there was a tale in the making.

"Lincoln isn't much to look at, unless you want to take a laugh or two at his own expense, I give you that my friends. But to do that is to do the man a grave injustice. You see he is one of the sorts that is more than meets the eye."

"He is a man who pulled himself up by his own bootstraps. He came from little or nothing when he arrived in Springfield, but he made a name for himself in no time at all and all by his own means. Not many of us can say the same thing I think." Douglas cast a mean glare around before he continued.

"Now I know Lincoln a long time you see but I didn't know how he came here until he told me during one of the many nights we spent running the circuit before either of us became prominent citizens and the like." He looked over at the New York City Reporter looking perplexed.

"You didn't know that now did you?" Douglas asked. Then he continued, "Yes, the two of us knew each other quite well for over a dozen years before we became political enemies though we always remained friends. We even had to share a bed once or twice when circumstances dictated it. He might think one way and I another but there is no other man I would trust more than Abraham Lincoln. Just don't let that filter down into your paper." He said with a meaningful look at the NYC reporter.

"I'm only repeating what it is I read from Lincoln himself," retorted the reporter a little defensively then continued somewhat apprehensively. "His own autobiography emphasizes his lack of education and exceedingly poor background."

"Indeed it does," agreed Douglas now in his own element, having led the reporter unwittingly into the main points of his narrative. "Lincoln remarks upon his family's limited means as a way of giving weight to his remarkable feat in educating himself with the barest of support. He has expressed this to me on numerous occasions during our many long discussions."

"I believe he had perhaps a half dozen books he could call his own starting with a Bible, I believe it was the King James version. Included in his library, if you could call it that, was the Revised Statutes of Indiana & John Bunyan's Pilgrim's Progress. Aesop's Fables & William Scott's Lessons in Elocution completed his meagre store of written works, but a most worthy starting point for any would be orator if I do say so myself."

"From this humble beginning he began to explore the world of the written word and from then on he would procure any and every tome he could lay his hands upon, at times walking miles or offering manual labor for the opportunity to borrow the book for a few days, sometimes only having the briefest period in order to consume its contents. And consume them he would! Lincoln has a remarkable memory. He may be slow to learn, by his own account and no doubt due to the late start to his education and paucity of formal training. However, once he digested something it would indelibly stick to his brain like dried sap to a tree."

"Among other books Abe read were one or more ancient histories, a history of the United States, Kirkem's Grammar and the Arabian Nights. He later found in his small library the great fable Robinson Crusoe and a story of the Life of George Washington. All of these are worthy books and ones he made the most out of his reading of them."

"Through them he learned turns of phrases that you will note when you hear him speak and uses them to great effect. He in turn discovered the basic foundation of the laws of God & Man to the mysteries of the world and beyond into the realm of myth and fantasy. You will clearly see the pattern of biblical nuances and even some expressions that come straight from Aesop himself. Since his youth he has read extensively and assiduously from such great writers like Shakespeare and our own Edgar Allen Poe, and from these he has taken what he could and made them his own."

"Often times one might wonder at first what Lincoln was getting at with his tale. It may seem to be completely off kilter but by the end of it he would have made his point. And that point was always relevant to the circumstances and he was quite often bound to be right in the end, however much you might not like it. Perhaps not as correct as one such as I, but at least so frequently as to entrance the less refined to believe that he held some superior wisdom along with common sense."

"Now to get to my point without belaboring it any further. As I said young Lincoln would walk miles to get a book if he found one available and do whatever work was required to lay his hands on them. This was how he got his hands on many of his books, and I will tell you about two of them."

"His father didn't take too kindly to Abe's reading though he may have been more inclined to deal with it if he didn't often find Abe neglecting his daily chores or work in order to catch some time reading. His father, Thomas by name, would become infuriated if he found Abe regaling his coworkers with tales he picked up from his reading when they were involved in jobs together. Tom felt he was not only delaying the completion of the work but taking out from the time for whomever the job was being done and leading others to take up Abe's lazy habits. Not to say the boy was lazy. He wasn't but it could seem that way at times."

"As I said, if Abe found a neighbor had a book he would walk miles to his house and see what he could do to borrow it. That was mostly true when he moved out on his own. He would often read the magazines and periodicals he would be delivering to farmers outside New Salem when he was Postmaster or while tending shop in that self-same town long since abandoned. He studied law mostly by the reading of dozens of law books from such eminent writers of the time like William Blackstone and Joseph Story."

"Before that time, he found it troublesome to find any books to read and ponder. Books were not so readily available as they are in our big cities or anywhere out east. In the backwoods of Kentucky and Indiana they were hard to come by indeed. But Abe would find them when he could and read them as often as possible. Every night when he got home from farming or working as a hired hand, or if he stayed over at a neighbor's farm because he was hired for a job that would take more than a few days and the trek was long from his home he would be reading. Sometimes he would read when he went with his father to town for some business, but most often at those times he would play with other kids because he didn't see them often and he loved to be in a group usually entertaining everyone."

"One time he got real sore at his father. Abe was working at a neighbor's home and he finished the job early. Since Abe was already there and rather than have Abe just walk home since his father would be coming to get him later the neighbor wanted to keep Abe working. Abe was such a good worker the neighbor knew he could get a lot done. So the neighbor asked Abe to do some extra work. Now Abe knew the neighbor had a book he was itching to get his hands on so Abe said he would do it if the neighbor would let him borrow the book."

"The neighbor knew a good deal when he heard one and immediately agreed. Abe was so happy he did the job quicker than a hare with a cat on its tail and then helped with some chores and still was able to get to reading some of the book before his father ever got there."

"Now when Tom got there the neighbor was happy to have had Abe do so much work and wanted to get the boy for another even bigger job of clearing some of the woods to fence in another large part of his land. Then he let slip that he got Abe to do some odd jobs for borrowing a book. I guess the neighbor couldn't pass up and opportunity to let Tom or anyone else for that matter know when he got a good deal."

"Tom was none too pleased about it since that was money or barter he could use for the family. So he immediately got to arguing and knowing of Tom and his way with words he got the neighbor to give up some corn for the extra jobs Abe did and Abe had to give the book back."

"Now Abe was awful sore but Tom was in the right there. Abe was his boy and couldn't be making deals with his time without his Father's say so. Now Abe knew that in his heart, but he never could set it right with himself that having to give up his own hard labor for someone else."

"Lincoln might have been the best at menial work among his peers, and when he got to doing work he sure worked harder at it than anyone but Abe didn't like to do work with his hands. He didn't like it one bit. He thought it better and easier to do work with his head, and far more lucrative. He was surely right, as we all can agree."

The car burst into hearty laughter with much nodding of their heads in sycophantic agreement.

"But it just wasn't right for him to do that without his father's say so. His father owned him until he reached twenty-first year. His father knew what was best for Abe but more importantly the family. Abe wasn't looking out for the family when he made the deal. Tom was always looking out for the family. Abe would do anything for the family, but he had a mind of his own."

"Abe thought he was a bit better than everyone. It's true that he was better at working, at sports and he could speak and knew things better than most others, but it wasn't right to think that way. As our Founding Father Thomas Jefferson stated in words that every true American knows "All Men Are Created Equal", and so it is true."

More nodding with a few murmurings of, "Hear, Hear."

Mr. Douglas never got to the rest of his story of Abraham Lincoln's reading for just at that moment the train lurched, spilling a drink or two of those gathered and stirring up a string of oaths all around. A train attendant soon emerged from the forward cabin to announce they were nearing the next stop, and this broke up the impromptu gathering as all went back to their respective cabins or seats to prepare for disembarking.

For his part, Douglas went to his specially prepared parlor. He was expected to give a few words before the morrow's debate and he needed to prepare himself and his appearance so as to offer the greatest spectacle to those who would greet him at the station.

*asking for something to be kept under ones hat these days doesn't have as much meaning today as it did in other times. Nowadays getting clicks online will drive even the more scrupulous pundits to ignore such a plea and even if demanding they not be recorded their words may often filter down through "anonymous" sources. This, however, was a time in American history where such a soft request to keep something confidential was honored for the reporter would know if he didn't he may never get an opportunity to speak with the celebrity and by granting their request they would often be privy to benefits their rivals would not receive.

A WAY WITH WORDS

"There was many a time when Abe and me would be working the fields together. Oftentimes we were working our own field or one of our neighbor's, some of whom were relatives by blood or marriage. But there were many a time when we were hired out a bit away from home or even into a nearby town itself to do some work for a wage to be given to father Thomas." John Johnston was speaking to a stranger while standing on a street corner in St. Louis. He had been engaging in a scheme to get some investment money for a plan he and one of his many partners had to start a ferry service across the Mississippi river.

John Johnston had wished on more than one occasion to leave his place besides his family and his father in law to pursue a course similar to Lincoln's but not within the same profession. He wished to pursue a course in land speculation or working mines and/or seeking his fortune in California in search of gold.

Now Lincoln was not keen on these ideas for the reasons, as he explained that those pursuits carried much risk that far outweighed the potential rewards. He felt John had a better chance of making his mark by working his farm, or if he left that work to his father in law and John's son, then John could hire himself out and make money while still being close to home and tending to his family's needs.

When John wished to move with his immediate family from Illinois to Missouri and start afresh on a new farm but needed such sums as he felt he could only get from Lincoln. Abe dissuaded him from doing so by commenting he didn't think he could find a better farming opportunity in Missouri as he already had in Illinois and leaving his father in law in a lurch. Abe had even offered to match any money John could make by staying home near the family from his own purse, but John never took his step brother up on that offer.

For some time, John D Johnston was resentful of his brother in law. He didn't understand how Abraham felt perfectly comfortable leaving his father of blood knowing he could be cared for by his cousin and brother in law, while when John wished to do so knowing that Tom had other relatives living with him that could tend to him and his farm, he was advised against this course of action by Abe. John had a family and needed funds in order to guarantee they could live a while with bare necessities until he could lay in a crop or begin work. Abe had left as a young man, alone, so needed little in such a way as he could readily find enough to get by until he could have a stable occupation or start a farm. Abe also spent some time speculating and failed, when he tried his hand as a merchant, then spent decades before he could repay. He didn't want to allow John the same opportunity perhaps in fear that John would be successful where Lincoln had failed, or so John liked to think.

John was a flashy dresser, spent more than he earned and was always on the lookout for the quick way to strike it rich rather than earn his keep. He was a good worker when he did work but often found ways to shirk his responsibilities. He was quick to point the finger at others rather than take the blame himself.

His mother loved both Abraham and John dearly but clearly thought that Abraham was the better son both morally and intellectually. John couldn't help but notice for his mother was an honest person and this led to a resentment against his brother and a belief that Abe had abandoned his father because he knew that John was there and less able to fend for himself in his own, all of which was partially true. Abe did send money to help his father on occasion and did visit them though this was infrequently and never with his own family.

After Tom died John ventured with his new wife to Arkansas but soon failed at farming there and returned shortly to Coles country Illinois before he decided to try his hand at farming in Missouri but he lost everything there. After this failure he then tried his hand at getting a ferry service started in the bustling city of St. Louis amidst much competition.

The stranger had expressed an interest and while not rich, he did have ready cash and that was all John needed to know. The stranger had heard Abe speak once and was intrigued about John's association with Lincoln and this led him into a long monologue about his step brother. The stranger had always lived in big cities so Lincoln's method of oratory was alien to him but he found it mesmerizing. John was hoping to bedazzle the man by his relationship with a man the stranger clearly admired and through it to "cash in". He tried to affect Abe's easy way of speaking, at one time he had had a bit of the gift of gab himself, but a hard life and lack of education had an ill effect on his once considerable skills.

"It was one of these times," John continued, "that Abe and me had work to do in town. We were hired out to assist in the loading and unloading of some wagons with feed for several farms that surrounded the town. Then we had to unload other wagons that were already hitched outside the general store and some other wagons that were due to come there that day and the next. Most of these had some provisions or other and it was quite a bit of work to be done."

"Both of us were young and strong and took to the task with gusto. I was considered a pretty strong lad in the area and hefted a sack of grain with ease, but Abe could lift two, one with each arm and walk them over. I do say this made my work a bit easier but Abe never paid that no mind and we were both paid the same amount for our work for the day."

"Not that the pay mattered to us since pa would be getting it. I didn't really care about that, pa being pa, but it always seemed to rankle Abe some. It never did set right with Abe that his work was paid to someone, even if it was his own father. Being the biggest and boldest gave Abe stronger feelings of his own ability and a higher standing of his worth as a person."

"Today's work was much like many another day but it was memorable to me in one way. This was the day the town all first got a taste of Abe's remarkable skill in speaking, his ability to spin a yarn. I've got none of this mind you but Abe got this ability from his father. Some say his grandfather also had this skill, Thomas being one, but none can say for sure since his granddad was killed before any of us who knew Thomas then were alive or acquainted with ole' Tom, as the townspeople and neighbors called him."

"Election time is rolling around in Illinois. Have you ever been?" John asked the stranger.

"To Illinois? Can't say that I have. I have never been more than ten miles outside St. Louis." John was answered.

"You aren't missing all that much. A lot of yokels in those parts outside Chicago but it's fun listening and watching the candidates canvassing for votes. I guess you never saw a stump speech then."

"What is a stump speech?"

"Well it's quite the lark I tell you. You get a candidate who sees a crowd gathering in a small town. It's usually around a time of a fair, after the harvest, or maybe on Sunday, any time when farmers will have the time to go to market or attend church services. The would be politician will find a convenient stump from which to perch themselves and start railing on about this and that."

"That's about how Abe started off himself. Now when he was still young, we both saw one of these candidates try his hand at a stump speech. It was right comical with his flailing arms and jumping up and down like a rabbit. But that was nothing until Lincoln got his chance at the stump. "

"Now see this man finishes up and gets off the stump and starts ambling away. He was roundly congratulated for his oratory and began to continue canvassing. People in them parts were quite amazed about nothing so to them the man spoke well. Then Abe pops himself up on the stump and starts off in a speech exactly like the one we just heard and he is flailing and jumping about just like the speaker but he exaggerated the motions and way the man spoke to make it even more comical."

"He drew such a crowd that you couldn't walk by, not that you wanted to. He had grown men rolling around laughing. But that was Abe's way. Now his pa saw how Abe had started on the candidate, how the man was agitated by the boy's mocking speech, and how the merchant Abe's pa was meeting to hire us out to was clearly not pleased. This led Abe's pa, Tom, to wallop him off the stump and cuff Abe on the side of the head."

"Tom then had to argue with the merchant for him to have Abe work. I think the merchant must have been a supporter of that politician. But it was clear from the beginning that Abe could stir emotions like none other."

The would be speculator chimed in, "Mr. Lincoln's oratory was something to behold. He had a way of saying things that made it easy for anyone to understand. It was as if he was in my mind a conjuring picture as clear as day."

John concurred, "That was Abe alright. He could pretty up a speech so's the high falooting educated lawyers and such would be there with mouths agape applauding his every word, or make his speech so easy on the ears even the simplest folk could make head and tails of it."

"Now Abe he could do all that see because Abe was good at mimicking. He could watch anyone speak and then he could repeat word for word what they said. What was more he could ape them. He was like a monkey imitating their gyrations while he spoke in the same manner they did. If that wasn't funny enough he did it with a comic way and that could get us all a laughing in seconds."

"He could mimic anything and anyone. He got that from his pa he did but Lincoln was even better at it if I dare say. You said you heard Abe speak. You must have heard the way he speaks in front of a crowd of educated men."

The man nodded.

"Well you know Abe could speak that way. But what you don't know is how he could speak so the poorest farmer could understand as well as the most educated man in all America. That was just the way Abe was. And this is how he learned it. He learned it by watching. He was always watching. He once told me he would watch his pa when ole' Tom was entertaining strangers passing through on their way to whereever they be going."

"Now at that time pa's farm was located along the old Cumberland trail, I don't rightly know if they still using it, not with railroads criss crossing the east. But being along a trail at that time it gave Abe many a chance for practicing and honing ability as a storyteller and mimicking. He could mimic a person movements, their accents and even their face."

"He learned all this from pa's storytelling and mimicking. He would watch each night as pa was entertaining travelers who would room and board with ole' Tom."

"When it came to speaking it was a gift Abe received from Tom and his granddad. Tom would love to listen to his father speak and he would watch and wonder how everyone just loved him.

Now Tom was able to do the same thing but better.

Tom was loved everywhere he went and lived. He could talk a snake out of its skin if he wanted. Now Tom would talk in a way that common folk could understand. It made people feel close to Tom. They never felt Tom was any better than them but they thought he was the friendliest man in the world. He could make them laugh or cry with a story and people would always stop and listen when Tom spoke. They still do I reckon."

"Now Abe would listen intently to the stories each night. After bed he would sit up until late and practice in his mind for hours. He would think long and hard over the words pa used. Most of those he didn't rightly know but he had a long memory. He would think about all the words and get to figuring what the words he didn't know meant by going over in his mind the whole story."

"He would change the words pa used and those who boarded with them used. He would mix them up and make the words easy for the other children who lived nearby. That way they could understand what the story was. The next time he would be with his friends he would go up on a ready stump or maybe have them all gather round him and mesmerize all of them by his ability to spin a tale and mimic the adults!"

"So it was from watching his pa that taught Abe the way of speaking so that his audience, if they were a farmer or lawyer, it didn't matter, they understand him easy like, like he was in their mind putting the words there himself. Abe became an expert through watching his pa speak."

"When he got older, and learned to read, he used to sit by the fire each night and read whatever book he happened to have. He would go over the stories and many a time I remember him telling me stories he used to read. I used to think most of them were silly. He'd be talking about riding magic carpets, or an ass talking to frogs and a tortoise racing rabbits. A whole bunch a nonsense I'd say and still do!"

"But Abe once told me it was these silly stories and learning how to read and from all those great writers that he learned how to change the way he was talking to anyone could catch on to what he was saying. Now I know this is true because you come to me now asking all about how Abe became so good at speaking. Maybe all that nonsense was a godsend to him."

"Now not everyone liked that and Tom being all practical minded he didn't like it one but when adults were around. Now Abe didn't have all that much time spending with people other than his kin so when he did he always tried to make the most of it. He was always the center of attention and there was nothing Abe liked more than being the center of the fun. And he always loved to have fun."

"Some people like to say that Abe was a sad man. Now he knew sadness maybe no one more, but everyone who lived out west knew sadness. Everyone had someone close to him die or lost something. Abe he lost his brother, his mother, his sister, aunts and uncles all before he became a man. Then he lost his little boy Edward not too long ago. So Abe knew about loss, just like we all did. I lost my own pa when I was even younger than Abe." There was a bit of resentment in John's voice, and he seemed to lose his train of thought for a moment, but it quickly passed.

"Always mimicking others he was, especially elders and one of his favorite pastimes would be to mimic his teachers and pretend he was one after class. He loved to jabber."

"You mentioned that already," the stranger was getting a bit antsy trying to figure out where John was going with his story. John didn't pay him no mind but nodded and continued.

"When he got older he would go to all the dances, he would, but didn't dance very often. Instead he would have all the boys gathered around him since Abe would be telling jokes, mimicking some one or such, turning handsprings or stretching all that way backwards until his hands touched the ground and generally being the center of attention. Oftentimes the girls would fret a bit since they couldn't get the boys to come over and dance with them since they was having too much fun cavorting with Abe and listening to his stories."

"Now here was the thing with these stories. You might wonder at first what Lincoln was getting at with his tale. It may seem to be completely off kilter but by the end of it he would have made his point. And that point was always right to the circumstances and he was most often bound to be right in the end, however much you might not like it."

John had gotten to rambling a bit and the speculator took the opportunity to interrupt. Informing Johnston that he had a pressing engagement elsewhere he took his leave and moved off a bit hurriedly. It was then that John realized he never had gotten the man to commit to any sort of investing, or even gotten to describing the great opportunity, nor did he get a card or any way of contacting the man in the future. That was John's way. He had the form of Abe's storytelling without the substance. He could never wind the story to a point the listerner could grasp or could help John.

Calling out to the gentlemen, it was too late. He had passed into the bustling crowd leaving John with nothing to show for the time spent except another reason, he felt, to resent his ever-successful stepbrother.

*While there may be little truth in the above depiction of resentment felt by John Johnston towards Abraham Lincoln there is every indication that having an exemplary example of his stepbrother to live up to from his youth onwards may have affected John detrimentally. Perhaps he lacked the physical and mental gifts to the extent that were so evident in his stepbrother, or Abe's great ambition, perhaps a little of each. Whatever it was John never saw his plans come to fruition and after a series of failed attempts he returned to Illinois, and eventually died penniless of unknown circumstances in 1860.

AMERICA'S HERCULES

Old Tom rarely spoke of his son, but when he did it was in glowing terms and one could always sense the deep pride that he had in his only surviving child. One occasion occurred in the winter of 1850, a few months before his death, as he sat with his extended family around the fireside.

Thomas Lincoln's voice had begun to fail him, but he lost none of his dazzling charisma that burst forth when he would spin a tale. Tom was as brilliant an orator as his illustrious son, though his speech was never as polished, and the subject matter was far more down to earth. Even so it took only a few moments of listening to the old pioneer weave a tale before anyone could easily see where the President had picked up much of his speaking ability.

Abraham had been a master of mimicry from a young age and his quick, fertile mind was ever ready to pick up any little thing that others did, remembering these quirky traits forever. His mind was like a steel trap with a memory like the proverbial elephant. Less well known was the fact that not only did he inherit his speaking abilities from his father but also his legendary strength.

Many thought the President gained his immense stature and herculean strength from his constant labor as a youth. This was true enough, he certainly honed his muscled frame from the unrelenting work he did for his family, neighbors and anyone who would pay his father. He was also certainly much taller than his father, and while having similar facial features, there the similarities ended. Lincoln was tall but lanky and rather thin for his height. His father was of more average height but stocky and built like a wall. His grip was like iron and in his prime he was every bit as strong as his illustrious scion.

Thomas leaned back in his small, roughly hewn but well-made chair, bound with leather, and smiled. The glint that was ever present in his eye when he told a story shone forth like a reflected ray of the sun. His younger kinfolk sat around him, some with legs crossed, others lying on their bellies with their legs bent at the knees behind them, feet in the air, and their little heads propped up by their heads. One of them had just had the temerity to boldly assert that one of his friends' older brothers was the strongest boy the village had ever seen.

This prompted the patriarch of the Lincoln clan here in Decatur to give the young lad a proper lesson in the family history.

"Well my little wolf cub," Old Tom playfully began. "That boy might well be said to be the strongest lad of this here village. But not the strongest the village had ever seen since last time I checked we Lincolns are a part of the village too. Or are we not of this town?"

The boy quickly nodded, having not thought about the situation like that before. Tom loved to engage his audience at various points of his story in order to draw them into the tale, and make them feel a part of it. His son did this far less often, in his speeches preferring to ask rhetorical questions for his listeners to ponder, and then answering them himself to unconsciously draw the audience to the conclusions he desired them to reach.

Tom continued, "I think you know fairly well who I am speaking of, but I could add that even at my advanced age I still have formidable strength in me. Come here my lad," He said to one of his niece's sons. The boy got up from his cross-legged position and scampered up to his grand uncle.

"Now clasp my hand, boy." The boy did so. The young lad was perhaps ten years old and was quite big and strong for his age, his hands well calloused from the many hours spent outdoors at various jobs but mostly due to wielding the axe, an ever-present tool for an enterprising young farmhand.

Tom seemed a weathered old man, much older than his 72 years, and a bit frail. However, he still had much latent power in him and his grip was like iron to the boy. The boy winced slightly and Thomas let go with a grin.

"You seem to have gotten to be quite a strong boy yourself. Maybe in a few years they will be saying the same of you! But for myself, I remember well my son, and Dennis here does likewise."

Tom nodded to Dennis Hanks, his "stepson" and only holdover

besides John Johnston, who happened to be away this evening, from the time decades ago when Abraham Lincoln had been a farmhand, much like the boy. It was not here but in Indiana where the two had labored side by side for years. Dennis was almost 10 years older than his stepbrother but even then young Abe was as strong as him, and Dennis was no slouch when it came to feats of strength.

Dennis had stayed with his stepfather after Abraham had left to find his own way. He had a farm nearby and was often at his Thomas' home, as this evening. He had watched and labored for Tom as his family grew from a small one of less than a handful when Abe had departed to now presiding over an extended family of over fifty members, one of the largest in the county.

Dennis nodded and smiled, always happy to be a part of Tom's tale whether his role be large or small. It always gave him a blush of pride that his father would include him in his stories. It gave him a piece of immortality, in his own small way. Maybe one day others would know a bit about him from the stories passed down from Tom and Abraham Lincoln.

"Now Abraham Lincoln as a boy that was bearing an axe the size of yours by the time he was six years. Before he reached his tenth summer he had grown to a height and had the strength and skill to wield that many an adult would have trouble hefting. And even the one of he used to cut his first tree would have been too much for any of the city folk he now deals with to handle."

The family had a nice laugh at that one. It was always good to joke at the city dwellers' expense at their naivety when it came to the tasks farmers found so simple at an early age. At one time it was rare to see any one from the eastern cities anywhere near their neck of the woods. Now it was becoming far more frequent to find one either passing through or seeking to settle nearby.

The land of the Near West and the country at large was becoming smaller with the invention of railroads. Populations were exploding all throughout the country as it approached its eightieth year in existence. This growth was due to natural causes but also in no small part to the vast increase of immigrants coming from northern parts of the Old World, and even some from southern Europe. Where once you would almost never see someone who had never seen the vast cornfields of Indiana except depicted in miniature on a painting at a home or museum to the east, now it was becoming far more common to meet those to whom farming was as alien as a tea shop in the Orient.

There were still not many railroads in the state, and connections between them were iffy to say the least, but it was only a matter of time before they stretched across the country. And if Abraham Lincoln had his way it would certainly be sooner rather than later. It was one of his pet projects to expand the infrastructure of his adopted state of Illinois and one of the main ways he sought to do it was by extending railroads wherever he could legislate to lay the tracks. A fair portion of his law practice was increasingly involved in cases related to railroads, and Lincoln was quick to see the advantages that lay in this new technology. Where once he saw the future in harnessing the power of river transport, now he was fully in support of the iron horse as the new means for American prosperity.

If there is another parallel between Abraham Lincoln and the railroad it would be in its test of strength. You could easily have substituted Honest Abe in place of Paul Bunyon in the fable of Paul vs. the Train. The only difference would be instead of hewing his way through a mountain, Lincoln would have cut his way through a forest.

"Now my boy Abe, it was said" Tom said as he cleaned and refilled his pipe, "was able at the age most boys would still be spending most of their time frittering away their time in the woods, to do the work of two or three men. It was quite a bargain for those who would deal with me for my son's labor to get him at an equal wage of one man."

"The first few times I asked for a man's price for the work of my boy some neighbors scoffed and felt I was trying to pull a fast one on them. I merely smiled and said if Abe wasn't able to pull his own weight during the course of the day then I would refund them the full price I asked. I am happy and proud to say I never once had to give one cent back for the work of my son."

"I remember there was one time when I came out to fetch Abe on an outlying farm. I came upon the farmer near the gate of his land. When I pulled up in my wagon I saw the boy just finishing up hauling a load of firewood as the farmer beamed up at me."

"'Why that boy is a monster of a worker! I came out to bring him some lunch as he was working off in the woods cutting wood. It was a ways off from the cabin so I thought I would save him some time and bring him some bread, cheese, nuts and berries. As I approached I heard such a din of cuttin I never heard before. I could've sworn there was three full grown men a hacking away at the trees and I seen them falling before I could see the workers themselves. I was even wondering if I had somehow got lost in my way coming out there because I had only hired your lad for the day. But lo and behold, it was just your boy, out there like a machine doin the work of three men."

"I thought when you set me that price I would feel lucky to have gotten the work of two boys out of him. By my word it was I that got the bargain out of you. That boy it worth twice the price you been chargin me!"

"Now that farmer was quite willing to give me twice the wages for my Abraham right then and there for the work he did, but as my boy strode up looking now worse for all the work he did that day, I said the price I set was the price I would take and not one penny more. Needless to say he not only didn't complain again about any price I asked but he was looking to get his hands on my Abraham any chance he could get!"

Tom had finished refilling his pipe and took a moment to set a light to it. Once he got it going good, with a nice red glow and a puff of smoke wafting out from it each time he stopped inhaling, he continued, "You might say, and from the look of your knowing eye, I dare say you will say it! Why I'm spinning a yarn! That don't prove nothing no how. You don't have to be the strongest man alive to be able to hack a tree with the best of them, and I dare say to you, You're right! That don't really prove anything."

"But I ask you, can you hold an axe upright by the handle with one hand and hold your arm out from your chest? As strong as you are little John I don't doubt you won't be able to do it with that small axe you have. Now our Honest Abe was barely out of his teens when he could do it with the great axe he used to use up until he was an adult working in New Salem and never touched an axe since. I would bet everything in our house he could still do it today!"

Legends of Lincoln

"But I do agree with you on one score. Being able to do wonders with an axe is one thing, and a big thing at that. But that don't hold that he would be the strongest Man in these or any parts. It was the tool he lived by as a young lad and we know we use different parts of our body when we have to do different work. We don't use the same muscles handling a plow, hauling wood or dragging a sled."

"Now I'll tell you some stories I had to hear from old Dennis here, or maybe from your Uncle Abe when he would come visit, though he hasn't done so in quite some time. But during the time he was in New Salem and then Springfield he was first itching to get into public office."

"Those parts then, like today, are full of its fair share of woods, and farmers had their work cut out for them clearing the land to raise crops. Now my boy Abe wasn't doing that sort of work anymore, at least none too often. He was minding a store or mill, or maybe he was surveying the land for speculators. You would have thought he lost that rough edge and the muscles that were once as honed as a newly sharpened axe had become as dull as a blade that had been spending the past week cutting down a few dozen trees."

"Not my Abe! To most farmers the worth of a politician lay in measuring up to tasks or feats of prowess they can lay their eyes on themselves. They felt any politician could spit out some fancy talk but could they back it up with the understanding of the trials that came with farming by being able to master the deeds a farmer had to do a dozen times a day or more."

"So they would look at Abe squarely and eye him up and down a bit. They would see he was tall as a tree verily, but as thin as a birch as well. To themselves they might be thinking that the lad could never measure up. He might look like a farm boy with his ill fitting clothes and down to earth demeanor, but that was just spit and polish, making him look that part."

"They would say to him, "Well you may look like you are salt of the earth but I don't care much for looks. If you can take this here log and throw it farther than any of us then you can have our vote." The others would nod agreement and look at my boy with a winning smile."

"Abe now, he took it all in stride. "Well," he would say. "If that's all it will take to win your vote I'm game." Then each of the fellers would take that log and hurl it as far as they could and some could pitch it a ways. But once Abe got his turn, he would outdo the best of them and then some."

"Others would bet their votes that he couldn't handle a plow like an old hand could then Abe would plough a line straight as an arrow without blinking an eye. I recall Abe told me it these were the easiest votes he ever got."

Looking at one of the boys he added, "Your father, John Johnston, once told me how he had picked up a whole chicken house by himself once and brought it to where it needed to go. Said it must have weighed four or five hundred pounds. I don't know if the chickens were still in it."

The children giggled immensely. One of them shouted, "Tell us more grandfather!"

"Well, right after we had moved to Illinois we had a lot of building to do. The neighbors had all pitched in during a Cabin raising bee, it seemed the whole community was there. The ladies had brought all their best dishes for the men folk who had chopped down enough wood, piled them all up nice and neat, cleared off a perfect square in a nice spot and had that cabin up within a day."

We still had a lot of work to do splitting more logs to make fencing, clear enough land to till the soil and put down a crop but we had to do that ourselves. The family was getting large then for we had Dennis here and his cousin John, Squire Hall, your Uncle Abe and your father John. We had spent one day felling some trees and began to pull all the timbers that were to be used to build us a new hog pen and get ready to lug them to the farm."

"Well we were all getting the timber all lined up to lay them on a sled for hauling. Then your Uncle Abe comes up and once the wood was all together and with a great heave puts them on his shoulder and hauls them all to the farm by himself using just an old rope to tie them together so he could prop them up onto his shoulder. I taught him that one but even I never had the gumption to carry that many."

"Another one he learned from watching me was instead of using sticks to pile wood upon and drag to where it needed to go, he would keep the timber's whole and lug them on his shoulder to where we would be building the fence or what not and then cut them there. It would usually take two or three men to carry that much and they would do it together. My boy could do it alone and quicker."

Tom could have gone on and told story after story of his son's legendary strength. How he once carried a man who had drunk himself unconscious three or four miles back and saved him from freezing. This had struck the man sober so afterwards he became a man of temperance. Or how lifted a wagon fully laden with goods so his stepbrother could change one of its wheels. But Tom began to cough and wheeze a bit, the talking turned out to be a little too much for him in his weakened condition.

Mother Lincoln had come into the room some time before but had stood in the doorway watching her husband. She always enjoyed listening to him speak. It was one of the many things that had endeared her to him. She had heard all these stories before, had been there for many of them when they either took place or when her husband had first heard them himself. It didn't matter. The sparkle in his eye and the way he wove a tale was a joy for her to watch and she felt that there may soon come a day when she would only be able to recall these moments and not relive them again except in memory. That had brought a tear to her eye which she quickly wiped away.

She took the brief respite as her cue and strode over taking the long since empty pipe from her husbands hand, "Ok little ones, your grandfather needs to get his rest. Now you all get up and get ready for bed. You can bother him again tomorrow after you do your schoolwork and chores."

Mother Lincoln's word was law in these parts and the children all jumped up and scampered off giggling and teasing each other as they prepared to get ready for bed, but not before each came over to their beloved grandfather and gave him a peck on the cheek and a hug. After this Tom's loving wife, Sarah, fixed his ruffled blankets, propped him up on his pillow and gave him some medicine before the elder patriarch drifted off into a sound slumber.

Sarah still had a number of chores to complete herself before it would be her time to join her beloved in slumber, but she was adept at her tasks and one of her older granddaughters was always there to help. Soon enough between the two of them they had all the other children tucked into bed and she was able to get herself ready to sleep. Within the hour she had joined her husband, though she slept in an adjoining room so as not to disturb him in his illness and drifted off to sleep herself.

THE BOUNTY OF THE RIVER

Abe sat in the small hotel room amongst his colleagues, as they often did on the road riding circuit. The room was sparsely furnished, though what there was of furnishings took up most of the room, while the half dozen men took up almost all the rest. There was barely room amongst them to walk from one bed to another without a bit of jostling between the men lounging upon them, but the jolly fellows would have it no other way. This was their time of freedom, such as it were for lawyers and judges in the wild western frontier of Illinois.

Seated there this late evening were a bevy of men who would later be amongst the most famous in all the country but here today were merely a gaggle of attorneys, all struggling to make their way in the world of American law, some a bit further along on the road to success than the others, but all still equals, at least in this room and in their minds. Sprawled at the head of one bed was Abraham Lincoln, the future president. Across from him was none other than Stephen Douglas, a good friend but once a suitor for the hand of Mary Todd, now Mary Lincoln, and later his rival first for a senate seat representing Illinois and later his primary opponent in 1860 for the office of the Presidency of the United States itself.

At the foot of the bed of Lincoln was his constant companion on the circuit, James Speed, a future Supreme Court Justice, while betwixt the two was Lincoln's later law partner William Herndon. Lounging on the bed with Douglas with his back leaning against the wall and smoking a pipe was Stephen T. Logan, Lincoln's current law partner and a state legislator.

Lying prone on the last bed and sole other piece of furniture in the small room was Judge Davis, himself a future Supreme Court Justice as well. He lay alone on the bed for his girth would allow none to share a bed with him. The one and only time this was attempted was on a large double bed and when Davis' happened to roll over his unfortunate companion found himself unceremoniously dumped onto the floor.

This group of strong willed and soon to be distinguished men, though all were ignorant of their later fame and fortune, were currently engaged in a rousing banter, trading stories of their past as they often did late into the night during their circuit of the courts. At this time in America, lawyers could often be found in hotels or boarding houses like this in small towns or bustling cities in their region plying their trade by day and enjoying their company at night. Many hotels didn't offer any meals so boarding houses were often required in order for travelers to get a decent meal and many residents frequented both if accommodations were sparse.

Very often they would room together to save money and for the comradery the arrangement would offer. Most of the time they would share beds since accommodations were frequently scarce in many communities where their cases would be contested. And at such times the courts were in session, many people from outlying communities would gather to hear their cases heard or just to hear the caes argued in general for distractions from daily toils were few and far between and the court could provide much entertainment. This was especially the case when a big case was to be heard or a famous attorney was in town. Thus, many a time opponents in a case would often be found, not only in the same room, but even the same bed that night.

Eating, sleeping and traveling together made many of them good friends and most would forget the daily grind at court, even if they were at each other's throats for much of the day. They would eat and drink together and spend much of the evening until the wee hours of the morning talking about whatever sought their fancy. This bedding and boarding together was a common phenomenon in the early days of the American Republic. Lincoln and James Speed's brother slept and ate together for better than three years while Lincoln first got himself settled into the bustling and prospering city of Springfield, the capital of Illinois.

Even amidst such illustrious companionship, Lincoln would dominate the conversation. His stories were always entertaining and the way he would tell them made it a joy to behold, no matter how many times he retold them. He was, at the moment, in the midst of one of his favorite tales, stemming from the Revolutionary period of his country's short but illustrious history.

"After that war, Edgar Allen took the opportunity to journey to England," He was saying in that country, high-pitched drawl of his that Easterners found very amusing and forced them to cling to his every word in order not to miss anything. His current audience knew it well and followed easily giving them a chance to enjoy the antics he displayed as he weaved his words in a spellbinding manner.

"While there," he continued, "the English never failed to find an opportunity to poke the old war hero about his colonialism and their supposed superiority, the recent conflict notwithstanding. Edgar was not one to take the bait offered and always was nonplussed by their antics."

"One day his erstwhile companions had hung a portrait of none of than George Washington himself in the privy, knowing that when Edgar went to use the outhouse he would not fail to notice it in its rude location. Once again Edgar rose to the occasion. When he returned from using the privy he made no comment. The English were a little perturbed by this and asked him if he happened to notice the portrait. Edgar answered yes he did."

"Well, what do you think about having your illustrious George Washington's portrait located in the privy?" one asked trying to contain his laughter.

"I believe that's the perfect spot for the picture," was Edgar's reply.

"Why?" they asked much perplexed and a little disappointed.

"Well," Edgar said straight-faced. "Nothing could make an Englishman shit quicker than seeing George Washington."

Lincoln's companions never failed to set the walls shaking with laughter with the telling of this well-known, but much enjoyed joke. And Lincoln led the rousing roar of their laughing himself always enjoying tales immensely, even when he did the telling.

The laughter produced from his stories shook more than the timbers of the hotel sometimes. It would often bring a measure of rebuke from several of the other guests. However, this did little more than give the merry making men a brief pause in their musings and mirth, to the consternation of those who's rest was disturbed.

After one such complaint this same evening, from an oddly attired fellow with a scarf draped around his neck, drew the usual apologies, along with a number of snickers, Judge Davis began the conversation anew with a topic that became the highlight of the evening's discussion.

This topic was the money making schemes of their youth, successful or otherwise. Some of those gathered were wealthy from birth, while others were considerably less fortunate, but none more so than Abraham Lincoln. This combined with his never-ending font of tales and engaging wit had him dominating this conversation once again, as he did the others.

"Come now Abe," he contended. "All your work must have given you some opportunities to squirrel together some cash when you were a spry youngster."

"Indeed it did!" Abe leaned back uncrossing his legs and grinning from ear to ear in a way that was infectious. The others grew more attentive knowing an entertaining story was about to burst forth from their giant companion.

"When I was a scrawny lad of seventeen summers, I found myself hired out by my father to work as a laborer on the Ohio River for a whole summer. This was the first time I was away from home for such a length of time and let me tell you it was a wonder for a naïve youngster like myself. Everything was new and fresh, and the labor was just the type to keep even a curious fellow like myself entertained from dawn until dusk."

When the others embarked on their stories they were often interrupted with snarky remarks or playful jibes but it was rare for this to happen with a Lincoln tale for he had a way of entertaining the spectators with his frequent gyrations and remarks that kept the attention of all who were privy to it on the tall gangly speaker so they missed none of the show. In an Age before TV and radio, storytelling was a primary form of entertainment and for those with the gift, it was like they were a full-blown celebrity in their own right.

Lincoln was such a man and none seemed to enjoy his stories more than himself. His ringing laughter could be heard quite a ways and all within earshot would be drawn to him eager to hear a humorous anecdote, poem or story.

"Now I was just loading and unloading boxes, crates, luggage, barrels and other odds and ends onto a local skiff to ferry them across the river," Lincoln continued, "but even a mundane task like that took on a whole different meaning when plying it on a boat."

"If I was merely lugging wood up to a cart and piling it on or unloading some corn to store the work would be mere drudgery. Now I had myself the chance to speak with people from far off places, lands I had only heard of or more likely as not read about from a magazine or some book I managed to get my hands on. But these people actually saw them, or even lived there, and now I could through their eyes. Such wonders they spoke of was beyond my wildest dreams."

"The ferry was frequented by many an Easterner moving west, and many western merchants or store owners would trade some livestock or agricultural produce to the districts just south of river, and more often than not bring back whiskey, cotton or tobacco. Then there were whole families from the south moving into Indiana, Illinois or one of the territories."

"I enjoyed the tales from the Easterners the most. Many were journeying from big cities like Philadelphia, New York, Boston or even the Capital! Then there were some from smaller cities like Richmond, Charleston or Atlanta. Most were on their way west to St. Louis, Chicago but some were looking to settle in Indiana."

"To hear them speak of cities like New York and Boston, places so old they seem to come out of the mists of time, was a tonic to me. To them to talk of the sights and sounds of their harbors or city streets, or old Federal Hall was old hat, but to me it was as if they came to life in my mind. I still cherish the memories of the talks and still harbor the desire to visit these places myself one day if I am lucky enough."

"The few from Philadelphia told me about Liberty Hall and the Liberty Bell itself, and one wizened old grandfather traveling with his family said he had once as a small boy even saw Benjamin Franklin. Then there were the stories of Washington DC. I always wanted details about the White House and the Capital where the House and Senate sat; to be able to go there even as a spectator in the galleries listening to the great law makers speaking would be even beyond my imagination, or to be privileged enough to enter the hall where the Supreme Court met and hear the likes of Daniel Webster plead his case to the venerable Justices sitting in judgment."

"But often it was the most mundane looking gentlemen who proved to be the fruitful, especially financially. For it was here working the ferry that I first began to make real money. In the towns I grew up in there was no real cash to speak of, if there was it was horded like some treasure and never used. We had the simple barter economy of the time, ones you still see if you travel off the beaten track or head out to the more western parts of the country. But here working a mere thankless task of a hired hand I would get tips now and again. Tips! Real hard cash! Mostly coins of the lowest worth, pennies and nickels but it was money and I was able to keep it so to me it was like the vaults of Solomon had opened for me."

"Once there were two gentlemen from Philadelphia who were on their way to Chicago as investors from an eastern bank. They were speculators I think, but they both wore finely woven, well-tailored clothes, sporting nice brass buttons and each had glistening pocket watches dangling on a golden chain. One had a monocle while the other sported a stove pipe hat, the first I had ever seen."

"After I had loaded a pair of sturdy chests they were hauling and then took them from the flatboat to the carriage that was waiting for them on the other side they each flipped me a half-dollar. I fished them out of the muddy track and stared so astounded by my sudden windfall that I can never recollect whether they paid me any thanks or spoke to me, or if I deigned to stutter some reply."

"I just stared at the two grubby coins I was holding, though in my mind's eye nothing had ever gleamed so brightly as those two glowing orbs in my hand. I held them up to the sun which had peeked out from a cloud as if to take a look at what I had gotten and each coin glinted a sparkling, dazzling light all its own."

"It was all these stories and learning to talk with strangers which began me on my path to become more aware of the ways of the world. It also gave me loads of confidence to talk to just about anyone. I think the fear of being made a fool keeps people from talking, but I had been a bit of a jokester all my life so having someone laugh with me or at me came naturally and never bothered me all that much. Always I was willing to speak in my little school and at any community outings, a bit too much for my father's liking sometimes."

"Well my dear friend," piped up Judge Davis still reclining on the bed. "What became of those two glistening half-dollars?"

"I wish I could recall," Lincoln laughingly replied. "I think it is far easier to recall the getting then the spending of one's wealth, however small it may be."

"Ain't that the truth! To the making and breaking of wealth!" The group laughed along merrily with their large companion and the talk slowly drifted along well into the wee hours of the morning.

*while it is highly unlikely, if not impossible, this event ever took place with this particular cast of characters, similar ones certainly did and adding this illustrious group together adds color and context to the story.

*Stuart had a successful political career as a state legislator and attorney. Davis and Speed were nominated to the Supreme Court by none other than Lincoln himself, Speed after political and legal success in Kentucky & Davis was Lincoln's campaign manager in his successful 1860 Presidential run. Herdnon was Lincoln's law partner and inherited the practice after his partner's untimely death. Douglas was a contentious and nationally renowned attorney and politician, known now more for the Kansas-Nebraska Act and the Great Debates with Lincoln than for the rest of his distinguished career.

ALL IN A DAY'S WORK

"Ah lads," Thomas called to the heap of boys gathered around the bucket. "This man here is a asking what's a day is like for the little folk in these parts. Any you wee boys want to give an answer to the man?"

The boys had been frolicking around the troth bucket, swallowing a bit of the water but wasting most in their mirth. Times of fun were not in ample supply amongst the settlers of the West, but when they came the people made the most of them, both young and old. A man had come from the nearby town of Decatur and had stopped to rest for a moment nearby and struck up a conversation with Tom and Squire Hall.

A couple of the boys moved up shyly accompanied by one of the bolder girls. Girls were infrequent on the outings boys were accustomed to, but not unheard of in the land bordering on the Wild. That was the land that old Thomas Lincoln always found himself living.

"we wuz yesterday, my brother Buck and me, xploring the land yonder for fruits and berries. My pa had looked over there and said there was bound to be some good wild vegtables there and Buck and I was itchin to find some we were!"

"Aw, you and Buck was just itchin to get away from somes work you were!" one of the other boys chimed in.

"Wasn't!", said Tim, a bit put out that the other boy was chiding him. Seeing the glint in old Thomas' eye gave the boy the confidence to go on and confide in him his tale.

"We goes there but we wuz smart this time and took us a nice goat to graze there." Tim looked over at Thomas leaning back in his chair, as if for permission to continue. Thomas bright stare was enough to egg the young boy on to impress the legend of Bethusula's Berries.

"We tied up ole' Bethusula when we found us a bunch of bushes full of berries all ripe and just waiting to be picked! Mum would be so pleased and we would be eating pie for a week with all the blueberries there! We had ourselves a nice stash between us..... both our sacks nearly full when he come onto us...."

Tim had been watching old Tom and begun to catch some of his storytelling skill. He hung his tale for a moment, just enough for one of the other boys to plead, almost beg,"Come'on Tim, what? What wuz it?"

"Well," Tim added, obviously relishing his time in the spotlight. "Buck and I looked at each other smiling, I think we both wuz thinking of a nice slice of blueberry pie, when all of a sudden ole' Bethusula starts a screamin'! Before we can even move we see a bear as big as a boulder leap onto her and start clawin' and bitin' our poor girl."

By now all the boys and girls were agape with horror and awe at the young boy's tale, while Thomas sat stone faced but with a sparkle in his eye that otherwise would have hid his merriment.

The boy with obvious glee that his tale had everyone's attention continued with gusto, "Buck and I were between the bear and home and we didn't know what to do. But I guessed the bear was too busy with poor Bethusula to worry none about us so I started to go around them. Buck and I walked past while that dang bear was a gnawin' and a munchin' but there was nothin' we could do!"

A little girl, barely able to walk, asked with wide, gleaming eyes, "What did you do next?"

"Well Buck and I skedaddled off back home as quick as you could wink and our Mom was cooking a scrumptious blueberry pie for us while ole' paw was wondering why he wuz one goat short."

Michael John Joseph Del Toro

That one sure got a laugh, even from ole' Tom.

"Well I am not sure that's how Honest Abe liked to describe things, near as I can tell. I'm no storyteller that's for sure but he is by God.", Squire Hall said in his own coarse way as he came up to the merry band. "I was thinking he would tell a story that could grip you by the heels and pull you in, I'm just trying to give it the best I can."

"But since you asking how's the work on a farm in these parts, I can answer how it was when we wuz young. Well I guess I can give you my best account of that cuz there wasn't much to talk about."

"We split the works amongst the girls and the boys and amongst the women and menfolk. I guess the women and girls had the most work to do but the menfolk and boys did the hardest jobs there wuz. We sure was tired when we got back each evening but the ladies they wuz workin' all evening and many times late into the night."

"I guess when you really thinkin' about it the girls been doin even more work than the boys, and the ladies they dun run the house. I never seen no man run a house, all single men go a' boardin'."

"I'm a thinkin' none of that means no how unless you ben there yourself beacuz' I wouldn't be believin' any of this unless I sen it meself. I tell you un think you don't be thinking is that it wuz the ladies that run the show. It wuz the ladies that did all the work an it wauz the ladies that told her Man whut wuz whut. At least that's whut I sen in my days on the farm."

"I mean who made the clothes? Who made the food? Who made ever dun thing that we needed and used that we didn't have to buy? It wuz the womenfolk. They dun it all."

"Maybe we give them the materials. We give them the wheat, the corn, the meat. Maybe we shorn the sheep, helped in fields, along farm, building fencing, chopping wood, hauling goods, stores, feed and crops, clearing land, pulling stumps, harvesting grain, oh so much harvesting crops. If we didn't have the things we needed then we would be off yonder to buy them from town."

"Now when one of us goes a hunting what do we come back with?" First they shouted, "Pork!" which brought a chuckle from Squire and Tom.

"Well we don't rightly hunt for the pork, 'cept on ocassion, since we have a pen full of them right here. Can you think of anything else?" Venison came the first responses, the deer meat was a staple as game was plentiful and was usually mixed with pork which was the most common meat. Others often eaten were turkey, chickens, ground hogs, bear, raccoon and squirrels.

"And what do we pick out in the woods or orchards?" This was answered with a chorus of apples, peaches, wild berries, potatoes, and such.

"Now can any of you tell me what crops we harvest?" Squire asked the children. They responded, chiming in back and forth with most of them shouting corn and wheat, a few said barley.

"I think you are all forgetting the most important one."

They all sat there thinking for a bit before one asked, "Which is that uncle?"

"Well, what are you all wearing?"

They brightened and all called out in unison, "Linen!".

"And how do you make linen?" The boys looked dumbfounded and looked at each other while one of the girls cried out, "Carded linen!"

Tom and Squire, and a few of the older boys got a big laugh out of that and the girl looked sheepish, then Sarah said in a quiet quizzical voice, "Flax?"

"That's right! And that's what the ladies were doing that day I fell sick and was bedridden for a week." He pointed to a barrel that was filled with water and flax. "Why it was sitting right there the whole time! Little do you know but that's what we'll be wearing come no time." The girls nodded slowly while the boys looked thunderstruck. One got up and peered in with wide eyes then looked back at his shirt and said, "Ewwww!" Everyone laughed.

"There wuz times I wuz a sick an I wuz watchin them all day an night. Not that I wanted to be doing it. That be sure. I can give you a good account of a week of their work right now if I had half a mind to but I'll just tell you a little of the things I saw."

"I was able to look out the window from my bed and saw them a pounding and scraping. It looked to be a whole lot of fuss and more work than I'd care to be doing. I asked them what they was doin' and they told me they were straightenin' out the flax fibers. I couldn't figure what it was for and asked them so. They laughed just like we did just now and said for the next shirt I be wearing."

"I was as amazed as you and so they told me how they would string out the fibers by puttin' them in water, just like you see there. When it was all stringing they would stretch them out and beat them and scrape them until they were all neat in a row. That's what they call 'cardin''. Then they'd be cuttin' and sewin' and a whole mess of other things I don't rightly remember but it was work work work, and then work!"

"I watched them doin' all this for a whole week. They got a whole set of clothes out of it but I dare say that was a lot of work for one set of clothes and somethin' I wouldn't be wantin' to do myself. But none of them complained one bit, they were talking about how the next batch would be a new apron and after that they would be makin' a nice new petticoat. They seemed awful excited about those, but not so much about my new shirt."

"Then they said they were looking to dye one of them purple or red, I forget exactly, and that they needed some berries and my shirt would be dyed with some bark. They then told me how they would make our pants from wool, or maybe leather made from the hides of the game we would catch. That would be used for our boots too."

"Now the lady folk did all the weavin', the cuttin', the cardin' and dyein' like I said. The did all the washin', which was an even bigger chore, and they mended all our clothes. They did the cleanin', the cookin'. But after those ladies were a pressin' an sewin' an weavin' an dyin' an makin' the clothes we wore to cookin' the food we ate they didn't stop. No siree! They did everythin'. They did the figurin', the countin', and told us Men what it was they needed and we just go out and get it."

"I told you what the womenfolk did, which our little princesses know since they be doin' it themselves now, and it was a chore an a chore."

"Now grandpaw, he'd make our three-legged stools; bedstead which he made of poles stuck between the logs in the angle of the cabin, the outside corner supported by a crotched stick driven into the ground; the table we eat off of, which was a huge hewed log standing on four legs. The pots, kettles, and skillets, and those tin and pewter dishes and what little other metal items were all bought in town."

"When I was out on the fields or in the woods clearin' ground or huntin' for game, I always felt it was the men that always did the work. I never really knew what the women did all day and I reckon I was a bit harsh on them and didn't give them any respect until I fell ill that one time. But after seeing them scurryin' about and even if they sat still they were always doin' somethin'."

"But the thing I reckon that sticks most with me is however much their hands were workin' or their feet were busy, nothin' worked harder than their jaws. Their gums were flapping from morning to night and I never once had a moment of silence with them jabberin' all day long. That may have done more to help me get well than any of them ministerin' to me did. That I tell you!"

That gave Tom a hearty laugh and even the children gathered about found something to smile about with that joke. At least the boys. Some of the girls were in high feather after that remark and Squire's wife was heard to say from the kitchen area inside the house, "You keep yapping like that and I'll be sure to see you be eating outside!"

Squire took his cue from his wife and got the kids and adults back to their chores before they all would settle down to dinner. "You all heard your mother. Let's stop with the jibber jabber and get ourselves all presentable for dinner. Now git!"

The children started at a run back to the house, the boys jostling each other as they tried to be the first to the door. When they got there, reaching the doorway about the same time, it was all little arms and legs as they squeezed themselves inside then disappeared into the aperture to get themselves ready for a nice family dinner.

Later, at the table, the large family of over a dozen were sitting, the adults at a large table, while the little ones were all seated at a long small table, all sitting nice and proper, at least for the moment. These dinners could turn out to be a rough affair but since today was a Sunday, Tom knew the missus wanted the dinner to be more subdued so after leading them in a short prayer thanking the Lord for their health and the bounty before them, he went about musing how he would spin a tale to occupy the children's attention long enough to finish their food without causing a miniature ruckus.

One of his granddaughters gave him just the sort of topic he could run a story with when she opportunely asked of him, "Grandfather? What is Uncle Abraham like and what does he do?"

A glint appeared in Tom's eye as he found the answer he sought in her innocent query.

"Well my little darling. If you and your brothers and sisters can sit still and silent long enough I think I can give you the answer you seek. Can you do that?"

All of them nodded their heads solemnly. They all loved dearly to listen to their grandfather. He could send them anywhere he wished with his magic words and charm, and always brightened an often dreary day or evening with a tale that could last long beyond the time it took for him to tell it as they dwelt on his words as they lay in bed, often murmuring to each other before they fell into a deep slumber.

"Let's see now, how should I begin? Well you recall your father Squire saying how your Uncle Abraham could talk the whiskers off a cat?"

A couple of the boys giggled while the girl nodded, her eyes as big as dinner plates.

"Well he got some of that from yours truly, and uses it to convince people to think like he does and help us right here, even though he is many miles yonder over the rivers and mountains where all the best men are talking and deciding what our great nation should do."

"Why aren't you there?" Buck couldn't restrain himself from asking.

"Why that's easy! Who's going to watch you and keep you out of the mischief that seems to follow you like that puppy of ours follows little Sarah here?" The children giggled as they were being passed their food and Marietta, whom the family called by her middle name, Sarah, blushed. Tom then continued.

"He wasn't always a politician living in Washington. He started out just like you and I, living on a little farm working all day long out in the fields or helping our neighbors like your brothers Abe & Tommy were doing last week. He did the same farm work that we men tended to do today, like pulling corn, reaping wheat, hunting, butchering meat, pulling stumps, weeding, splitting rails, felling trees, digging wells, clearing land, plowing and planting. Many of these required the use of an axe and Abe soon became a foremost expert in handling that tool."

"He even took to the rivers as I once did, first as a ferry man plying people and trade across the Ohio and once or twice taking a flatboat all the way down the Mississippi river to New Orleans!"

"But soon after he reached his twenty-ssecond year, he felt the outside world calling and got set in his ways to find a new calling for himself. He didn't know what he wanted to do but he knew that it wasn't here on our farm."

"After helping us settle in to our new home in the springtime after the Deep Snow, he got together all of his belongings, just enough to fill one of those handkerchiefs you use to blow your nose when its running, and wrapped them up in a bundle tied to a walking stick and went on his way to find out what the world had to offer, and what he could offer the world. When I think of all the occupations that we can hope for I always turn to my son, Abraham. He seemed to try his hand at every one before he finally decided to study law."

"When Abe left home he found himself still doing the same type of labor he did with his family. Soon he felt the call to arms and answered as all Lincolns do. This was fighting the despicable Indian race, a stain to all civilized folk. They had committed a number of atrocities and Abe went to serve. He didn't just pick up a musket but became a leader of men, a Captain like my noble father once was."

"When he returned from honorable service he ran for public office. He didn't have time to run for there were only a few days before the election. He had already made such a mark in New Salem that he won all of their votes except three but since nobody knew him outside of town he did not win election."

"After this defeat he found occupation with one Denton Offutt, as a clerk at his store. He was so good at this that he was soon running Offutt's mill too. Now Denton was a scoundrel, a man who talked more than he should and borrowed more than he could ever hope to repay. When his debts piled up he did what all scoundrels do. He ran. Who knows if he ever stopped running?"

"My boy was as honest as he was honorable and he took all the debts of Offutt on his own shoulders. He nobly strove to pay these off as he now not only ran the store as he was doing when Denton was there, but now he was owner and responsible for them as well. Unfortunately fate conspired to hamper my son's success and he was forced to close the store and mill. But he did not run as a lesser man would. He stood in town and fought tooth and nail by applying himself to many jobs to pay off this mountain of debt. He is still paying it to this day."

"What did he do next?" Abe found himself asking. He wasn't named after his uncle but rather his great grandfather, known to the family as Captain Abraham.

"Well he had to find some work. He still worked with his hands when he had to because he needed money and money was scarcer than it is today. But a neighbor took pity on him and seeing how he was the smartest man in all of New Salem if not the county he gave Abe a book on surveying and Abraham diligently applied himself to its study. Do you know what a surveyor is?"

The children shook their heads vigorously as smiled on.

"Well, that is marking out the land by using special tools and figuring with numbers so farmers and speculators can make legal claim to plots. He was able to do this figuring in his head as easy as we can count on our fingers. He marked off entire towns and most of the farmers tilling their fields in those parts these days can thank none other than our Abraham for their claim."

"He continued to do odd jobs in between his work as a surveyor, and by his hard work and friendly manners he made friends of all the residents in and around New Salem. This stood him in good stead on more than one occasion. I will tell you of two of them."

"His creditors were after him day and night. They were like bloodhounds sniffing out ever red penny he had but nothing could sate their thirst and greed. One even sought to take the very tools by which he could hope to repay him. Our poor Abraham was forced to auction off his tools he used to survey the land. Now he had no means to pay his debts and the insatiable blood sucking creditor still wanted more. If it wasn't for the strong bonds of friendship he formed in the community he would have been destitute.

"One man saw his plight and was charitable enough to aid my boy in his misery. He bought the tools at auction and gave them back to Abe on surety that he would help on a few odd jobs that were not close to the worth in the money he paid but to give my boy the sense that he was not a charity case and helped get him back on his feet."

"Now this was around the time after the great election of 1832. President Jackson became known for giving special preference to his supporters. Now Abe had supported the Whigs so it was understood that the new Postmaster for New Salem would go to a carpetbagging Jacksonian. But Jackson was as noble an American as there was and against all odds he handed the coveted position to none other than your Uncle Abraham. He had heard of our Abe's outstanding qualities and gave him the Postmaster position due to his merit."

"Now this wasn't a high paying position but the pay was higher than the money he could earn elsewhere and it was steady. It helped get Abraham back on his feet and even gave him enough to start paying off his many creditors. It also allowed him to start reading more and more."

"He hadn't been able to read much since his store closed down and this inspired him to begin his long study of law. It also gave him even more standing amongst his peers and he became the undisputed leader of New Salem and among the Whigs in Sangamon Country."

"Being Postmaster and surveyor for those few years gave him many chances to visit farms and residents who rarely ventured

Legends of Lincoln

to town. When it came election time Abraham felt confident enough to run again and lo and behold! He won handily. This began his run of several terms as a state legislator."

"His time in the capital of Springfield where he moved made him more well known. This gave him the ambition to try his hand at national politics and he decided to run for the House of Representatives. And again he came out victorious. He was now one of the representatives of our noble state, and still is today."

"So remember. You can be anything you want to be in life as long as you do hard work, be honest, god fearing and humble. Always respect your peers and good things will come to you. You only have to look to the example of your Uncle Abe to see that success follows by applying yourself to those simple rules."

"Now I dare say Mother is giving me the look so lets get yourselves ready to go off to bed. We have a bit of planting to do tomorrow and I'm sure our ladies have some of the many chores your father John told you about to do themselves. So let's git to it!"

With that the kids went off to bed, the boys a bit wiser to what their mothers, aunts and sisters were doing all day in and around the house and the girls to think about what their brothers, uncles and fathers would be doing tomorrow and beyond.

---

*It's possible Jackson wanted Lincoln to be indebted to Democrats hoping to lure him over in a fluid region where no party lines had yet been drawn or to make it seem that Lincoln was beholden to Democrats and decrease credibility. It's also interesting that while Lincoln was Deputty Surveyor John Calhoun was County Surveyor. Calhoun was a political opponent of Abraham Lincoln and Lincoln had said he was the best orator he ever debated. Whether or not any of this was the case neither happened. Lincoln was forever a Whig and his constituents always supported him.

AN ABE OF ALL TRADES

A creditor had stopped in to speak with James Gentry, now the lone merchant of New Salem. New Salem was in the doldrums but Gentry's Store still thrived. He had put paid to all his competitors and was the dominant trading force in the town and surrounding region.

Lincoln had been among the first to pack up his tent and move on from there. This was why the creditor was there now. He was looking for Abe and after Gentry said that Lincoln was out of town the creditor told him why he was there. The man had accumulated a large amount of the debts of Lincoln and was pestering Gentry as to Abe's character and how likely he was to pay.

Gentry was a bit put off by the tall hefty man. He was a friend of Lincoln though also a rival, politically as well as in the trading business, but that didn't make him dislike Lincoln. Quite to the contrary, Lincoln was of a type that could make friends with a surly badger. That's why Gentry wasn't taking too kindly to a stranger questioning Lincoln's character. He would set him straight.

"Lincoln? You couldn't find a better man in all the states of the Union." He said looking he man squarely in the eye. "There isn't a dishonest bone in the man's body. I can tell you everything you need to know about the man and then some."

"That's what I'd like to hear," the man answered with a curious look. "I'm needing to square up with these debts. They are quite substantial and from the looks of it well beyond his means. I even heard he almost had to sell his surveyor tools in order to make a payment on those debts. This was before I had acquired them of course." The man added the last when he saw the baleful stare Gentry gave him.

"Indeed he did. He couldn't have met that payment and it was a friend of his who saw to it the payment was made so Lincoln could continue surveying. That should give you some indication of the esteem with which he was held here. If you need more along those lines you can look no further than the fact he was the postmaster of New Salem."

The man was confused. "How does that make any difference?"

"Well then. You can square it by the fact he was given the post by none other than Andrew Jackson. Now it's common knowledge that Jackson favored his supporters with so many posts in and out of Washington that his administration coined the term "The Spoils System". Now I'm a Jacksonian myself and Jackson knew Lincoln was a Clay man, and an outspoken one at that. Lincoln was one of them who had been stirring up all the Whigs to vote against Jackson. When it came time to divvy out the postmaster position to Sangamon Country he gave it to Lincoln even though there were plenty of worthy democrats here that coveted the job. If that isn't enough to convince you then "honest" is the name he's known by in these parts."

"I heard some about that and was thinking on it myself," the creditor added.

"Now speaking of his time as Postmaster. A mutual friend told me this story about the time after the New Salem Post Office was closed down and a federal agent stopped by many months later to collect the outstanding fees that Lincoln had been entrusted. My friend knew that Lincoln was in debt on account of his store's failure and was about to call him aside to loan him the cash. He knew how difficult it was to get cash and since Lincoln was in debt he figured that Abe would not have any ready cash available to pay the fees."

"Before he could do so Lincoln asked the agent if he would be willing to go to his boarding house with him. The agent agreed and my friend went with them, since he didn't finish his business with Lincoln yet. When they got to the boarding house Lincoln asked the agent to be seated for a few moments. Then he went over to his trunk and pulled out of an old blue sock a bit of silver and copper coin that he had been keeping in it. He proceeded to count the coin, and counting it up there was found the amount, to the exact cent, of the fees owed, and in the identical coin which had been received. He never used, under any circumstances, trust funds. The agent was amazed and seeing his look Lincoln just offered that he never used money that didn't belong to him."

"That's but one of the things that made him stand out in the crowd of clerks who worked at a general store. Some were good at one thing. A few were good at some things. Lincoln was good at everything. He excelled in all aspects of a rough and tumble occupation. The wonder of it was that he could never put it all together."

"Most people call Lincoln a sad man. You get that from first looking at him. He has a sad face. It's his natural look. Melancholy some call it. Melancholy was but the surface mask of the one basic characteristic which defined Lincoln as a person, his mirth. His practicality, conservatism, wisdom, circumspection and melancholy all derived from the unrelenting hardships of his childhood and tempered his jovial humorist tendencies. But he was as happy as can be and that mask of sadness would drop the moment he spoke. And within moments you would find out about his main trait, his humor."

"Lincoln's humor could take a malicious bent if he felt it was warranted. When he once borrowed a book he had carelessly kept it between a couple of logs in the cabin. When it rained the book became all but ruined. Abe went to the Crawford farm and offered to work off the cost of the book. Farmer Crawford forced Abe to work two full days harvesting corn."

"Abe did as was asked and pulled corn until the entire harvest was completed. He didn't feel the book was worth that much work and took it out on the hapless, greedy farmer by referring to him and his large nose as "Josiah blowing his horn" ever after to friends and even writing poems and songs with that turn of phrase."

"But that was rare and only when the person deserved it. I mean there was no more congenial or friendlier person in town. Being in good spirits and jovial was Lincoln's natural state. His good humor was infectious and made him a most desirable companion. Lincoln was friends with everyone and anyone. He was respectful to all and had the respect of each of them in turn. He was always ready to lend a helping hand be it farming, helping someone build a fence or cabin, haul or chop wood, carry groceries or even aid a drunk in their time of need."

"He brought this friendliness to his store and added to it his honesty and fairness in all aspects of the business. I don't think he ever tried to sell someone something they didn't want or need or overcharge for an item. I don't think he could do it even if he wanted to, which he didn't."

"Well that seems a bit of a stretch don't you think?" The stranger asked skeptically.

"You would think so if you didn't know Lincoln, which you don't so I will forgive you for your incredulity. But it's the truth. If my testimony before didn't convince you then here are a few others. Besides helping elders bring groceries and produce to their home even when they lived miles away, he would go out of his way to make sure everyone he dealt with was not only satisfied but pleased with his service. He would steer people form buying something from him if he didn't think it was good for them, even if it was all but sold. He just didn't feel it was right to sell something they didn't really need. That may have had something to do with his shop failing. He would forgo ready profits in order to please his customers."

"I trusted him enough to allow him to keep shop here when I had to leave from time to time on business. I trusted him even more than my own son, who is a good man. Lincoln just had a way about him that lent one to trust him and he never let anyone down and he certainly won't let you down. Mark my words!"

"I am beginning to think I may have misjudged him, but will he remember to pay these debts. So often the cares of the world weigh one down and make otherwise good men forget their responsibilities." The stranger mused.

"Well I dare say you won't have to worry about that with Lincoln! He is a man who takes his responsibilities seriously. And if he didn't take him as serious as he did, he has a memory like an elephant. He recites entire passages from the Bible by memory. He can remember a person he met a dozen years past by name, how they met and every other particular. He still can remember the smallest details of conversations we had and I am sure he can recall the exact amount owed to you even computing the interest."

"Did you know he was quite remarkable with numbers?"

"That I did not know please tell me more." The stranger was

beginning to realize that while Gentry may have once been a rival to his debtor, Gentry valued the friendship more and really relished in relating tales about his friend.

"I certainly will!"

"Abe is brilliant at adding and subtracting. He never made a mistake I know of. He could compute up in his head and doing his figuring there quicker than anyone on a paper with their pencil. It took only a few days before Abe became a clerk at store. He did all the packing and unpacking. He took in the money. He kept the accounts. He made sure there was enough stock and he would do the ordering. He virtually ran the store even before he took on all of the store owner Offutt's debt after that villain gone and run off. I will tell you the whole tale."

"Now when Lincoln first came around these parts he had just came back from taking a flatboat to New Orleans for Offutt. He had a little mishap around these parts and some still remembered it. Now Lincoln was about as tall as you but he was lanky and looked a bit like a birch tree."

"They might have called him a long armed ape. He was long armed no doubt about that. His arms were so long and so strong. He could pick up just about anything and with one arm or two just as easily put it up on the top shelf about six feet from the floor as you or I could hoist up a baby into your arms."

"An ape he was not! He was one of the ablest and most brilliant men I ever met. He was a slow learner but if you were patient with him and explained things thoroughly to him he would never need you to tell him again. He was so smart once he learned anything he could teach it to even the simplest child in such a way that it could come easily to them."

"Offutt had Lincoln doing all his calculations. Any sums Lincoln could whistle up in moments. Abe was practically running that store by the time he was not there three months. He did it a sight better than Offutt himself he did!"

"Offutt saw he could get Abe pretty cheap. Abe didn't know his worth when he first came to town so Offutt was putting jobs on him and getting pennies on the dollar. That was until Abe wised up and then Offutt was stuck doing work himself again."

"He even got Lincoln running his old mill and Abe had that

Legends of Lincoln

running along nicely as well. This got Abe to thinking what's the point of him doing all the work while Offutt got all the rewards."

"Now Offutt was always looking for a quick buck and he spent way more than he ever made in every little wild scheme, not the least of which were the boat trips he signed off on to New Orleans."

"It came about that Offutt's creditors wanted to start seeing some money flowing their way. Offutt didn't have the means to pay them and he wasn't about to get stuck with the bill, which was substantial. Lincoln by this time had caught onto Offutt and knew, quite rightly he could run the store much better than he. So Abe and his coworker, one Berry, decided to pool their meager resources and together, take on the debt and run the store themselves."

"Berry was long gone after just a season or two leaving poor Abe the entire debt in his lean shoulders. But Lincoln's store had one thing going for it. That would be Lincoln. He was such an entertaining person that he always had a handful of locals there just to listen to him. This took a lot of time from him being able to mend the store and the problem was that these folks would spend hours in Lincoln's store but when it came time to buy something, more often than not they would buy them at one of his competitors, including me."

"We had long standing relations with many of the leading manufacturers in St Louis or the big cities to the east. This gave us the inside track on the best produce and the best prices to boot. But this wasn't the biggest point that favored us. The most important point in our favor was that while he was in debt, we were not. This allowed us far more leeway in being able to extend credit to our customers and in turn receive credit ourselves when need be. Lincoln could not match this advantage."

"Add to this that there were several stores all in this area. Believe it or not but New Salem was once a thriving town and all thought the sky was the limit. Once they could get the river cleared up in these parts then the money would be flowing right in here. I believed it too at one point. Lincoln had some ideas about how to be doing that and was so confident he even bought one of the stores when the owner decided to give it up. This was while Berry was still his partner."

"But the river was not going to get cleared enough for boats to make it down here, at least not yet. Lincoln's flatboat and one other boat were the only ones to ever make it and it was only because of Lincoln's smarts that his boat managed it."

"After a while, Lincoln caught wind about how things were and with his debt just getting higher and higher on account of the interest he knew it was time to call it quits. But he didn't run off like his partner and Offutt. No siree. Lincoln kept his honor and swore he'd pay off the debt whether it took ten years or a hundred. But you can bet it will be sooner rather than later if you knew Lincoln like I did."

"And I will add that he may well be resentful to have people like you pestering him for a debt he is not only willing to pay but compelled by his own good nature to pay, but his humor is such that he will never hold any resentment towards you or anyone else for that matter. I have never met a man who was more willing or happy to forgive and forget than Lincoln."

"He has many reasons to be resentful at times and even to hate but that was something that could never enter his mind. He was constitutionally unable to bear ill feelings towards people. His compassion was such that he would always put himself in another man's shoes and try and feel what they felt rather than let his baser emotions get the better of him."

"He was also one who always sought to better himself and I think this stands you in good stead to be patient with him and you will be well rewarded."

"How is that?" The stranger pressed.

"Well he is of the type who has an ambition to succeed and better himself in every way possible. This can only be beneficial to you in that he will find a way to increase his means. This will make it easier to pay you off and probably quicker than you anticipate."

Now Gentry leaned over a bit in a confidential manner and the stranger did likewise so they were almost ear to ear.

"I tell you friend," Gentry finished. "You couldn't make a better bet than Lincoln. He is sure money and if you are patient you will find yourself as pleased as any of his many customers were within. That I guarantee!"

The creditor stood up from the stack of boxes he had seated himself.

Holding out his hand to James Gentry he said, "Well sir, I must thank you. I admit that when you first began your tale I believed you may be trying to spin a yarn to deceive me. But I now see that you hold this Abraham Lincoln in genuine respect. And I also see that there is no way you could have made that yarn up yourself. The stories are just too many and of different character other than that the man you speak of is one of honor and fully deserving the moniker of "honest".

Gentry took the man's hand and shook it, "I'm glad you feel that way and I assure you that Lincoln will not disappoint."

"After speaking with you sir, of that I have no doubt. No doubt at all. Please let Mr. Lincoln know I stopped by and I will come around again in a few months just to see how he is doing."

"I will be sure to do so, sir." Gentry replied.

And with that Lincoln's creditor left the store, none the richer in money but much fuller in confidence that the money owed was in as good hands as his own, and was not a debt but a capital investment that was sure to pay off better than most far riskier ventures.

CASH OR KIND – THE FRONTIER ECONOMY

Jane Doe was dressed in all the finery her meager household could provide, her Sunday best as it were. Fitting it was a Sunday and she and her husband were in town with her children in tow to attend church services, a rare occasion for an outlying farming family. This gave it much fanfare for herself, her husband and their seven children. She had borne eleven children over the last 17 years but the Lord called four to join him in watching over the others. Her fourth child was stillborn, one (the second) having died in childbirth. The other two were taken by tuberculosis and a fever in their first and fourth year respectively.

Death was a burden all families had to endure. God worked in mysterious ways but she felt blessed to have such a large, loving god fearing family. The eldest, her daughter Sally, was now in her seventeenth year and recently betrothed to a fine young man from a neighboring farm. She was due to be wed in the coming month. The youngest, a swaddling babe nestled in her arms, was a mere seven months old. The others were staggered in age between 14 and 3.

Wearing their homespun dresses, her three girls looked like miniature versions of herself. Each dress was of an earthy tone, but still vibrant in colors the family presented a veritable kaleidoscope of browns, reds, pinks and greens. The men, her husband and two eldest sons, were garbed in browns, grays and the ubiquitous butternut that would become world renowned a few decades hence as the predominant color of the western confederate soldier.

They were outside the small, modestly designed, but finely built church, the services having concluded a short while ago. Her husband was from Tennessee, like the pastor so found the sermon pleasing. She was from Kentucky and while neither of their families were slave owning, his was sympathetic while hers was not. They dwelt on the north bank of the Sangamon River. Most of those that did were anti-slavery, her husband was a rarity being sympathetic towards the southern affliction.

Being a Sunday during election time in Illinois, there were a number of candidates for the state assembly who were gathering for their stump speeches. Two were arguing as to who would speak first and it seemed likely it would resort to fisticuffs, as these "discussions" so often did, Lord's Day or not, when a tall gangly man stepped forward from the crowd and got between the duo. Within moments he managed to quell the argument and one of the two then proceeded to get atop the stump and begin his address.

Jane was much intrigued by the tall man who so easily broke up what appeared to be an inevitable altercation that could have done much to darken this holy day.

Her husband, John, identified him as Abraham Lincoln, the leading Whig of the neighboring county. Illinois had a heavily democratic leaning, Lincoln's county being the sole exception. Her husband guessed he was here to support the Whig challengers to democratic dominance. He had been speaking with some of the other farmers. Lincoln wasn't due to speak, he was here in the capacity of lending his presence and giving some weight to his colleagues and by going amongst some of the neutrals seeking to sway them by his words or deeds. He was accompanied by a few of his fellows. John indicated they were his political gang of toughs that often journeyed with him from town to town during their electioneering.

Jane didn't get to town as often as her husband, so she leaned on him for knowledge and while it was considered unladylike to partake in political conversations, listening to speeches were not taboo and John knew full well of her interest. They had many a discussion over the dinner table. Her husband was hoping to hear from John Calhoun, a leading Democrat from Sangamon County renowned for his oratory, who it was said was going to be speaking today. A distant relation to the nationally famous John Calhoun of South Carolina, he had inherited both his oratory and democratic leanings from the great man, though a Bostonian by birth and now a resident of Illinois.

The first speaker was an inexperienced politician running in his first election and it showed. He was cumbersome on the stump and what little he said came out in a gnarly disjointed fashion. As one of the few Whigs in a democratic stronghold he wasn't likely going to last long in the rough and tumble western political landscape. The second wasn't much better though at least he had the becoming trait that he was a staunch democrat so the locals didn't hoot and holler as much. The next two were nondescript and were running for re-election so they kept their speeches to their main talking points in order to not create any mishaps.

Jane was very interested in the fifth speaker. Her husband had gone off to the stables to take a gander at some draft horses before Calhoun would be speaking. It was the big purchase he was looking to make. He wouldn't be able to make it today since the stable master was very religious, so business was not done on the Lord's day but, he did allow prospective buyers the opportunity to take his horses out for a viewing or workout. Farmers didn't have too many opportunities to get to town so there needed to be some leeway with strictly following the Lord's Day of Rest in order to keep his business profitable.

By the time Jane was able to quiet her babe down a bit and move amongst the other bystanders to a suitable position in which to view the speeches, the fourth one had already completed theirs, and the fifth was just then finishing his opening greeting.

"...The society we live in is one that allows our people to live but not prosper. The Declaration of Independence clearly states that all men are created equal and are bestowed upon their creator life, liberty and the pursuit of happiness."

"Can anyone claim that we who live in this fine, bountiful land do not have life? Can they question that within the bounds of this fruitful society whether we have liberty? But can we at the same time proclaim within the bounds of reason we have attained happiness?"

"On this latter point I think not! And I dare you to proclaim otherwise! Look to me my friends and fellow citizens! Ask yourself those questions and look into your hearts. You know this to be true!"

"Now I am not a man of words like our brother Abraham Lincoln. I have not the ability to speak as he does and to reach into your minds what is your utmost desire. But I preach as he does! I speak as he would without the eloquence but with the same emotion to you! Believe what he does and when you vote on election day vote with him and set your tally to my humble name and allow us Whigs to bring your voice to the legislature as one!"

"Now there are a number of ways the river can improve the lot of all of us. I will illustrate this to you point by point so that you will fully understand the import of developing the Sangamon to its fullest extent."

"First there is the cost to the seller. Let's compare a seller moving their wares by road or by river. When moving by road a seller often confronts communities that charge tolls for entering their territory. There are also tolls for going from state to state. Now there are many are many many products that are in demand due to short supply in one state while in no demand in the state in which they are grown or produced. Sometimes a seller has to go through several states to reach the desired market. Each of these states charge tolls and many of the communities in between do as well."

"What does that have to do with you, you rightly ask. Well I will tell you. Do you think the seller will put those costs to the side and only charge you what he would charge if he was selling the item near his home? No! You as the buyer will have to pay these added costs! He will add a little to each item for each toll he has to pay. It is you who will have to pay extra and the seller will be hurt by not being able to sell as much as he could. Why? Because the cost of his goods are now too high for everyone to afford, even if they need it!"

"But you're a Whig! You are supposed to want tariffs!" one of the bystanders chimed in and many agreed, laughing incredulously at the politician.

"Quite right my friend!" The politician answered. "But I am not speaking of tariffs. Tariffs on one good are all well and good to favor our domestic business in the face of goods coming from outside the state. And these should be charged upon entry of our border ports and paid to our state coffers where they can be used to benefit all, like in the very improvements I am promoting."

"Tolls are charged by towns just for entering and they are charged for everything, even if they are made in the state and charged in every town even if the cargo is not meant for sale in that town."

"Now you will rightly ask yourself: how does a river make this easier to bear? There are several reasons. We have the fact that river transports are bigger than a wagon so a seller can fit more on one, especially if he owns the boat or barge. Next you have only the port where the seller goes to sell his wares that will charge him a toll but is true that sometimes a city will charge sellers a toll for their product passing through even though the seller has no intention of selling there but the smart seller will avoid those ports since there are many landings outside towns or cities that can be used to spend the night."

"Now think about time. What does time have to do with anything? Well time has everything to do with it! Traveling by water has always been faster than by land. Even in ancient times of our forefathers on the Old Continent traveling by water was always faster than by land. But still you ask why this matters? Well if you think about it, the more time a seller is away from his shop or farm the more time is wasted idly traveling with no profit to himself or his family. More time also means more money. Every day away is a day spending tradeable goods or hard cash on food and lodgings."

"There are many ways a farm can find itself falling into disrepair. Every day a shopkeeper is away from his store he loses customers and profits. A good river to transport goods makes these lost profits a thing of the past! Progress is the key to prosperity, and it is by developing the Sangamon that we will all find our prosperity."

"Now I bring you to the biggest reason why opening the Sangamon will make us all prosper like we never had before. Cash! I know you are thinking what do these bits of paper and coin going to bring us that good products don't? That's an easy one to answer. Cash brings opportunities. Cash brings options. Now here is why."

"Think on the many tolls you need to pay for transporting your goods. You might not realize it but when you are forced to trade a good for another good you will pay more than you would pay if you had cash. Why? Because the seller can only sell the goods he receives from you to a limited number of buyers if they don't use the goods themselves. Cash gives the seller the ability to buy more things for less and these savings are passed on to you."

"You have all had to pay up to a quarter of your goods at a mill or through tolls in order to get your grain ground or goods to market. Or maybe you were expecting some good in payment but were only offered another less valued one in compensation. Am I right?"

A few call out in agreement.

"You would only wind up paying a tithe of that if you had cash to use and would never have to settle for something you don't want. That would now give you extra cash you could use for a host of other things. The possibilities are endless!"

"I can't relate as well as some the limitations of bartering since my circumstances afforded me opportunities to gain ready cash easier than many of my good hard working peers. So I will use the example of my good friend and brother Whig, Abraham Lincoln who many of you know. Please stand up Abe and take a bow."

The tall gangly Abe stood up for a moment and waved to the crowd, most of whom cheered lustily for him. This gave Jane another chance to look him over. He didn't seem like much but had a confidence and bearing about him she found most intriguing. He quickly sat back on the fence and Stuart continued his speech.

"Many of you know of Honest Abe's hardworking past and the many jobs he held in New Salem before earning his law degree and entering politics but many do not know of his hard past. What I can say is that through that period in his life he, like many of you, found it difficult to earn ready cash for your labor. You would receive items in kind."

"If you farmed you could barter your produce for items you may need or sometimes you could be offered a line of credit that was granted only with the merchant, millkeeper or neighbor with whom you contracted. Most often you would receive goods or services that were deemed equal to the amount you had earned by working or bartering goods."

"In either case you can only receive goods or services they offered. Your options are limited. If you wanted something that was only offered for sale elsewhere you would have to try and barter the goods and services you had and if the seller didn't want any of that you would have to go to a third party to barter for other goods the seller might want."

"This is a hard, laborious process that took much time and was always susceptible to the changes in fortunes and needs. What if by the time you acquired the goods the seller originally wanted he was able to procure them elsewhere and no longer desired them. Where would you be then? Has this happened to you before?"

Many in the audience including Jane nodded in agreement. Some called out "Yes!" or "Hear Hear!"

"How many of you have wanted to clear unused parts of your farm but haven't because you can't find ready buyers for the surplus grain you could grow so you only grow what you can easily sell or use yourself?"

More nodding and cries of agreement.

"Of course you have! We all have. With cash this becomes a thing of the past. With cash all the vistas of opportunity are open to you. You can go where you want and buy what you want. There are no more middle men. There are no more running back and forth trying to find what someone needs so you can get what you want. With cash you have the chance to get what you want when you want it as long, as the price is right."

"Cash all allows you the chance for speculation. You can use you cash to make more cash and you don't have to work to do it! You can do what is called an investment. By giving your cash to someone who has a business idea and is trustworthy you can help them start their business, and when it succeeds you will reap the rewards!"

"Now I'm not talking about confidence schemes or get rich quick scams. I am talking about sound speculations like buying land or providing money for a partner to set up shop or buying the tools needed to expand an already successful business."

"All this can become a reality through improvements to the river system which would bring an influx of cash that will increase the prosperity of all. When I first entered town I saw in a merchant's store a sign that read "Cash is Accepted". This shows how rare money is in these parts and how those who have an eye for business understand and desire the liberty to choose what to buy and who to buy from."

"I see everyone is out today in their Sunday Best. Now I know many of you here would like to get the missus an extra something or two. Maybe a new bonnet or dress, or one of those fine silk shawls I saw on display in the general store window. Cash gives you the chance and the river can provide the means to gain cash."

"We have already seen The Talisman make a successful run on the Sangamon all the way to the Mississippi. Now with a few more improvements we can see more boats floating down a ready made artery to prosperity and have your own goods shipped to St. Louis and New Orleans for profits the likes of which you could never dream of before!"

John had just returned and only listened for a few moments before he scoffed and got condescending about the speech. He thought the improvements were a waste of money, especially the river ones. He stated flatly to Jane that no amount of dams will ever make the Sangamon navigable and there are no need for major railroad and road projects that demand state funding. Any needs can be met by private firms. Asking people to pay more taxes for things they may never use or need is a waste of money from a people who have little enough of it to start. Tariffs were even worse in his mind. It was just another tax. If a business couldn't survive on its own it shouldn't. Jane knew all this before since they argued it countless times over dinner.

John Doe was a staunch democrat and didn't want Jane to be uppity in public, so when she wanted to continue listening to The Whig speaker, who seemed to have just been getting started though he had been speaking for a good thirty minutes, John demanded they leave to return to their farm which was a few hours away by wagon. When she began to argue that John Calhoun hadn't spoken yet her husband simply replied that Mr. Calhoun was detained in Sangamon having some business to complete.

Knowing how much John had wanted to hear the famed orator speak and understanding his disappointment, Jane said no more and left with her daughters in tow, still holding her infant, and clambered up onto the wagon. Without looking back she sat calmly beside her husband as a good wife would. He reached out and grasping the reins with a flick of his wrist, he called out, "git, git, git now". The horse began a slow walk while the wagon lurched forward in the direction of their farm.

FUN & GAMES OF ABRAHAM LINCOLN'S YOUTH

I came upon this man alone on his porch, sitting on a non-descript chair smoking a pipe and staring wistfully out across his overgrown patch of field. A small portion of it had the remnants of some recently harvested corn and some other type of crop. I was a city boy from Philadelphia and didn't really know too much of farming. I could recognize the corn stalks but that was about it.

I had come out here from my home city to find some people who could tell me about the great Abraham Lincoln, who had been killed the year before by the wicked scoundrel John Wilkes Booth. I had seen President Lincoln in 1863 when he spoke at Gettysburg a few months after the historic battle there against the rebel hordes of Robert E Lee. I had been a student at the time at a nearby university and when I heard that the great orator Everett would be speaking at the memorial for those that had fought and fallen at that great battle I, like many of my schoolmates, took the day off from my studies to hear him speak.

I didn't even know the President would be speaking that day. I was a student of English Literature and had read all the great speeches of the day, but Everett was my favorite. Gettysburg changed that for all time. I was a $300 man but favored the Union. I really didn't have a say in the matter. My father wanted me to continue my studies. We had wealth and like many of those of my class, we took the opportunity to pay what was a small sum for us rather than risk injury or death by battle or disease.

My father did other things to assist the war effort, one of which was donate large sums of money to help clothe the soldiers. He said that the shoes ole' Henry Heth of the Confederates was looking to confiscate for his soldiers were ones that he had purchased for Union troops. I don't know anything about that, but I do remember hearing the cannon and muskets firing those three days from the house we had fled to a few miles from my college.

That was the only time I was directly affected by the war, but the roar of the cannon is still etched firmly in my memory. It was something I will never forget. I remember thinking about those poor souls fighting and dying out there and I wanted to join them in their struggle. The cannons' rumble drained my will, even at that distance, and my courage was not the equal of my desire, so I stayed with most of my fellow students huddled in the home.

We barely spoke to each other until after the battle but then some of us went to the field in the days after to assist with the wounded. I lasted at that for but a day, my constitution wasn't cut out to see so much blood and I had become faint and nauseous and soon left. I wasn't proud of that moment but I don't dwell on it much, so it has affected me little.

Everett that day at the Gettysburg memorial fulfilled the promise of his previous speeches, and he went on with power and feeling for over two hours. It was quite an oration, but his effort was humbled by the two minute speech of his successor. In those few minutes Lincoln seemed to capture everything I felt from the speech of his predecessor, and it amazed me that someone from the prairies of Indiana and Illinois could capture so much feeling in so little words that it dwarfed the achievements of an eminent scholar and orator that day.

I had determined to find out what I could of the President. I didn't graduate from college until after the President was assassinated so it was the only time I had ever seen the Mr. Lincoln but his words stood with me always and inspired me. After graduating, with the help of my father I took a job as a journalist for a local newspaper. Father wanted me to join him as a banker, but my love of words was too strong for me to go into that line of work. But I soon became bored at the drudgery of writing about local events.

I was a restless soul. I wanted to do more when one day staring out the newsroom window it came upon me. I would find out all I could about Lincoln and write a book about him.

Father was none too pleased about this turn of events and thought even less of my idea to go out west to see the land of

Lincoln's youth myself. He just didn't see the point of looking out over endless fields and what it could do for me. He didn't have that sense of creative spirit that drove me here. He was a man of numbers. I was a humble man of letters.

My first stop had been Lincoln's boyhood home.

I had come out here to find out what made Lincoln tick. Maybe it was to figure out what made myself tick. I heard from one of my teachers that a man often puts things about himself into what he learns of great men, seeking the similarities that may inspire him to great things themselves. Perhaps it was that way with me.

The thing was I wasn't finding all that much to help myself so far. Maybe father was right, and I was wasting my time. I could probably find all I wanted at home, or maybe I just wasn't cut out to write about this sort of thing. Or maybe I wasn't very good at investigative reporting, or writing for that matter, since I wasn't learning much at all out here and what I did learn came out dull and mundane when I put pen to paper.

Then I stumbled upon a farm one evening seeking boarding, and hopefully a room to spend the night. Otherwise I would have been doomed, as I so often was, to sleeping outside under the stars. The residents of the farm were curious what someone was doing out here and I told them my story. They said they happened to know an older man who claimed to be a boyhood friend of Lincoln. Maybe he could help. I jumped at the chance, found out where the man lived, and the next day I went to seek him out. Now here I was looking at the man himself. Well at least I thought I was.

The man gave me a cold hard stare but brightened up when I told him why I had come. He said he thought I was a traveling salesman at first looking to sell him some books or a bottle of cure all. But I guess I seemed harmless enough and he seemed to want to speak, or maybe he was just lonely and wanted some companionship. Anyway, it was but a moment before he began to weave his tale in his country bumpkin sort of way.

"I knows Lincoln a long, long time," the middle aged man said as he puffed on a small, well used corn cob pipe. "We was friends," he continued, "when both of us were wee lads but I don't think ever was Lincoln a wee boy. Mayhaps he was born tall. He certainly was when I knew him. Tall and thin, but strong as an ox."

"We was both Indiana boys. Growing up in Indiana at that time was hard, not like it is nowadays. We kids spent most of the time working in the fields or around the cabin, doing things our father's or mother's didn't have the time to do so we didn't have much free time for games and such. But any time we did, we had fun with what we could get and find. Most of the games we found ourselves playing were simple and most of these games we played with the children in our own families."

"Sometimes we would have some fun with kids of the neighbors. This was mostly if we happened upon them on our way to school. We would toss a rock or ball between us, if someone had brought a ball with them, or we would race or see who could throw a rock the farthest but we rarely saw anyone when we were walking to school, even though it would take a couple of hours to get to school and back each day."

"I do be remembering another time we went playing a game of "Ox", least alls this was the one time Lincoln ever played it. Abe hitched himself up to a sled and hauled around a couple of the girls including his sister around a bit. It was all fun and games but some of the other boys got wind of what Lincoln did. Now Abe was a sweet soul and would never really harm the hair on your head, but these boys took to calling him a bunch of names, like a beast of burden and such, and well Abe lost a bit of his legendary patience. Let me tell you how he took to whupping those boys some. I'll say they never once called him anything like that again, that be sure!"

"Lincoln's pa, ole' Tom, now he was a carpenter of some repute. He used to make Abe and his sister the best toys. I remember I was over at the Lincoln cabin one day and in the corner I saw some of the most beautiful stick horses I ever saw! I asked Abe about it but he was a bit shy about speaking of them for some reason. But Sarah she wasn't. She told me how her pa had made them for her and Lincoln. There was three of them, all made of wood with some wool attached to the backs of the heads like a sort of mane. One was obviously made for a girl but the other two were more manly. Why to me, the wee lad that I was, they looked like they were made for a prince!"

"One was of a wood that looked chestnut brown, while the

other was a bit gray. Sarah told how Lincoln had named them Blueskin and Nelson, after the great George Washington's horses. And she said he would love to go prancing about on them reliving the great battles Father George fought upon them. Sarah said when they would race Abe would like to saddle up ole' Blueskin but when it came to 'a warrin' then he would only ride Nelson, just like Washington himself. She giggled as she said Abe would play with them even though he was much too big for them and looked a bit silly riding about with them around the farm."

"Lincoln reddened a bit after that but when I went to touch one and asked if I could play with it, big Abe said "No" in no uncertain terms. I guess he prized them still to that day."

"Sarah was real good at calming her brother down when he done got a little riled up but she needn't do that very often. Abe didn't get heated about too much and it was rare he would ever get mad, even if he was poked at. It was only when something touched him dearly he might get angered but he was quick to forgive and forget."

"This time around I remembering she started talking about how she liked to play Cat's cradle. She said she usually played it with her mum when she was very little but sometimes Abe would play. She asked if I wanted to play and I said sure would. I didn't like to see Abe get all ruffled so I went along with his sister."

"She took out a long string many feet long and we sat cross legged on the ground and started weaving the string between our fingers to make a cat's cradle out of them. After a few moments of this Abe ambled over plopped himself down and joined in the fun. We played that a whiles and forgot all about the horses. We then played a bit of hopscotch with his sister and we all soon came to laughing until her mother called us all in for a bit to eat. Sarah was a real saint, God Rest Her Soul."

"But as I says their pa Tom could make just about anything out of wood and he loved to carve up some toys for his kids. My favorite toy that ole' Tom made for them had to be Jacks. Now Sarah was a real whiz at Jacks so Abe most often wanted to play dominoes but their set of Jacks was the best in town. Tom had a wit about him, and he was pretty creative, I guess that was why he was some storyteller and his son certainly got that same sort of wit from him. Well this set of Jacks was like no other one I ever saw then or since."

"Tom, well he made the jacks and he crafted them of different sizes which Abe and Sarah gave different points. It all depend on how hard they was to catch them. If you was catching different sizes you got different points. I think she did that so Abe would play them more. Abe was a wiz with numbers and figuring so he did pretty good at them and his large hands made this the game he would win other than the other types of Jacks they would play so that was the one Abe often want to play. Sarah enjoyed the company of her fun loving brother so she usually did what he wanted. I think she let him win more too so he'd play it more. I never could beat her. I didn't care since I just liked to wonder over them and sometimes I would just pick them up and stare at them a whiles."

"I was telling you about them dominoes and I think that was Abe's favorite game. Tom made them a bunch of sets of these. Now you be thinking dominoes was a pretty easy to make but Tom made each one with a different carving on the one side, and I says he was a great carpenter so you couldn't tell which was which underneath. I remember one set had a crescent moon on the one side and the other side had all stars instead of dots. That was one of my favorites but Abe liked the one that had a beautiful cross on one side and miniature crosses just like the big one instead of dots."

"Sarah took a shine to the one she called the "Princess" dominoes. That one had a girl a kneeling down in prayer on the one side while the other had stars instead of dots. I knows there were more but my remembering isn't as good as it used to be."

"Abe, if he didn't have a book to read, he could often be found whiling away the hours playing cup and ball, sometimes alone and sometimes with his sister or me and I guess others. I remember sometimes I used to be playing Jacks since Abe wasn't always fond of that game and I liked to ogle them some and whiles I was doing that Abe would be playing ole' cup and ball. Just tossing the ball up on its string and catching it in the cup. He really like that one."

"Now the one I remember the most was pick up sticks. Tom again gave his little ones a fine set and he made them of all different sizes and shapes carved from natural shapes just like the branches you be seeing in the trees or lying on the ground. Again Abe was always tinkering away in his head and he gave a different point to them since Tom didn't color them. When I first saw them I became awful jealous of them and begged and begged for one like theirs from my own pa. Now my pa couldn't make anything like that so he came to asking Tom to make one for him. My pa even offered to pay some corn for it but ole' Tom was always nice to us and we was always helping each other so he just made up a set and gave it to me as a gift. I did hear he made some for other kids but most of those he charged a wee bit to help him get by."

"When we got older we grew into the games the bigger boys would play. Lots of them would be something about the work we did, we used to play those to show off who was better at what but Abe pretty much always won at these. It didn't matter if it sprints, running a course with all different things to jump or crawl under, stump tossing and we sometimes put stump tossing or chopping a small pile of wood in the middle of the race but Lincoln he usually won all those. Especially wood chopping. Abe was a wonder with an axe. He could chop anything with an axe and he was using a man size axe when most of us were still using the ones they gave to the lads. We was always amazed at Abe's skill with and axe and how he was always the best at all sports. But he was never one to rub our faces in it. He would just beam from ear to ear for a moment and then we would move on to the next game."

"His mother Sarah often teased young Abe about his lanky, tall frame, claiming that he'd better "keep his head clean, or she'd have to scrub her whitewashed ceiling." One day, Abe watched two small boys play barefoot in the mud, and he got an idea. He invited the boys inside. One by one, he lifted them up, flipped them upside down and had them walk on his stepmother's beloved ceiling. According to the story, Sarah Bush Lincoln took it in good humor, although Abe did have to whitewash the ceiling afterward."

"I do remember that he wasn't too fond of any card games. Most of the boys would be gambling away but Abe always shied from that. I think he never wanted to be under account of someone and owe them any time or anything and I'm sure his pa would be none too pleased if he did."

"We did do a bit of barrel rolling when we was getting up to our man years, and once or twice did some tar and feathering to a roust about to teach them a lesson but this sort of rough housing games we only did if we caught someone being rowdy or we would stick someone in a barrel who had too much to drink and was soused then roll him down one of the hills. That brought a laugh until one of them came flying out and broke his arm. We all got in trouble for that."

"The biggest game that Abe was probably the best at was his wrassling. Nobody ever beat him at wrassling. Never saw one person ever get the best of Abe at wrassling and he would wrassle boys almost twice his age and when he was still in his teens he was known to have beaten grown men. There wasn't one person from town who could beat him and Abe even wrassled strangers and never lost once. He was strong as an ox and wily as a coyote. Couldn't throw him and once Abe got you down on the ground there was no coming up until you cried uncle."

Now the old feller winced a bit as if he remembered one time he may have tussled with Lincoln. I spoke with the old man for quite a bit more, but he kept going back to the games and such and it came to mind he might be a little crazed in his old age. He said he wasn't yet 60 but he looked like he could have been over 70. I guessed his life was a bit hard and maybe it was rough on him since he was all alone now. He said his kin had all moved away or were killed in the war, so he was stuck by himself. I gave him a few dollars for a meal, which wasn't very good, and for his time and story. He perked up a bit after that and thanked me several times, but soon enough I was well on my way and off to the next town.

It was when I got to Illinois when I heard another fine tale of one of the pranks Lincoln played on some young kids that almost blew up in his face literally.

It was in the fine city of Monticello, Illinois where the townsfolk witnessed another one of Lincoln's supposed pranks, maybe it was a tall tale but the townspeople insisted it happened and is now a legend of the wit and often mischievous bent of the mind of Abraham Lincoln. This one almost backfired on Honest Abe in the worst way and set the Tenbrook Hotel on fire.

Michael John Joseph Del Toro

While he was staying at the hotel, Abe scared a few kids by getting them to heat up an inflated pig bladder, which kids liked to fill up with air and bounce around to throw to each other like a balloon. Like I said he had them fill up the bladder with air and heat it up in the hotel fireplace telling them it was a trick to make it float in the air. The bladder soon expanded and burst, as Lincoln knew it would and gave him quite a chuckle by startling everyone in the hotel, but it also spread hot coals and embers all over the room. Lincoln then offered to sweep up the debris, but in doing so, he set the broom on fire. This wound up startling Abe for a few moments but someone managed to grab a bucket of water and doused the broom, and drenched Lincoln, making the future President look like wet muskrat. The water succeeded in putting out the flames but not the President's mirth even though now it was at his own expense.

I did wind up learning a lot about Abraham Lincoln in my long travels and spent a couple of years longer than expected wandering around the Western countryside, but I never got around to finishing my book. I got a little sidetracked myself when I met a fine young woman in Springfield, Illinois who eventually came back to Philadelphia with me and we were wed. By then I had gotten over my reluctance to work in the bank with my father, and lost my itch to write, but I couldn't help but cherish the memories of my time searching the past of Lincoln, for through it I might not have found out about myself, but I did find my future in a loving wife and eventually a fine family. And for that I will always thank our dear President and the inspiration he gave me that one fine day at Gettysburg.

DUTY, HONOR, FAITH & FAMILY

Abraham Lincoln's eldest son, Robert was home on vacation after his most recent term attending the prestigious Harvard College. Unlike his other boys, whom Lincoln poured adulation and leniency to the point of being subservient and deferential, his relationship with Robert was of a distinctly different nature. Cold and reserved would be an apt description.

Perhaps it was the gap in age between Robert and his siblings and the circumstances of the Lincoln family during Robert's youth compared to his brothers. When Robert was a young boy Abraham Lincoln was still in dire financial straits, with a looming debt that hung over him like an albatross or a monkey on his back. When Thomas & William Wallace were born the Lincolns were in much better financial condition, the debt had been all but paid off and his law practice was prospering like never before.

Whatever the reasoning behind the treatment of his eldest son compared to his younger ones, Abraham was a bit stricter and less forgiving with Robert than he was with either Tad or Willie, especially as Robert grew older. This became even more pronounced after Willie's untimely death in 1861. Thenceforth Abraham lavished more warmth and affection on Tad, even going so far as to have him sleep in the same bed in the evenings, and disciplining the child was a non-starter as Lincoln's assistants, aides and government officials soon found out much to their chagrin.

Tad was given free reign of the White House and had no high opinion of books or study, and absolutely none at all of discipline. He was allowed to do virtually anything he wanted and if Lincoln was informed of any transgressions, rather than punishing the child the President was far more likely to take the boy in his arms and lead him out while chastening whomever was so presumptuous as to inform Lincoln of the youth's misbehavior.

Robert, on the other hand, never had as free a reign when it came to his studies or free time. Lincoln didn't ride him hard, but he did make sure Robert always did his work, had the schooling that Abraham never had himself, and was expected to be an upstanding and upright man from an early age. Now Lincoln may have been a bit stricter with his eldest son than the others, that being said, Abraham was still a very lenient father and Robert was never very diligent in his studies.

He was proud his son was getting such a fine education and presumed his son felt the same way. Thus it came as a rude awakening when Robert suddenly informed his father he wished to discontinue his studies and join the Army. This was the last thing on earth his father had wanted to hear, and he was sure that if Mary caught wind of it she would fast lose her mind through worry and disappointment.

Now Lincoln could understand why his son would like to serve his country. It was the same reason he, his father Thomas, and his grandfather Abraham had done so. To serve one's country is the highest civic virtue, but it didn't take into account serving one's family in their time of need. It was this point Abraham wished to stress to his son and in his first distress on learning of Robert's desire Lincoln found himself having difficulty formulating words that were often so readily on his lips.

Abraham's first thoughts went to Robert's mother and his brothers, and he began with those.

"Robert, you understand mother's condition. You know her conniption fits have become stronger and more frequent. You know why these fits are recurring. She misses our Willie. We all do. I know you do. I certainly do all the time."

"I thought about our Willie for days and weeks on end after he passed. I would go and visit him as he lay in his little casket and I would weep upon it for hours at a time late at night."

"You did so too. Mother did so as well as did our sweet Tad. We lost much with our little Willie but none of us lost as much as dear Mother. Your mother has been beside herself after the loss of our Willie. She has been near hysterical on many an occasion. You really need to understand your mother's situation before you decide on your current course of action."

"Add to these the trauma of a trio of deaths that afflicted her soon after and while you were still a young lad. Losing her father, and grandmother who tended her in her youth and then the loss of our beloved Eddie shattered her frail health and affected her for years. This past year she lost our beloved friend and Eddie's namesake, your Uncle Edward Baker and then your brother Willie."

"Please bear in mind how having you join the army, where brave Uncle Edward found his fate leading his regiment in battle would be disastrous to her failing mental stability that is only just recovering from Willie's death. In your times of longing for distinction, excitement and adventure in the lure of the din of battle recall the misery you would bring to mother and the responsibility you have to her and myself as a dutiful son to complete a first-class education."

"You well remember your mother just after the death of our beloved Willie. However, you were in school during the worst of the ordeal, which still flares up from time to time. She was beside herself for weeks barely eating and rarely leaving the White House. She wallowed into a melancholy I know all too well, she became inconsolable and was almost lost to us."

"You know full well that even now she will not even enter Willie's room. She still refuses and it still is as it was while he yet lived. We at one point considered sending her yonder," his father gestured out the window towards a large lonely looking building that housed an asylum. "If you left Harvard and went off to War you would bring on her affliction yet again, and this time I feel we could not bring a semblance of stability back to her. Is this what you would want?"

"I don't want you to feel you bear responsibility for your mother, but she cares deeply for her children and the press treats her with scorn. She has borne much to be here and losing you to the vagaries of war after also losing our beloved Willie would be more than I think any woman could bear."

"Think of your friend and my clerk, Elmer, beloved by all of us. and how the young lawyer had so endeared himself upon the family Remember your mother's lamentations when it was learned he was killed in Alexandria. That was almost a year ago and still she cannot speak of him without tears."

Lincoln was becoming a bit inconsolable himself and could

barely string the words together.

"Try my son, try and understand the trials she is going through right now and maybe you can understand why we need you to stay where you are and complete your studies."

"Your dear mother has gone through much in her life. She married a poor man. Of this you know little for we tried to give you every luxury of life, and I am sure you understand now how you were not granted the benefits a wealthy family would have. You can readily note at Harvard how we lack the means to provide you with luxuries your fellow students take for granted,"

"I know that, and I beg your forgiveness. I also ask you to understand your mother and where she came from and her standing in society and how much she sacrificed as my wife and as your mother. My social standing forced her to do things she never thought she would have to do. She was not just a southern belle. She was THE southern belle of Springfield and she gave all that up to be the wife of a lowly man from Illinois."

"She had to do tasks she had never expected to do. Have you ever been to a stately manor in Kentucky? The ladies there would never in their darkest day for one instance think about having to do any sort of manual labor like washing clothes, cleaning dishes or even taking care of their own children!"

"Your mother took upon herself all of these tasks and she never once begrudged her choice. Mayhap once or twice she may have expressed her displeasure at having to be subjected to such menial tasks as no one of the blue blooded Kentucky hierarchy would do, but those expressions were voiced at moments of high pique and never an indication of her true thoughts on the matter."

"On occasion I would hire out help, when I had the means to do so, and once your cousin Harriet Hanks came to live with us for a time. Harriet was here to live with us while she went to the Springfield Female Academy, though to Mother I said the young girl would assist her in the daily chores when she was able. This was due to my strained finances as I could not at the time afford a hired servant. Thus, Mother would at times take out her frustrations on the poor girl."

"It was a trial on your mother having servants from the north, because an Illinois girl would talk back where no southern girl, free or otherwise would ever have the gumption to do so. She would rail at them to no avail and desire their dismissal, even Harriet, our own kin."

"These incidents would occur most often when I was spending time away, sometimes months riding circuit around the state. Often I would stay at the office working very late into the evening leaving your mother all alone. At times she would become frustrated at my wayward ways and lock me out of my own house. I understood how I was not the most expressive husband and often didn't take into account her needs as much as I should have done."

"Your mother is one who has the highest virtue. Of that you surely have no doubts. She has done her utmost to raise you and your brothers. Your success is her success. Her life is lived through you."

"Your mother deals with the daily strain of having to live within her means while being vilified in the press and Washington circles for every little action she takes in public and rumors swirl when she is in no position to respond. You know this all too well from your time with her in New York and it has only gotten worse since that time. She misses you dearly and our situation here in Washington does not help."

"Mother is constantly beset by Northern papers declaring she is supportive of the rebels and some declare she is even a traitor due to a slew of her relatives serving in Confederate ranks. She is despised by eastern elites due to her western heritage. Think of her condition if you were in the Army. She would not be able to bear the increased strain on her nerves that are already taxed to the breaking point, if she was bereft of you, her eldest son, and if you joined the army she would be thinking upon that day and night."

"Perhaps you do not remember the time when we first moved to Washington in 1847. Mother was left all alone tending to you and Eddie. Though barely four years old, you would run rampant through the hotel causing all sorts of havoc and your mother would bear the brunt of the abuse your innocent racing caused. All the while she was beset with the caring for young Eddie."

"Remember well she had no female companions in which to draw solace and I was away on business all day and often far into the night. These are the trials a wife must bear but you as a loving son should respect her wishes and try to not draw too much emotional distress from her in selfish desires."

Lincoln now began to ramble causing Robert to look upon him wide eyed. The boy had certainly not expected this reaction from his father. Robert felt his father was reflecting the strain of his office. The boy was perceptive to others feelings like his father. He began to doubt the wisdom of his desire to leave school.

"I think you take for granted the situation you have been given and all the sacrifices we have made to put you there. Don't think on me but take your mother's situation when she first left the life of her youth to join with me, a poor struggling lawyer. She came from a family that was at the pinnacle of its local society. Her surrogate father and family were the de facto rulers of Lexington Kentucky, the foremost city of Kentucky, our homeland."

"Now she was by herself for much of the time. She had to do all the work she had normally had slaves or servants to do for her. She didn't know how to do it. She had to learn how to do it. She did every single chore she would normally have considered beneath her. She was a good Whig. She was always a good Whig. She took all of this and had no problems."

"Now think about this my son. She had to do all of this without me to support her. I was often either on the circuit, which would take me all across the southern districts of Illinois, or I was as often staying late at my office trying to prepare a case."

"You were of an age where you could begin to understand of sacrifice and struggle after our return to Springfield after my term in Washington ended. She was unflagging in her support of me through my many failings, especially in the turbulent 1850s when the nation began to fracture. She was steadfast after my failure to attain United States Senate in 1856 & 1858, my failure to argue the major Reaper Trial that would have done much for my standing, all due to homeliness and lack of legal refinement in both appearance and argument. Such setbacks could tax the patience of many a forbearing woman, but your mother always remained true."

"Mother's belief was that I would someday hold the highest office in the nation, she believed I towered over my great rival, the late Stephen Douglas, intellectually as much as I did physically. Mother was always there to pick me up when my confidence was at the lowest ebb, even momentarily and her support never wavered and this unflinching devotion helped me persevere throughout the darkest days of my career when I felt every barrier to success had been placed before me thwarting me every time, even as I left no stone unturned in my hopes of prospering."

"She was the only person to never lose faith in me and through her diligent efforts to succor me and gave me the patience to weather the storm and eventually turn failure into a stepping-stone to success."

"We both have this same faith in you, and we are sure you will have a future any father and mother would be proud to witness. Would you sacrifice such a bright future for your mother's failing strength?"

Abraham was visibly distraught by now. His compassion for his son was great, as great as that for Mary. He was torn between the two, but he knew the only honorable way for his son. He just needed to formulate the words to impart his wisdom to his firstborn. He stopped for a brief moment in order to regain his composure. Robert was about to speak but his father held up his hand. Robert remained mute.

"You know this full well," he continued. "You as a young boy and young adult before you went to Harvard were witness to this and you should understand how this affected your mother."

"Don't misunderstand me my son. I know how you feel. You have no idea how I understand your feelings. These are selfish desires you are harboring and let me tell you a tale when I had similar thoughts, for similar reasons and how I successfully dealt with them. If I didn't my family may very well have perished in the ensuing winter. Your feelings are akin to mine when I was about your age. The circumstances that created this feeling were very different, but it doesn't take away from the fact that there was an acclimated feeling of wanting to leave our families, and yet I remained."

"I never spoke of this before to you or to anyone else, but today I will impart to you this story of the time when I once deigned to run away from home, and why it was I determined to return and fulfill my obligations to my family and kin."

"Around my nineteenth or twentieth year, my father had hired me out to a neighboring farmer for some chores. I had completed them early, as I was wont to do, and the farmer asked if I could assist on some additional tasks. We agreed on a price and I did the tasks required. When my father came to fetch me the neighbor innocently mentioned the extra tasks in the course of his congratulating my father on having such a fine son. My father did not accept the price I had reached with the farmer but took a different fee."

"When I learned this, I was angry. I felt that the time after completing the first chores was my own and I could then offer my services without having my father set the terms. I was so bothered by this that I determined then and there to leave home and find my own way in the world."

"The next day I was still hot from the incident the night before and left our farm, winding up some miles away at another neighbor's farm that evening. I asked to stay there. The farmer was a friend of the family and agreed. He then asked why I was not at home. It was an understandable question."

"I described to him how I was abused by my father and how I was determined to leave the family and find my own way in the world. The neighbor set me straight. He rightfully informed me that as I was still not yet twenty one years of age, I was legally bound to my father, and therefore my father was perfectly in his rights to make any price he wanted for my work. He also gave me a talking to in stating that shirking the responsibilities to my family at this time would stand with me forever. It would stain my reputation and follow me wherever I may wind up, for it would become a part of me and once I became a shirker it would be easier to shirk again. I would be a shirker for all time and slowly but surely would lose all the honor I had until I became as worthless all the time, as I was that first time I didn't not uphold my responsibilities to my family."

His father was such a master wordsmith that Robert had never heard him use the same word three times running. This drew the boy in and made him think that word "shirk" had a strong meaning.

"I took his words to heart. I knew what he said was true and it took me only moments to realize that his dire warning would undoubtedly come true if I continued on this dishonorable path. I told him I agreed with him. The farmer said I could stay the night since it was late. I declined and said I would make my way back home and inform my father of my thoughts as he had a right to know."

"That is exactly what I did. My father said he understood why I would feel that way, but the farmer was right. I was bound to him until my twenty first year. When I became twenty-one and decided to leave home my father would not try to stop me. We shook hands and never spoke of it again. I didn't leave home until my twenty second year, until I helped my family through the ordeal of The Deep Snow and aided them in their move to Decatur. It was only then that I made my way to New Salem and began my new life, alone but with honor."

"I understand full well your desire to make your mark in your own way in this conflict. But I beg you to think upon your mother and how it will affect her. I think your desire outweighs your family responsibilities."

"My son, please understand. I promised Mother you would complete your studies. We don't know what fate lies before us but while we have the means we wish beyond all the trials of life for you to be granted the best education possible."

"My son. Understand this. If you complete your studies and if the war still persists, I will do everything in my power to ensure you will play your part in it. But please my dear son, do justice to your mother. Make sure you graduate college and become a man of education for her. The rest I will do my utmost to make a reality. That I promise you. You have my word and my honor depends upon it."

Robert looked upon his father. He was much like Abraham, not the least of which was in compassion. The boy was distraught himself by this time. He looked at his father who had tears in his eyes, and Robert's eyes began to well too. He was clearly disappointed, but he knew that he couldn't dishonor his father and mother, even though it would be dishonoring himself not to take part in trying to heal their bleeding nation.

His father bore great responsibility in trying to unify such a divided nation, and now he understood his mother bore an equally strong responsibility in showing a brave face to the nation. He would be less than a loving son if he begrudged his parents their wish in this, at a time when they could control so little of the world around him.

Robert would stay in school and complete his studies and do honor to his parents, and then, Lord willing, he would do honor to himself and his nation by fighting to preserve freedom for all Americans.

Robert agreed with his father's wishes and the two weeping, embraced.

It wouldn't be until late in 1864 that Robert completed his studies and was able to join the Army that winter as he so fervently wished to do. He was appointed onto Lieutenant General Ulysses S. Grant's staff as a Captain and served honorably until the end of the conflict.

*history is replete with ironic twists of fate and Robert Lincoln is no stranger to them. Most people know that Abraham Lincoln was assassinated by John Wilkes Booth. Far less known is that around the time Robert graduated but before his father's tragic murder (the exact date is uncertain and unimportant), Robert was at a train station and slipped and fell onto the tracks as a train approached. A man leapt onto the tracks and aided Lincoln in getting back onto the platform. The man who saved his life was none other than Edwin Booth, the nationally acclaimed actor and older brother of John Wilkes Booth.

THE WINTER OF THE DEEP SNOW

Abraham looked out towards the lightly undulating plain of southern Illinois, his adopted homeland. It was one of the nicer days of this winter, if a day where the temperature barely reached the 20s could be considered nice. The sun was out this late afternoon affording the young man a picturesque view of the surrounding landscape. And what a view it was in this year that became known in these parts for all time, as the Year of The Deep Snow.

The winter of 1830-31 became a great leveler of Man, while few of the wealthy succumbed to the bitter cold, all were subjected to great privation in the Deep Snow. Such was the pain and horror that it could truly be said it was the time when Hell froze over. Those who survived this most intense of winters bore the marks of their trial upon their souls. In time a prestige was placed on those who could lay claim they had settled southern Illinois prior to this forbidding winter.

The Lincoln family was one of these early settlers, Thomas having brought them to this part of Illinois just prior to this legendary winter. His young, able son, Abraham, became a hero of Sangamon County for the help he willingly gave to all his neighbors in their time of need. His youthful vigor and great strength made him one of the few men able to sustain themselves in this bleak winter, where the snow was as deep as a man's chest and much of the land glazed with an ice so hard and deep, man or beast could walk unhindered atop the surface without fear of crushing the glazed over snow beneath them. It was a permafrost that was said to be found only in the farthest north or the great barrens of faraway Siberia, yet here it was, on our own doorsteps.

As seen from the hill upon which young Abe stood, the undulating plain spread before him on his way back towards his family's home took on the appearance of a white sea with small mounds, each spewing a bit of brownish black smoke interspersed around 3-10 miles *apart from each other. These islets were the homes of some of the Lincoln family's neighbors, one of which nestled behind Abe within the confines of surrounding woods was the one where the young man had recently departed. This peaceful scene belied the hunger and danger that persisted within each of these homes as the families huddled within struggled against the biting cold for survival.*

"That's the way my father would recite the tale he heard from Abraham Lincoln one day while at the General Store, first owned by Offut, then later by Berry & Abraham Lincoln himself. I remember the beginning by heart for I used to hear it often. Now I'm not much of a storyteller and neither was my pop but when you are sitting in a cabin huddled near the fireplace, where you can feel every draft through three or four different cracks in the walls, you cling to every word in order to forget your own hurts and wants even if it only lasts a few minutes. We had many a day or evening when we needed to while the time a bit before sleep would come over us and as young curious children, my sister and me would always be asking pop to give us a tale or two."

It was late in the winter of 1875, a new election year was about to come into full swing, and always around this time people would be reminiscing or wondering about the man known as the Great Emancipator. They were curious about what he would do if he were still President, and for many Lincoln was a man who could do no wrong. The stories and legends were told in their thousands and already many a story or legend, true or not, had blended into one and with each retelling became etched into the minds and souls of Americans until these tales were as true as the blade of a newly sharpened axe.

Now the residents of Decatur, Illinois held Abraham Lincoln in particularly high esteem and laid claim to their town being the birthplace of the great American's political career. It was here after all that the Lincoln family first settled in the great state that eventually propelled Abe to the presidency, well less than a dozen miles to the west. And it was here where young Abraham Lincoln was said to have made his first speech on his first election campaign.

While Abraham failed to get elected in that fabled campaign, he did make his mark with his neighbors. They were almost unanimous in voting for him in that election and most others up

Legends of Lincoln

through his successful reelection to the Presidency. The speech was also noteworthy for its brevity, folksy manner and policies he would follow throughout his political life.

Most of the residents choose to forget that the Lincolns only spent the one year before moving back east. They chose to remember that the most famous of all Americans lived there and many of what are now elders of the community or descendants of those who were proud to be called his friends.

Byron didn't know Abraham Lincoln firsthand, but his father and mother, God rest her soul, both laid claim to that distinction. His father was a man of moderate wealth and standing in the community, while Byron was not wealthy, he was highly esteemed due to his military service during the War to Save the Union. Many people in these parts chose to call it by that name rather than some of the others that gave credence to it being a War to end slavery or secure the rights of the Negro.

Byron was in a local drinking establishment and this new election was bringing a lot of the same animosity and questions he felt were already firmly and forever answered by the great victory of the North. He had learned quickly that these feelings had not succumbed but had merely milled about just under the surface and would often reach a boiling point to rear their ugly head whenever an opportunity presented itself. He knew this full well, so he preferred to use the less partisan phrase for the war when he was in public places, especially one where people's sensibilities were more easily offended or if he was hoping to gain a free drink or two by his stories as he was today.

Byron himself, while not an abolitionist per se, was firmly in the camp of abolishing slavery. He hadn't always felt that way, and most of his family members were even now still avidly pro slavery. This section of Illinois had long been one of divided loyalties when it came to the slavery question, and had been since the township's founding, which happened to be just before the Deep Snow he was in the midst of describing to his audience.

There was a time when Byron, just like his father, was an unrepentant supporter of the Southern Affliction, as many northerners called the institution of slavery. He joined the Federal army soon after Lincoln's first call for 75,000 troops during the furor surrounding the firing upon, and subsequent surrender of,

213

Michael John Joseph Del Toro

Fort Sumter in Charleston, South Carolina.

His reasons for joining were simple and had nothing to do with the Negros. He certainly didn't want them to be placed on equal footing with hard working, law abiding, good white folk. His reasons were simple. He wanted to support the Union and punish the rebels for disrespecting the flag, and just as importantly he wanted to ensure the safe and free navigation of the Mississippi river. The river was still the life blood for most of the families in Decatur, even while the railroads were making their way through Illinois and beginning to spin their metal webs in and around the state much like the navigable Illinois rivers themselves.

The rivers were a viable trade route and often cheaper than the railroads, which were under the whims of railroad owners, many of them proving to be quite unscrupulous in their search for profits. But railroads were an all-weather trade route to the east and from there to other countries. His family hadn't done much trading and when they did, they used the Mississippi, the Old Man was navigable all seasons. Many of the rivers weren't. One of Lincoln's pet projects during his first years of a politician was making the Sangamon river navigable. It never panned out and he paid the price when the expenditures were blamed for causing a recession. This wound up knocking the wind out of the sails of both his river improvement legislation and the Whig party itself. The once unsinkable island of Whig dominance had become a bastion of the Democratic party, virtually overnight.

This eventually had the county changing hands several times, and in recent years it had become one of the many counties supporting the successor to Whig ideology, the Republican party. It was now again becoming a battleground for party dominance and it was expected to have a significant part to play in the upcoming election.

At the time of his service to the Union all he knew was that the rebels were blocking the use of the Mississippi and they must be stopped. This fervent desire inspired him to re-enlist for three years or the end of the war. He still had no love for the Negro, that came later. It was when he was struggling with his division of Grant's army digging a canal in order to come to grips with the Rebels holed up in the fortress of Vicksburg that he got his first taste of the inhumane conditions a slave lived with every day.

They were stuck in the middle of nowhere on the other side of the river facing Vicksburg. His company had commandeered some slave pens to use as their quarters. When he first caught sight of the pen he was to spend the next month in he almost vomited.

But the alternative was to sleep in the mud, so he made do with what he had in the realization this is what a slave had to live in their whole lives. It was this and the cheery disposition the "contraband" slaves who were given shovels, and many of whom wound up working beside him, displayed that made him reevaluate his earlier convictions. Now he never became an out and out abolitionist but his first experience with the Negro and others during the rest of the conflict made him accept that the Negro was due his freedom and the rights of other Americans, if not the vote.

None of this really mattered to Byron at the moment. He was enjoying the temporary celebrity he had as he held court with his tale of the Deep Snow. There were a few residents in the county who could remember that fabled time but most living in Decatur had settled afterwards and lacked the prestige that came with one who could state he was one of the pioneers who tamed the land before that harrowing winter.

Byron was now giving a vivid description of the winter itself, while adding bits and pieces of the stories he had heard of the Lincoln clan from his father, "Larger game like deer was easy to catch as the ice frozen over the snow was strong enough to bear the weight of man and game, but after a few bounding strides the deer would crash through and be unable to escape. A great many were slain in this way and this game was never plentiful after the Deep Snow for over a decade. Men would sometimes be caught far from home and be forced to kill and disembowel their horses, then let the guts spill out in order to sleep in the cavity formed until morning."

A few scoffed at what they thought was an obvious tall tale.

"You may laugh, friends," Byron cast them a hard stare. "But find any true blooded Old Settler and you will learn I speak the truth. We lost old Bessie that way when my father was caught out one windy evening and got lost. Almost froze to death he did and if he didn't take out Bessie he would have!"

All it took to stop any murmurings of disbelief would be to invoke their claim as an "Old Settler", such was the esteem of these early settlers. Abraham Lincoln himself had helped form the Old Settler Society, which celebrated their past every October 20th starting in 1859. Having any ties to the most famous American of all as a founding member virtually guaranteed one to be held with a certain amount of respect if not awe.

"Both my family and Lincoln's arrived prior to Winter of the Deep Snow, but the Lincolns were caught completely unprepared for such an ordeal. They had arrived later in the season, so they had to hurriedly lay down a crop on a small amount of cleared land. This was before we had begun to use the prairie for anything other than grazing. We never suspected the prairie would be better farmland than wooded areas. The Lincolns could only clear a small area and so they ran short of corn."

"I remember my father telling me a story of how Abe Lincoln and his cousin John Hanks journeyed through the ice encrusted snow and then over the frozen Sangamon river to a mill located on the south side. Drawn by horses this mill was sought by all far and wide to make meal from their grain, mostly corn."

"The two boys were allowed by the owner to open the gate and gather enough of the remaining corn to fill a sled which they proceeded back across the river to their new home. This helped them have enough food to last the rest of the winter and into spring, but they were haggard and more likely to get the shakes because of their weakened state."

"Old Settlers used oxen, like those used to draw the Lincoln's sled, to pull ice scrapers to cut through the great snow drifts. This would make roads, but strong winds would create the drifts anew causing us to have to do it again and again over the next few months. Anyone traveling would have to plod their way over these temporary trails. Eventually we were able to pack the trodden snow into coarse ice roads. These "roads" lasted well past the time the rest of the snow melted away. Late that spring you could still see these as white ribbons across the vast brown-green, newly tilled fields like a giant net."

"Other game caught in snow were smaller but were very weak

since they had little to nothing to eat. Everything was too deep for them to forage under the snow. So we found it easy to get meat and we had plenty of turkey, rabbits, prairie chickens, ducks, geese, etc. These fell easy prey to hunters, wolves and packs of feral dogs."

Then came the inevitable question one always heard when telling the story of the Deep Snow.

"Now why did they call it The Deep Snow anyways?"

"The Deep Snow was caused by a huge blizzard that struck just after Christmas and lasted a week. It dropped several feet of snow across the land. This was followed by a rain storm and a cold spell that froze the rain on the way down. This made a sheet of ice atop the newly fallen snow. Then the next week or two was of a bitter cold which froze the snow on top into a sheet of ice so thick it could bear the weight of a woman or child, and even some men, with ease."

"If you think that was bad enough they said it snowed thirty times in the twenty eight days of February. You would be tramping in thigh high snow without even realizing under that snow was a sheet of ice you were walking on. There had never been anything like it before, and sure won't be anything like it again."

"It was so cold that winter the folk took to wearing their shoes stuffed with wool to sleep, not just to keep themselves a bit warmer but they learned that if they didn't then their shoes would be frozen solid next morning. I tell you that's that last thing in the world you want to be doing on a cold morning is stick you feet in some frozen shoes!"

"Now as I said the Lincolns had just settled in Illinois from Indiana the season before the snows hit. They never knew nothing like the snow that year, and for all they knew every winter was like that in Illinois. It wasn't even the snow that made the Lincolns want to go back to Indiana. That snow was something else, but they were a pioneer family and tough as nails. It was those "Illinois Shakes" that first fell winter that did them in and made them start longing for warmer places."

"If you never had those shakes I can't tell you how bad it was. I can only say it didn't just rattle your teeth and body, but it addled your brain! We all came down with them and to top it off we then had this fever. So for a week or so we were cold all the time and our body never stopped shivering. Then we were sweating and out of our minds from heat the next week. It drove us all batty and when the snow finally broke and you could get along the roads ole' Tom decided it was time to call it quits and seek greener pastures."

"Now the Lincolns were well on their way back to Indiana when they were convinced by some friends to give it another go. They were told the winters were never that bad before so if they could get through the worst of that then everything else would be easy. This convinced Tom and so they stopped in their tracks and made a new claim then and there, and they be there still!"

One of the other patrons issued a "Three Cheers for the Lincolns!" This led to a rousing chorus of cheers interspersed with many clanging glasses until some others started a series of bantering songs and Byron was lost again to his musings and all but forgotten to the boisterous crowd singing and carousing late into the evening.

HONEST AMBITION & COMPASSION

William Seward had always been a jovial and entertaining man. He once had had many guests over his homes daily whether at his mansion in Auburn, the hotel he resided while governor of New York, or the stately house he stayed in while Secretary of State in Abraham Lincoln's talented cabinet. However, the combination of a carriage accident that shattered his jaw and left him a broken heap followed by the ghastly neck wound from the near fatal attack coinciding with Lincoln's assassination in rapid sequence that fateful spring in 1865 robbed the once hale man of much of his vitality.

He could still entertain in a most hospitable and cultured manner, but he tired easily and had begun to show his age. His once nightly after dinner parties were now few and far between and he spent much more time with his immediate family who tended after him in a most loving and gingerly fashion.

Tonight was just such a night. After ministrations from his granddaughter to help him relax, he settled in his luxurious chair beside the fireplace. He was propped up on many pillows and enjoying his cigar and a glass of wine, reflecting with his eldest son Augustus on what made a man great.

Naturally considering the close association and reverence Seward held for the President, Lincoln dominated much of the ensuing discussion. Augustus was not present with the family during most of their time in Washington, as he was an active officer in the Union army during the conflict between the states. He spent most of the war as a paymaster serving in New Mexico and the Arizona Territory though he had been reassigned to the capital late in the war and was present during the attempted assassination of his father, which he helped thwart. During the altercation the would-be assassin had stabbed the younger Seward seven times and it took a long time to recover from those wounds.

He was still serving in the army, now as a colonel, and was on leave to visit his family. William himself had recently just returned from a trip around the world and his son noticed his father was noticeably weaker than he was the last time they had seen each other about a year earlier.

Seward was using these discussions to serve as a reminder to him in a series of notes that he was hoping to later develop into his memoirs. This reminiscing helped keep up his spirits. Thinking of his service to the late great President and the war effort was the highlight of a long illustrious career. This was a career that spanned several decades and was intimately intertwined with the state of Slavery and the Negro, which William Seward championed for all his adult life. Seward was understandably quite proud of the very important part he played in one of his country's most trying periods.

Seward was telling his son about Lincoln's own progression in the political arena and the *Cause*, as abolitionists referred their quest to ban slavery from the country.

"Now his speech at Cooper Union in New York City just prior to the start of the 1860 Presidential election was said to be the pinnacle of the art of the spoken word. So mesmerizing was it, much like that of the esteemed Edward Bates' in St. Louis around a decade earlier, that none, even the correspondents covering the event, had the presence of mind to record the words. It was a magical moment that was said to have eclipsed even his "House Divided" and Gettysburg speeches and catapulted Lincoln into national prominence in an instant."

"I do believe that it was that speech in conjunction with the series he gave in his debates with Douglas that allowed him to gain the nomination over both Chase and myself. It added a luster that Bates couldn't circumvent as a Dark Horse Candidate, like Lincoln. Besides Bates was never a true Republican and would have stained our platform with the taint of a former slaveholder however repentant he may have been."

"I think it was the compelling oratory of Lincoln that put the fear of God in Douglas and forced him to dishonor the office he sought by personally campaigning and I think that the precedent he set will forever degrade the Presidency into the sullied ranks of a mere office much like a Senator or congressman."

"Douglas had felt the full force of this oratory in their highly publicized debates. He knew better than anyone that ability of Lincoln to speak in a manner that best resonated with his audience. This was proven in those debates and proven again in his Cooper Union speech which was delivered to the far more refined Easterners, many of them who had been or were going to be office holders at the municipal, state and federal levels. If Lincoln could draw that much applause and renown from one speech, Douglas was forewarned he would have to go to extraordinary lengths to counter him, though Lincoln would never stoop to campaigning personally. Many of his speeches were readily available in print and that alone would be tantamount to a personal campaign. Plus, of course, he would have the full support of the legions of Republican party supporters, including yours truly, to back him with active campaigning. And behind it all we held the truth of the evils of slavery and the moral superiority intrinsic in such truths."

Augustus didn't wholeheartedly agree with that assessment, "I agree that with the likes of Lincoln's, Chase's, and Bates' supporters, combined with the party bosses of Simon Cameron, Curtis and of course your mentor Thurlow Weed that was a most formidable combination, but I'm not sure if it was not the splintering of the Democratic Party which was the death knell to their campaign."

"Well if you look over the election results you would see that even if all the anti-Republican factions closed ranks under one candidate, they still would not have mustered enough electors to win. The backing of slavery was their death knell, the Cause was justified by the Lord and the Will of the American electorate."

"Lincoln stood as the standard bearer of the moderates of the country. He was known to back the Cause, but not as wholeheartedly as the radicals. This was appealing and the correct formula. While it may have disappointed radicals in not fully backing the abolition of slavery, they would close ranks behind a Republican candidate. All the other platforms they would find disgusting."

"He could relate to the average American whether that American was a farmer, laborer, merchant, landowner or doctor or lawyer. He was many of those things and lived and worked with people from all works of life. Not many of us could say the same and this made everyone he ever met believe that Lincoln could understand their condition and desires better than any of his rivals."

"His greatest gift was to be an Everyman. He would often declare himself of the humblest of origins and circumstances to appeal to the poor and downtrodden while offering policies that could appeal to those from all walks of life. Depending on his audience he could in one moment speak in common phrase and then speak using the lofty terms in vogue with the more cultured electorate."

"We both had the same Whig views throughout our lives. We were Clay men through and through and espoused the beliefs of Henry Clay, so we naturally gravitated towards the Republican Party when the slavery question reared its ugly head again after the monstrous Dred Scott decision of the Taney court."

"When it came time to nominate a candidate for the hotly contested 1860 election I was deemed too much the radical to please our esteemed colleagues gathered under the great wigwam in Chicago, as was Salmon P. Chase who later earned distinction as Secretary of the Treasury under Lincoln and later as Chief Justice of the Supreme Court. At the same time Edward Bates did not draw satisfaction since he never committed himself fully to the Republican cause so was deemed unreliable to both the Whig faction and radical alike. Lincoln also recruited him to round out the most distinguished cabinet in our history, and he did fine service as our Attorney General."

"Lincoln was always smarter than any of us when it came to picking his battles, though not infallible, and making himself known in the major national issues. I learned this fully when he became President and working closely with him and fellow cabinet members as his Secretary of State. Others took a little bit longer to learn, but we all eventually came to understand he was our political master and a genius of the highest order when it came to statesmanship. His loss while in the fullness of his power was perhaps the greatest blow to the nation in all its history."

"Unlike in New York and other eastern cities, in the West there were no national parties when Lincoln first became politically active. The success of a candidate was based on personal popularity and their ability to connect with the voters. This helped Lincoln, and was a positive advantage that he quickly mastered and stood him in good stead from the very beginning of his career as a public servant through his time as President."

"My first meeting with Lincoln in Tremont Temple in Boston, Massachusetts was a memorable event for both of us though he doubted it had as much an impact on myself than it did on him. This is entirely understandable as I was already a rising star in the Whig party while Lincoln had scarcely begun to soar before he had his wings clipped by his overreaching ambition for distinction."

"We were spending the night in the same room and I recall asking for his thoughts on slavery. Lincoln described the witnessing a slave auction on the wharf in New Orleans and seeing slaves on a chain along the Ohio river. He then asked me how I came to my views on slavery."

"I told him my stance had always been anti-slavery but I think what really galvanized my hatred to that accursed affliction of our country was when we decided to take a long vacation touring the South, if you recall. That route took us through the Allegheny mountains, an area with a nary any slaves, but many low income white residents. But even there the decrepit roads, dilapidated buildings, no commerce or travelers, the economic stagnation everywhere was already readily apparent. It was as if time stood still and if I could compare to anywhere, the only country in a similar state was France who had been rocked by a generation of almost continual warfare. The south had about the same amount of time of uninterrupted peace yet it looked devastated."

"That night I suggested to Lincoln he should galvanize his position in slavery. Instead of taking a middle road of straddling the fence between being for or against the institution he should formulate his position in clear terms that people can get behind and lead instead of follow. I said he was one who could convince anyone."

"I didn't tell him anything he didn't already know. He can speak in a way that audiences can readily understand and support. He can sway people in ways I can't. I can make those who already support my views more strident in their desire to see those views materialize, but at the same time I would entrench those who disagree into their own, while the undecided often viewed my manner of expression as divisive. Lincoln can march the undecided down a path of logic and morality due to his understanding of their language and background, and lead them, believing of their own accord, into the anti-slavery camp. So I said that fateful night."

"But Lincoln vastly miscalculated the public temper when it came to the War with Mexico. Even when he realized the error, he stood upon his principles of an honorable war, like I did when it came to slavery issues at the same time. I could sympathize with him on the abuse that was heaped on him and pushed him out of the public eye as I was a few years earlier."

"Lincoln took his principled stance on an issue that was more easily forgotten than the issue that inflamed public opinion the most and this helped him get back onto the main stage and made him a much safer bet as a moderate than I was when it came to slavery and had the radical tag hung on me like an albatross and I was proud of it. Lincoln made himself acceptable to all. Often times he may not have been the first choice but was the more palpable one when it came time to vote."

"Early on in local, state and national politics Lincoln was an aggressive politician, and in his speeches often spent as much time attacking select opponents of himself or party as in reflecting on his achievements or policies. He continued in this vein throughout the 1840s up to his abrupt temporary retirement from politics, and avoided great attachment to the slavery issue., with one notable exception."

"While agreeing with my argument of taking a firmer and more positive stance on the issue of slavery he stated his preference to refrain from doing so in his speeches for the remainder of his term in Congress. But I did sway him in some small way."

"Due in no small part to the influence of my arguments that fateful evening in Worcester, and no doubt due to the knowledge he would not be returning to Washington for another term, if ever, Lincoln introduced a bill to outlaw slavery in the capital. This was neither the first of such measures or the last, but it highlighted his practical mind that would be a hallmark of all his approaches to the issue of slavery while President."

"He tried to deal with every possible element that could raise concerns in a reasonable manner that reflected favorably to both sides. He misread the tenor of that House which was so disturbed by this question that his attempt to be reasonable and compromising was felt by each side to submitting to the opposition on the very matters he felt compromise would bring them together."

"This ignoble failure ended his one and only term serving as a congressman from Illinois and national legislator, and began his long sojourn from politics. Perhaps he would have remained on the outside, content to work behind the scenes but events transpired to bring him back into the fold."

"It took the moral outrage brought out by the Kansas-Nebraska Act and the Dred Scott decision to bring Lincoln's natural indignation over slavery to the forefront of his political agenda. He still attached a strong constitutionality to his brand of anti-slavery policy. For him it was only the territories that slavery should be forever banned, not the country as a whole, but these factors made his views of slavery a major facet of his political views. It gave him the ambition to help found the Republican Party in Illinois, and incidentally this moderate view on slavery is what made him more palpable as the 1860 candidate to the Republican Party as a whole."

"I was too much a radical in the minds of the delegates. They felt they would lose too many of the Whig voters who were not so anti-slavery if they clung to a more positive abolitionist agenda, as well as the moderate Democrats who found the popular sovereignty dictums of the Douglas camp repugnant."

"Lincoln at one time remarked to me that in the one and only election he lost by a direct vote, incidentally his first campaign, he won his own precinct with 92% of the vote. This was even though his own town was heavily in favor of the democratic presidential nominee Andrew Jackson, while Lincoln voted for Henry Clay. I think that goes a long way in showing how he was a person who people that knew him could get behind and trust even though they might not agree with everything he stood for politically. It's a shame that more people in the south were not aware of him more intimately."

"Lincoln was more attuned to the pulse of national feeling. He took a constitutional stance up until the middle of war and the south's intransigence forced his hand towards harsher measures. He originally felt that he could only ban the spread of slavery into the territories, and had no constitutional right to affect any change in states where it existed. His emancipation proclamation was a military measure he knew could not stand against constitutional scrutiny. His hope was the people would either abolish it of their own accord in the border states where it still existed, or an amendment would be enacted that banned it forever throughout the whole of the United States which after victory would affect both north and south. We see now he was right in that assessment."

"Now I had put some of my thoughts, related to above, to writing and wanted to hear your criticisms to what I believe is a fitting prelude to the war years. "

"Of course, father," Augustus replied.

Seward coughed to clear his throat and then began, "The Kansas - Nebraska act was the Bolt out of the blue that struck Lincoln and caused him to return to the fight he swore to lead so many years ago to himself. It was the fire that lit all our hearts. Every man and woman who believed that all men and women were created equal were smote in their breasts by this infernal Act that."

"It was like a tonic for us, a most bitter pill to swallow but once we did we all were galvanized to fight stronger than ever, by any means necessary, to demolish the evil of slavery from America forever. We began to marshal the forces of freedom from around the country and from these humble beginnings, the remnants of the Whigs, Free Soil and Independent Democrats, came together to form the fledgling Republican Party with the sole unifying factor of defeating the spread of slavery from our sacred soil and complete the process begun by our Founding Father's but left incomplete. Our divine purpose needed to be consecrated through four long years of blood and sacrifice in the crucible of war, but consecrate it we did."

"The Republican Party didn't last ten years before fragmenting in the furor of war, before again transforming into the Republican Party we know today, but it served its purpose. In providing a banner to form around the rallying cry of freedom, and with that as our sword and the Constitution as our shield, we sprang into a battle that brought our country to the brink of ruin before we succeeded in freeing the Negro from the shackles of servitude to take his rightful place beside his fellow citizens, and our beloved nation to be truly free not just in theory, but in fact."

Seward looked up to his son for his thoughts and advice.

Augustus thought for a moment and stated, "I believe it is perfect but why give Lincoln the more exalted status than yourself who had fought longer and while not paying the ultimate sacrifice, it was not from our wayward southern brothers from want of trying to extinguish your life?"

Augustus was referring to the attempted assassination of Seward on the very same evening Lincoln himself was basely murdered.

"I was pondering this subject myself. I feel the best way to express it would be as follows in some notes I have written." The elder Seward cleared his throat again, '…debates on the merits of the pro-slavery position and the anti-slavery camp were taking place in every senate floor, fairgrounds, church, market, store, even every dinner table. The greatest orators of the day were lined up and squaring off against each other whenever and wherever common folk and statesmen would gather. These were epitomized in the great debates between Honest Abraham Lincoln & the author of the Popular Sovereignty view enshrined in the Kansas-Nebraska Act, The Little Giant, Stephen Douglas himself."

"These encounters began at Illinois' State Fair of 1854 and did not end until Election Day 1860. For better than six years whenever Douglas spoke, Lincoln would follow. The two became inseparable in the eyes of the nation and each became the standard bearer of their respective Parties."

"The contrast between the two were as extreme as the ideologies they expressed. One was short and dapper, with a deep voice that carried far and wide, and graceful yet forceful gyrations that could bring his supporters to a fever pitch, and even those who were staunchly against his stances would be hard pressed to find themselves unmoved by his oratory. The other was tall and gangly, awkward in dress and expression, even his high pitched and hesitant voice displayed this sense of intrinsic uneasiness. But his well reasoned arguments expressed in a logical sequence in language all could readily understand would make even his most ardent critic doubt their deepest convictions after listening to one of his speeches."

"A complicated set of events conspired in early 1855 to keep Lincoln from gaining the US Senate seat he covered so much. This in turn create the backdrop that brought Lincoln into contention with Stephen Douglas, as he had not been in open confrontation with The Little Giant in 1856. Sacrificing his chance at distinction to guarantee at least one Senator from Illinois would be an anti-slavery man, Lincoln guaranteed he would have no such obstacles in 1858 for him being the only choice for supporters of the anti-slavery agenda to back against the pro-slavery Douglas Democrats."

"This setback also led to Lincoln honing and refining his already large backroom political machinery, which led directly to his formidable challenge to Douglas in the next Senate race and then to creating the perfect storm that brought Lincoln the Republican nomination for President in 1860. Hindsight provides a fitting backdrop of the hand of the Divine leading Abraham Lincoln to become the Man of The Hour at the greatest crisis in American history."

"Lincoln's attendance at the celebrated Reaper trial' had a lasting positive affect on him. Seeing the refined oratory of some of the eminent lawyers from the east, such as the future Secretary of War, Edwin Stanton, implanted the view that he needed to polish his own speechmaking in order to hold his own against them in both the legal and political arenas. This return to study of law and history to enhance his rhetoric was the last important impetus to elevate his speechmaking to the highest levels of eloquence while retaining the down to earth phraseology most commonly associated with him. Through it Lincoln became the United States' most accomplished wordsmith and attained a seat atop the pedestal of orators above the likes of Paine, Henry, Adams & Webster."

This blend of eloquence and down to earth rhetoric was reflected in his political views that stood in marked contrast with the likes of Salmon P. Chase and William Henry Seward who, as the nationally recognized standard bearers of abolition were held to be too radical to be elected to the highest office in the land." Seward looked over to his son.

"I think it is a wonderful summation that just needs a bit of tidying up before being able to be presented in a form that can be published. But what of the character of Lincoln? Don't you think that should be addressed as well?"

William Seward smiled at his son, "You read me quite well my boy. I have cobbled some notes on this as well." He then continued.

"Now Lincoln got the nickname of "honest" as a boy. He first was called it because he valued the truth so highly. If he heard someone speak an untruth, whether a child or an adult he was apt to correct them. He was so outspoken in this regard that it often got him into a bit of trouble. We all know children are meant to be seen and not heard. So if you were having to hear some whelp correcting you, it was not something you wanted to hear more than once, or at all for that matter. It took some doing for his father to get him to hold his tongue and most often he never was able to get him to curb this habit altogether. Abe always felt the truth must be told."

"His honesty evolved as he grew older and found expression in his dealings as a clear, merchant, surveyor and postmaster. Most recollections of his honesty regarded this trait when it came to money but it was also evident in correct assessments and his duties as a postmaster."

"We all heard of this through the example of the money he held for months after he was no longer postmaster. How he once overcharged a customer for sugar by an error when weighing the amount . How he made an error in his calculations and traveled for miles to return the correct change."

"It is exceptional to note he didn't carry this honesty over to his politics. At least regarding promises kept. He would to some extent do this but there were times when it was politically advantageous to himself to not do so and he would feel little compunction to keep the promises. This was most evident during the Civil War where he often would say or do something, but later when he felt it would not be to the best advantage to himself or more importatnly to the country to maintain this, he would quickly change his tune. This led many to refer to him by less complimentary terms like slippery, two faced or unscrupulous but he was no worse than the average politician by these actions and didn't create a general feeling of ill will towards him."

"Between the time of his election and inauguration Lincoln was disingenuous with me but I understand he did so in order to take office with a clean slate, beholden to no policy or any one person, while maintaining as many states in the unruly region of that South as possible. In this he was mostly successful."

"His compassion was always evident through the war years. I remember well visiting the injured troops. Whether they were from the North or South, to Lincoln they were all Americans, and he showed the greatest compassion towards them all. I remember how much he detested the military laws that required the death penalty for falling asleep on watch and for desertion. Many of these were appealed to him and he looked closely at each and whenever he saw an opportunity to remand the sentence he would. I remember he often expressed the opinion that it didn't make sense to kill a boy for deserting while letting the politician who convinced to desert go unpunished. He meant the Copperheads of course."

"He showed great compassion and sympathy to all men and animals. There were many tales of his going out of his way to help animals that were suffering. He was known to scold his peers as a youth when he found them torturing defenseless animals, or he would stop what he was doing in order to aid an animal in distress. He was known to be unwilling to kill another animal and there are countless occasions of his remitting the sentences of malefactors in order to relieve their pain. This compassion was among his greatest traits and most endearing ones. He once help d a drunkard who likely would have died if not for Lincoln's timely interference."

"Reflecting on Lincoln's compassion is well represented in the face of office seekers and how his humor masked his disappointment he couldn't please all of them. Now he felt awful about not being able to satisfy them. They seemed innumerable and would multiply each day. He would become down right miserable about it, and I often felt that did more to darken his mood than any reverse the army might encounter. There were too many pigs for the teats was a jibe he would often make in connection about these men."

"I, going to see him one day, during the time Chattanooga was besieged and right after his Gettysburg speech, and he was being looked over by a number of doctors. I remember him remarking in jest when they declared he had a malady, I believe it was some variant of smallpox, and needed to be isolated."

He looked them over and said, "Now I have something I can give everyone."

"I think Abraham Lincoln's compassion could best be exemplified by the restraint and effort to understand the slaveowner on the same plane as they understood themselves. He once told me, "In order to win a man to your cause, you must find a way to reach his heart for that underlies how he reasons the way he does." The contradictions of the South were readily apparent if they looked to their own past. It was many southern leaders who led the way in banning the piracy of the high seas represented through the slave trade.

"Thomas Jefferson himself, though remaining a slave owner broached the subject of banning the importation of slaves in America once that provision was constitutionally acceptable. He promoted making slavery illegal when he first introduced measures for the state constitution of Virginia. The former ideas gained wide acceptance both north and south, while the latter was objected out of hand by Virginia's residents. Jefferson was pointing the way and he was just one of many who recognized the basic incompatibility of slavery and freedom. This was a refrain Lincoln would turn to again and again as he sought to reason with the South in its illogical continuance of the evil affliction."

"Lincoln was among the most ambitious of men. He always felt since he was a young boy that he was meant to make his mark upon the world and always strove to match his success to this otherworldly ambition. However, he tempered this enormous ambition with his compassion. He could be the most aggressive of speakers in his rhetoric, but his wisdom tempered this as he grew older and more experienced. His compassion to the feelings and sensibilities of others intensified so instead of appearing as a broadsword swiping his opponents pride and stirring forever their resentment, it became like a rapier that dealt telling mortal blows to their reasonings without fatally severing the individual from ever treating with Lincoln in the future."

"If there were two traits that could compare to his compassion they would be his humor and his melancholy. The sadness he exhibited throughout his life manifested itself early and was likely due to the hardships one would encounter in the circumstances of his situation, of which many of his peers were experiencing."

"Melancholy was the surface mask of the basic characteristic which defined Lincoln as a person, his happy, merry disposition. His practicality, conservatism, wisdom, circumspection and melancholy all derived from the unrelenting hardships of his childhood and tempered his jovial humorist tendencies."

"The death and suffering of friends, family and strangers left their mark on him for all his days. The plight of the slaves he encountered at various times in his life. The massive suffering he witnessed by the soldiers and civilians affected by the Great War whether they fought or sided with the Union. He felt all their pain and it manifested upon his visage."

"But his way of countering it was unlike many of his contemporaries. Where they would harbor resentment or express anger, Lincoln responded with compassion or with humor. Many times when the sadness directly affected himself he would deal with the sorrow with self deprecating or light humor and what was most remarkable was the transformation this reaction would make upon his visage. Where once one could note the myriad of wrinkles marked upon him by these heart wrenching moments, these would disappear suddenly and his face would take on so evident a joy, happiness and hilarity that it became instantly infectious. All around would be unable to resist joining in this mirth and it was what made him so popular with all. It was guaranteed that spending time with Abe meant you were sure to spend a good portion of it doubled over with laughter or cracking a smile that would remain long after the joke ended."

"People often ask me why Lincoln received the nomination over me", Seward looked up and noticing his son about to begin to defend him, he quickly continued. "Now I am not bitter about it. Far from it. Lincoln did a better job than I could have. I learned quickly he was a man who was more than the sum of his parts and the best of us. I am proud to have served in his cabinet. Certainly when compared to his successor."

"But I am often asked. Just like you my son, they usually have a ready answer themselves be it luck or the advantages accrued to be ideally placed in party appeal or location of the convention in his home state which was hotly contested in the election. I don't see it either way though I am sure they helped."

"What I think is it was the actions of others that was the primary force that catapulted our late friend to the Presidency.

Grant once said Lincoln admitted to him he was never in control of events but events controlled him. He meant military events, but I think it was the same in the nomination. The first two votes during the nomination in Chicago had given the clear advantage to me, and if in the first vote a few more went in my favor I would have surely won. But Bates, Chase and I made many, often crucial, errors. Some at the convention, but most before. Our biggest failing was Lincoln made himself available to the nation at large prior to the election while we did not. He was in the public eye and memory and that was the blow that struck us the hardest."

"All is well. I have no regrets and dear Weed had always done his best for me. I don't regret taking his advice in going on a months long tour of Europe prior to the nomination, for the nation was led during its greatest trial by the one man who could have seen it through successfully. I believe the Lord gave us Lincoln and who is to question the Lord."

"Now Augustus, I did want to address some common misconceptions about Lincoln and his plan for slavery before the war erupted. I believe many southerners did and still do err in his ideas on the subject. I wrote the following about it."

"Now people have long been saying that Abraham Lincoln wanted to strike down slavery and that was his intention when becoming President. They say it was why he ran and they had been saying like things even before he was elected, especially down south."

"If one ever heard him speak or read his speeches prior to the election they would have known differently. I certainly did for I spent many a long evening with him as he ceaselessly toiled during the War that seemed without end."

"I do know he believed he was fated to strike a blow at that infernal institution, and he dearly wished to fulfill that fate but it never came into his mind he would be in a position to deal slavery its death blow as President. He didn't for one believe he had the Constitutional power to do so. He even believed his emancipation proclamation was unconstitutional in peace and would have been struck down after the war had not the Union proved victorious."

"However, he did know that he could do things in war not

normally reserved for the Executive in peace. He did have an earnest desire to ban slavery for all time in the territories. He believed that was within the scope of the powers of the President and he believed it was why he was elected as it was part of the Republican platform in 1860."

"I do know, as sure in my heart, the first inkling in this desire came within his vision to strike a blow at slavery and one he hoped from it that the institution would never recover. He spoke of it several times to me and I will relate one instance of the time the kernel of making the Negro free first nestled in his breast."

"There is great irony in that there was a previous amendment that had passed both houses before the Sumpter furor, and Lincoln would have signed and it only needed to be ratified and it would have kept slavery forever in the current Southern states that had it at the passing of the amendment. It would have only banned it in the territories. The south refused wanting to have full control of their own destiny. They also knew an amendment could be rescinded and if the election of 1860 taught them anything it was they no longer had any more political clout as a region. They needed a coalition if they were ever to have any say in the union and in doing so would have to compromise which might mean losing the right to slaves. The south wanted to have their cake and eat it too, and by doing so they lost both."

Augustus smiled, "I believe that is the best passage so far."

His father fairly beamed at his son's praise, "I also wanted to add a bit of the following I had heard just after Lincoln's death in reference to Mrs. Lincoln. I believe they have merit enough to warrant inclusion."

"Mary's redecorating efforts were not unwarranted or unappreciated by the more refined of the city. She truly transformed the White Houses appearance from that of a second rate, well worn, even dilapidated hotel to that of an executive mansion that any European prince or ambassador would be proud to call their own. That was one of the few endearing traits I found in her."

"I do recall some stories I heard from Lincoln's young personal secretary John Nicolay on the extraordinary and somewhat dubious means she went to pay for her extravagant renovations.

Mary, whom they lovingly referred to as "the Hell-Cat", would use the influence of her patronage with creditors to have the costs reduced, hide the expense under departments that were ostensibly under her employ. He had said on one occasion she had even gone so far as to ask Lincoln's other assistant, John Hay, to defray some of these costs under his own account to which the young man replied, according to his colleague, "Kiss mine, First Lady." Oh how I would have paid dearly to have witnessed that and I do say I would have had some choicer words from my overwhelming font of obscenities to bestow on her for all the trials and tribulations she cost me."

"Mrs. Lincoln was adamant in her belief that I was constantly attempting to control the President, and was largely successful in this endeavor. It was a persistent theme in the Press that was fully embodied in Mary Lincoln. It became an almost hysterical jealousy that thankfully she was never able to manifest in the President. He was far too wise to fall under sway of that sort of gossip and I dare say I would flatter myself to think I ever held any more of his ear than any other of our worthy cabinet members or advisors."

Augustus didn't agree. "I think it is best to leave any mention of that sort of reference towards the First Lady out of any work. Most know of the contentious relationship between the two of you and how she believed you were pulling the strings behind Lincoln, so if you wrote anything like that it would just present you in a mean spirited way. It is best to let others take up that cudgel and leave you free from taint."

Seward looked up from his musings, "Yes, I do believe you are right Augustus. That shall be stricken. I did add this so far."

"Lincoln was far and away the best of us and he was guided by his own star. Anything he took from ours only added a greater luster to his own and we gladly, most of us anyway, took the brunt of criticisms that were directed towards him unto ourselves."

"I think that would be a fitting way to end your discussion on Lincoln," Augustus observed then added. "It may well be best we also end tonight on that note father. You need to keep up your strength. We can talk more of this on the morrow."

Seward smiled agreeingly and allowed his eldest son to assist him in getting to his room and then to bed. Afterwards Augustus himself retired for the evening and the only sounds that could be heard was a light pitter patter of the rain falling on the roof.

*William Seward was a master orator, as much the equal to Abraham Lincoln himself, and full of anecdotes as well, but he far surpassed the President in the liberal usage of the wealth of profanities at his disposal and once, while on a carriage ride the President was heard to have asked the driver, who was in the midst of a tirade chock full of swearing, if he was an Episcopalian, to which the driver responded in the negative. "Oh," Lincoln quipped. "I figured you must be as you swore as eloquently as Secretary Seward and he's a warden!"

*technically, Lincoln did try to remain in the political arena on the state level as an administrator after his term as a Congressman. He applied for the Illinois Commissioner of the Land Office believing this was just spoils for his aid in bringing Illinois into the Whig camp in the 1848 election. The post was granted to another and Lincoln duly retired from active politics much chastened if not embittered, and remained a loyal Whig working behind the scenes to assist his fellow party members in their political careers.

LOVES WON & LOST

I have learned over the years that the best method for me to work out issues that have caused me undue emotional trauma has been to write the issues out and through exposing them in written form to wrench these thoughts from the risk of them overwhelming me causing me untold harm and possible permanent damage. It took me a long time to learn this and only more recently have I used it to great success.

I will start by going over the greatest losses in my life, one by one, from the first to my beloved son. I hope this will allow me to focus my energies on reunifying the nation by relieving a small portion of my pain in order that it may not unduly distract me from the tasks at hand. I pray for myself and the nation that I am successful.

The first death of a loved one was that of my young brother, Thomas. He was such a beautiful baby, and the first I had ever seen with my own eyes though I remember naught of him. Yet his life was not meant to be a long one. He died after just three days and I never was able to gain more attachment to him as I was three years old myself.

Death was something that struck frontier families frequently so it was something one would think we would get used to through long association, but my character was not so stern. I never could get over death or understand its meaning. I remember the pain my mother experienced for I often found her weeping quietly from time to time when I was a bit older. When I would ask her why she said she was weeping for little Tom. I was so very close to my mother so I felt her pain and it made me sad that she was unahppy.

My mother's death was the first that ever struck me that I could remember. Her death coincided with the deaths of my aunt and uncle. Father told me that she went to join the Lord, but I could never under-

stand that and it yet perplexes me. But the Lord works in mysterious ways and it is not for us to question Him but to try and learn what we can from misfortune, perhaps to make us stronger when it strikes again as it is bound to do.

These three deaths had struck our family to the core. Now there was myself, my sister, my father and Dennis Hanks who had joined the family with the Sparrows who had passed by the same milk sickness that struck down my mother. I remember crying for many hours for many months. I would cry often when I lay in bed, trying to keep my sobs from waking my cousin who slept in the same bed as I. I would weep when I was alone doing the farm work each day. It was difficult in that my father was gone for many months. I had wanted to ask him so many questions, to partake in his wisdom but he went to fetch another wife and by the time he returned the questions had abandoned me.

I know this had a traumatic impact on my life and my treatment of death, and I have never fully recovered from the horror of that time, but I think it was through those hardships that I was inspired to do great things. I hoped that through great things I could attain such heights that my mother could see me and that by doing so I could make her proud. Maybe one day I will know, though I have never really believed in the afterlife so many say is our lot. I pray to the Lord I am wrong as I have been in many things over the course of my life.

This event did one thing that was a great boon to me for the whole of my youth. I became very close to my sister. We would talk and cry together. Dennis was gone many long hours and for much of the winter I was in the home with just my sister. We discussed many things, mostly about mother and when father would return, what our new mother would be like, etc. We never had any doubt father would return with a new mother. He was liked by everyone. It never entered our minds he would not, and of course he did return with a wonderful woman who afterwards I loved as much as my first mother. I was perhaps as close to her as with anyone in the world except my beloved sister, Sarah. Those months created a bond between us that we felt could not be broken.

Michael John Joseph Del Toro

Yet broken it was, for in my eighteenth year she was called to Our Lord through complications arising from childbirth. I was almost a man now, but this blow struck me hard. I was a pale shadow of myself for quite some time. I remember sitting on a log and crying for what seemed like an eternity. She was the one person I could always turn to about anything and now she was gone forever. I felt I had nobody to love in my life. I felt perhaps I shouldn't love anyone closely since they all seemed to die. It remains to this day difficult to discuss or think of my sister for the pain is still strong. I believe it may never go away and perhaps it shouldn't. Maybe some deep part of me believes if I lose the pain of her loss I will lose her forever.

I loved my father, but it was of a different sort and we were never close. We had some hard times, but I cannot help but think that it was the death of my sister that caused me to seek to leave the family. First was about a year later, but a neighbor was able to talk me out of such foolishness. It was a good thing too because I still had much to learn from my father and I believe that without me my whole family may have perished during the dreaded winter of the Deep Snow.

I always kept up a jovial appearance and an outward air of friendliness, but from this time forward the trait of melancholy that always lurked underneath the surface became an indelible part of my nature. I was marked by an outward appearance of care until I would speak then my normal friendly visage would reappear as if by magic.

I never felt I would ever love again, nor should I. That is until I met and fell madly in love and had my first real romance with a wonderful angel named Ann Rutledge. She was a delightful young woman, as intelligent and compassionate as she was beautiful. Everyone said she was the most beautiful girl they had ever seen. She was of average height with lustrous blue eyes and auburn hair. Very beautiful face especially when smiling, which she often did and with my humorous nature I was always able to coax a laugh or smile from her at will. She had a friendly outgoing and expressive personality as befitted the daughter of a tavern keeper and was beloved by the entire community. Her vibrant personality was complemented by a keen intellect, quite philosophical, and a witty sense of humor that matched mine perfectly.

She was already engaged when we met. I met her from boarding at Rutledge's tavern and would find any excuse to tarry there whenever possible. Often I would go with my best friend Joshua Speed. I would frequently go with her to a wooden knoll and read poetry and stories from famous authors together, or sometimes recite those of my own composition. Many were written of or for her.

We seemed an ideal match, and though she was already betrothed she was planning to call off the wedding once her fiancé returned from visiting his family in New York. Prior to his return, Ann caught an affliction that devastated the entire community that fateful summer of 1835 and was stricken down within a month.

Thus by my twenty sixth year I had lost a brother, my mother, my sister, an aunt, an uncle and now my first love. It seemed my lot in life to lose those I loved the most in the world. Anne's death so shortly after I first met her, and after such an intimate time, was soul wrenching to me. I lost all will to live and merely existed for a time. I would forget to eat, would walk listlessly through life and could scarcely remember what I had done mere moments before. I took to wandering aimlessly in the woods for hours on end all alone with my thoughts and wallowing in misery. I was certainly off kilter a little and out of sync, maybe even temporarily deranged.

This shattered me, leaving me in such a state of depression that friends had to watch out over me for a time believing I might end my own life. I think I wouldn't have, but who can tell what one will do when madness takes hold of them. I became moody and never smiled anymore, never laughed or joked.

I understood my friends' concerns and eventually shook myself out of it. But Ann's death affected me for years, and was likely partially responsible for pulling out of not one but two engagements. I think I believed I would never desire to marry or love again, nor should I since all the women I loved in life died early, except of course my beloved stepmother.

I recall that when it seemed dreary outside I would be off the track a bit and almost besides myself with the thought of rain or snow beating down upon her grave. Though I eventually reverted back to my normal self enough to earn my law degree and enter into a prosperous law partnership I never truly recovered a real semblance of my old self until I met my Mary.

My wonderful Mary Todd Lincoln. I struck the surest gold when I courted Mary Todd. She came from the preeminent family in all of Springfield, the Todd-Edwards-Stuart clan. Many had dubbed them the aristocracy of Springfield not meant to be complimentary in the democratic west. This was more from jealousy and their inability to wed into the clan, for if an eligible bachelorette settled in Springfield from their relations to the east every Tom, Dick and Harry was sure to come a calling or show up in their Sunday finest in the hopes of attracting the new belle's eye.

How I ever managed to win the hand of the most eligible girl in all Springfield was an ever sense of wonderment and amusement to both of us. Now while she was of a social class much higher than myself, and by marrying her I immediately catapulted himself into a circle I could only have previously viewed from the outside, even as a law partner of the eminent attorney John Todd Stuart, for long I felt an outsider.

It was in the sphere of romance where my awkwardness would always manifest itself in ways no other emotion could inspire. It made me wonder how it was I was able to attract one such as Anne in the first place. I could not even when away from my dear wife during our longest time apart express my feelings of longing for her in writing the way I could any other feeling. The words would come effortlessly and eloquently when I desired to explain fear, outrage, awe or excitement. But when it came to love then my hands would tremble and my mind would draw a blank, leaving an empty page or one filled with words devoid of a tithe of the extent of the emotion I was feeling at the time. My loving Mary understood that in me and found it both touching and endearing.

Our relationship was contentious indeed and almost ended before it began. I was always self conscious of my shortcomings at each event hosted by the Edwards at their beautiful home. My lack of social grace, normally disheveled and homely appearance, and my country bumpkin like manner made me stand out in a most embarrassing fashion even to my own eyes, perhaps more so than it really did, when compared to other social rivals most vividly epitomized by the young Stephen Douglas.

Stephen Douglas was a sprite man, undersized yet a bit portly even at his young age, but he was as polished in the social graces of the time as I was lacking. Douglas could hold court with any one of any standing and always looked dapper and completely at home and at ease with the finely attired and richly garbed members of the Springfield elite. He was also a successful lawyer, while I was still getting established, and was something of a politician himself.

However, there was one thing that stood me in good stead. That was my political affiliation. It was ideally matched with the young Kentucky belle I was courting. That a young woman was politically aware was something of a novelty, but Mary was able to stand her ground with anyone in conversation, though she always maintained the proper deference that was required of one of her station. It was in more private encounters when her ward was otherwise occupied that she would revel her courtiers with her vivacious wit and political acumen. I loved her for it as her intellect was a perfect match for my own, and her outgoing character complemented my more reserved manner in these events. We were so in tune that she often completing my own sentences.

But still I had managed to ruin my chances with the most prized catch of Springfield or so I thought. We had become engaged and were due to marry when I suddenly called it off. It was the sense of doom and my sense of unworthiness which caused me to doubt the wisdom of the match.

I remember the time I broke off the engagement with Mary and how since it came hard on the heels of the recession that temporarily derailed my budding political career made me quite miserable to the point of insanity. My friends once again became worried about my mental health and Mary herself was not mentally stable, and was overly distraught over the break up. I was at an utter loss of what to do. My affliction was commonly termed as "the vapours" and both of us were a bit off kilter if not suicidal.

At one point I was so distraught I remarked to my boon companion Joshua, "I wouldn't mind dying, but as I had done nothing to make any human being remember that I had lived, and that to connect my name with the events transpiring in our day and generation and so impress myself upon them as to link my name with something that would redound to the Interest of my fellow man what I desired to live for."

Michael John Joseph Del Toro

Ultimately I wound up renewing the engagement with Mary. It was by offering advice to my good friend Joshua Speed when he himself was estranged from his fiancé that I found the will to seek to resume my courtship with my beloved. Through that advice I determined that I actually did love Mary and then began to pursue her again. Thankfully I did for she was the best thing that ever happened to me, and I have never regretted my decision, and love her today as much as I loved her when we first met.

My advice to Speed was for him to be more realistic in conceptualizing love. "Your hand must follow your heart." I believe this still, and it has stood me in good stead through many of the most trying periods of my life. This advice I almost didn't heed myself. Once I proposed to a fine woman named Mary Owens, though I soon regretted it, but felt compelled to consumate the proposal though my heart was not in it. But luckily she eventually rejected my proposal.

This helped me in my own troubled courtship, and by advising Joshua I brought myself to realize I did love Mary and should marry her. Thankfully she forgave me and together we have led a bountiful life.

There were hardships, no doubt. Amongst the hardest before the war was losing our dear Edward. Once again one of my loved ones was struck down by illness. He was but a few years old when he was taken from us. It was a low point in my life, as it coincided with a fall in my political fortunes. He was a wonderful boy named after my good friend Edward Baker.

Edward Baker himself was killed this past year, and combined with the loss of my clerk Elmer, both at the head of their troops it was a horrible loss. Losing Ed Baker was a tremendous blow, and was one that struck me dearly. Believing we were winning a battle and then to hear we lost it, and my dear friend was hard. Compounding this was when the General in Chief laid the blame squarely upon the shoulders of my dead friend.

This brought the worst element of my party to take measures in directing the war through the creation of the Joint Committee on the Conduct of the War. This was the start of a number of Congressional committees on all aspects of the war effort. There was even a secret committee to investigatge treasonous intent in the North. This committee even had the temerity to begin to investigate my dearest Mary.

That is until I went before them of my own accord and stopped them from their machinations that were purely political. I would not allow my wife's name to be besmirched if I could do anything in my power to prevent it.

But Willie was a blow that struck us both so deeply. Mary has so many cares upon her in trying to maintain her dignity in the face of a hostile press and Washington's elite. I believe this will never leave her. She has been most hysterical for weeks now. I fear for her sanity. She is a strong woman but so very passionate. It is her passion that is driving her now and has taken hold of her reason.

I must be stronger. I must master my own despair for the loss of our beloved boy so that I can be a rock that can steady her during the most trying moments of her affliction. I must be more understanding of her needs. I must realize that she cannot take on all the burdens that have been tossed upon her. I can do more and I must be more assertive in doing as much as I can to relieve her.

This must take the form of being stronger in the face of the nation. I have been as accommodating as I could in trying to keep the states from fracturing further. I have been holding one hand back, while extending the olive branch with the other. The rebels have had their way much too often. The forces behind us that have been succoring the rebels have had too free a hand. I must take these matters unto myself and use the strength that lies in the Constitution to combat both the rebels in our front and the Copperheads in our rear. Letting either get away with fomenting rebellion may yet cause us to lose everything we still hold, much less regain and redress the losses we have incurred thus far.

Yes, I believe strength is what is called for from all of us. I must have more strength if we are to persevere. I must believe more strongly in my conviction to prosecute the war more vigorously. I have given McClellan too much of a free reign, and by doing so he has the audacity to feel content to delay any forward movement until he has the numbers he believes necessary. I shall start there by disabusing him of that notion. He has more than enough to start now and I believe I should more strongly convey this thought to him. General Meigs and Secretary Stanton are correct that I need to take control of the tiller and steer the ship more convincingly. I believe I will take Stanton up on his idea that to close all recruitment will provide the necessary stimulus to McClellan that he can't keep depending on getting all the recruits he wants before setting off. Spring is upon us and now is the time to move forward and nip this rebellion in the bud.

This letter has proven a boon in both relieving myself of these burdens of guilt and pain and understanding that there will be more deaths in this war, but if we don't prosecute it strongly the war will not end. I have always wished to have my name linked to some great event and I will do everything in my power to ensure the Union will continue and my name not linked to its dismemberment. Writing these words have cemented my resolve and through this resolve I hope to revive our fortunes.

*Lincoln often would write letters that he never intended to send, some as a way to vent his spleen and allow him to resume his work with a clearer mind. He used this method of self-therapy numerous times over the course of the war, especially when dealing with political and military individuals. I took these instances to concoct one such letter that in this instance is being used to help him to get over the tremendous grief he has over the loss of his favorite son, William. Over the past year he had dealt with the loss of many loved ones and Willie's was by far the most unbearable, but Lincoln had to continue to perform the functions of his office during this most trying period. This necessitated some drastic measures. It is evident by many of his actions directly after Wilie's death that he was greatly affected by it and it took himself and the nation a long time to get over the results of these haphazard actions, at great cost to each.

*this taking unto his own the reigns of military strategy, especially in the region around the capital, brought several disasters in the Eastern theater which culminated in Robert E Lee's Army of Northern Virginia's first invasion of the North in the late summer of 1862. It took years to recover from those early fateful decisions and was never fully redressed until Lieutenant General Grant was given overall command of all the Armies of the Republic above the head of Major General Halleck and Lincoln resumed a more hands off approach to military matters.

TANGLING WITH ONIONS & MOSQUITOS

Excerpt from Springfield Daily Herald:

William Butler served during the Black Hawk War with Lincoln. They first met when Abraham Lincoln was working the flatboat down to New Orleans for a man known as Denton Offutt. William was initially unimpressed by Lincoln, as most were upon first meeting him because beyond his size his physical presence was unremarkable. He was never dressed well and didn't take care of his appearance and came across as a gangly unsophisticated fellow. They would soon become good friends, political allies, patriots serving in the same militia company during war, and Butler became one of Lincoln's best supporters during the latter's successful run to the Presidency. Here is Butler's story of Lincoln in his own words.

Now Lincoln used to say that he was elected captain of our militia company during the Black Hawk War by us spontaneously, but that isn't rightly true. How it came about was the fella who wanted to be captain was one who owed Abe some money. Now Abe wasn't one to hold a grudge, but he didn't take kindly to people shorting him on money. Money was always a sore spot with him on account he never did have much of it, even later in life. It took him years to pay off the debts for his old store so it wasn't until he was running for Senator against Douglas that he really began to see some money, and his wife was not prudent with the money they did have, that I can tell you.

Anyways on that fateful day when he became our captain, Lincoln leaned over to a couple of us who knew about the debt that was owed him and said, "I'll square with him alright." So he walked over and said he wanted to be captain too. Right he was for when the voting was taken Abe got more than twice as many as his would be rival and Captain he became.

In the end I don't know how square Abe got because he didn't turn out to be much of a captain. He wasn't much on discipline or rules. Once even the boys almost mutinied on him when they were in the middle of nowhere and thinking they were lost and since it was close to the end of their service they were wanting to give up and go home right then and there. Abe managed to talk them out of it that time.

The only rule I remember him knowing was the one he broke. We had passed over a makeshift bridge. It turned out it would have been better we didn't, especially for Abe, since we all wound up taking a swim it was made so badly, even Abe. Later on when we went to bed down Lincoln realized he forgot to clean his pistol. When he went to clean it he accidentally pulled the trigger and it went off right in camp. No one was hurt but when an orderly came up they demanded to know who did it.

We were all for protecting Lincoln and said nobody here did it, but Lincoln has his own sense of justice and couldn't abide by a lie being the leader and all. He admitted he did it straight away, and the general had his sword taken away for a week.

Abe confided in me one time while we were marching and had fallen slightly behind the others in the company that he was very pleased to be elected Captain. Now it wasn't just for the honor of holding the esteem of his neighbors, though that was a big part of the reason, and also gave him confidence that his recently interrupted campaign for the legislature would be successful. He later claimed it gave him much pride to have been elected by his peers. No, the main reason was he wasn't sure if he would be able to kill another man, even if it was in war. Now we knew from his tussle with the Clary's Grove Boys that Abe was not one to shirk from a fight, so I asked him why. He just said that he felt it would be a dishonor for him to not serve in the militia during a war since his father had served in the militia and his grandfather had once been a captain in the militia during our War for independence.

He knew it wouldn't look good if he shirked the obligation all Americans had to serve during a war, while he tried to start a political career and he thought that would be used against him. He just greatly feared when the time came he wouldn't be able to do his duty by killing another man since he only killed one animal on a hunt and even then he didn't like the deed. It would be far worse to have to kill a man. Now thankfully we never had the opportunity to prove him either right or wrong. We didn't find the enemy in our time in the infantry. When our enlistment ran out we had the chance to re-enlist in any company. Now both of us felt honor bound to complete our service while the war lasted and we hadn't once faced the enemy so we took the chance and both reenlisted into a spy company. This gave us the chance to ride a horse and since we were mostly scouting or reconnaissance as it was called, we thought we would be less likely to have to shoot at anyone in anger. We still never saw any Indians, at least not any hostile ones.

About the only Indian we saw in the whole was was an old one delivering a message for the general. He barely spoke a word of English, kept mumbling about "paper words" while holding up a slip of parchment, and all the rest of us was figuring him for a spy or maybe an assassin and were looking to kill him right then and there, but Lincoln heard all the commotion and came between us and the poor Indian and swore he would lick us all one at a time or all at once if we dared to lay a hand on the Indian. It was ironic since we had heard him tell the story, well many of us had, of how his grandfather was killed by an Indian in cold blood. If anyone would have wanted to kill that Indian I would have thought it would be old Abe but he really didn't have a mean bone in his body. He was a rare bird indeed.

As Lincoln liked to jest, our only charges were against wild onions and we were only attacked by mosquitoes. That does pretty well sum up our time served during the Black Hawk War. I did always find it odd that for a person who never wanted to kill another man he had to lead our country in the war where the most Americans ever were killed and were all done by their fellow Americans. I do know for certain that Abe would have done anything else than to have a war and tried many times to end it and bring peace to our nation. But he was constitutionally bound and honor bound to have peace as one nation and no other terms than that would suffice.

After serving together in Black Hawk War we rode back together. I secretly paid off some of Lincoln's debt, and brought his saddle bags back for him.

Now Lincoln boarded at my farm for first five years in Springfield. We were good friends for quite some time. My wife would even buy clothes for him as gifts when needed. Lincoln was a careless dresser at the best of times. It never seemed a concern for him. He never found his awkwardness to be a crutch for himself, rather he used it to his advantage. He would use it to disarm people on first acquaintance or to allow opponents to underestimate him due to his homely appearance.

Michael John Joseph Del Toro

We had a bitter falling out soon afterward, over what matters not now, but it would come back to haunt both of us, for when Lincoln served in the Congress I asked for a post in the Federal Land Office and Lincoln refused the request. Though a Whig, I worked behind the scenes to help deny Lincoln a place in the Senate during his famous candidacy against Stephen Douglas.

I since regretted my actions and swallowed my pride, put party over personal animosity and stumped for Lincoln in both the nomination process and the Presidential election which followed. I am as proud to have done so as much as I regret my previous actions against him.

When Lincoln first arrived in Washington as a freshman congressman, he brought his unrefined politics with him. This did not endear him to his peers in light of his questioning the legitimacy of the popular Mexican War and incessantly attacking President Polk. It showed Lincoln was immature when it came to national politics and by trying to distinguish himself immediately he allowed his ambition to overreach the pragmatic acumen that would later define his political career.

His father once told him "if you make a bad bargain, hug it then tighter". This stubbornness hurt him at times politically and this, like his views on slavery, modified as he grew older. He became less stubborn and more open to abolishing slavery by any constitutional means and doing so in territories regardless of the desire of its residents.

It was due to what some of us called "Lincoln's Folly" that we Whigs lost our district after Abe's ill-fated term as a Congressman in Washington. His ambition to make a name for himself lending him to condemn the wildly popular war against Mexico and then his attempt to ban slavery in the Capital both hampered us in the next election. Any Whig candidate in our district was bound to be tarred and feathered by the accusation that we stood for the same policies no matter how often we would refute it. We had been forced to support Lincoln during his term, so his law partner and successor as the Whig candidate, Logan was humiliated by losing the one-time Whig stronghold and was even crushed in the county named after him.

Due to a gentleman agreement, where each of the prominent Whigs would take turns as the congressional representative for the district, Lincoln had never intended to run for re-election though rumors surfaced at the time he considered breaking that promise. He never did and the rumors were probably unfounded, that was not the type of man he was and it would have cast him in a very dishonorable light and made him lose his prized moniker of "Honest". Lincoln was as shifty as they came as a politician but not in that way. It didn't matter since there was no way Lincoln was heading back to Capital hill.

During the long interlude between his congressional term and his return to the forefront of state and national politics, Abraham worked tirelessly to first help his fellow Whigs at the state and national level and later to reform the Whig party that was dying a slow agonizing death.

He took a firm stance on slavery and ceaselessly attacked Stephen Douglas. He used Douglas' fame across the state to propel himself back into the forefront of the Whig then Republican Party in Illinois. This was a slow process which picked up speed when the national legislature redefined the temporary truce afforded by the compromise of 1850 with the Kansas-Nebraska Act, and the notorious Supreme Court Dredd Scot decision of 1856.

In my opinion the fact that Lincoln was not even on the ballot in any Southern state worked to his advantage. It allowed his supporters to concentrate their energy in all the northern states and thereby guarantee a victory, which they would have attained even if all the northern opponents were counted as one, an astounding fact considering Lincoln only garnered less than 40% of the popular vote.

During the war he has been lauded as the key to our eventual victory over the rebels. I'm not qualified to give an accurate account of his actions during that time, nor am I one to be able to judge his merits as a war time President. The only real opinion I can offer is a simple one but I feel it is as just an opinion as anyone in my position can offer.

It is simply this fact. We fought a war where brother fought brother, father and sons fought each other and every household in the nation lost a loved one. Through it all Abraham Lincoln kept his composure, kept his sympathetic view that we are all Americans. He never wavered in this view. It is what kept him able to keep an even keel through all the trials.

He dealt with many losses, many reverses on the fields of battle and in the political arena. Yet he never lost sight of that basic truth. It was that wisdom, his political genius you might call it, that allowed us to persevere as a nation. Wars are fought on many fronts, not the least of which is the political. Throughout all the lost battles he constantly *came out victorious in the political arena and that was where and how we ultimately won. I think that is the best way to remember him.*

- *William Butler*

*The Springfield Daily Herald never printed any story like this from William Butler, nor do I know of the existence of such a periodical. It is being presented this way as an example of articles of this type which were printed during the time of Lincoln and after the War. The primary periodicals that did this can be best represented by the articles written by many ex-Confederate officers espousing the Lost Cause, which tried to romanticize the South and lessen the stigma attached to the Confederacy by the disgusting fact of Slavery. Various magazines would reproduce the opinions of officers and soldiers from both the Union and Confederates. This created a fulcrum where they could all air their grievances and attack both their enemies and fellow soldiers, all in the name of their respective causes, and continually fight a war honorably won by the North.

THE FIGHT OF THE CENTURY

Charles had had a hard time growing up in the streets of NYC. Charles, as he called himself now since it wasn't his original name, had been orphaned at an early age. He grew up in the ultimate melting pot of America during the 19th century, later famous, or more accurately termed infamous, as the notorious Five Points in Manhattan. Somehow surviving amidst the rampant disease and infant mortality, his childhood was spent as a street urchin who was cared for by various surrogates due to his skills in begging and thievery. When he approached his teens, he became apprenticed as a butcher, which gave him ample schooling for his later occupation.

He was brought up in an environment of hatred of immigrants who were flooding the various wards of the city, most of the poorest winding up from a variety of reasons in the Five Points or its surrounding environs. This hatred extended to the Negros, as Charles was born in the decade following the riots during one summer soon after the emancipation of Negros in New York state.

When the Civil War broke out, by his own reckoning Charles was perhaps twenty years old, maybe more. He really had no recollection of when exactly he was born, and no one was around to set him straight if he was wrong. He had become fully entrenched in the ideology of the anti-immigration, anti-abolition movements that had taken hold of much of the city and had been in his fair share of brawls, raids upon neighboring gangs, and took part in some arsonist activities and other crimes of the sort often perpetrated by his fellows in what became known as the Atlantic Guards.

He wasn't always engaged in acts of violence and criminality.

Most of the time he plied his trade as a butcher, but every so often he would join his compatriots in these activities in order to "cleanse the community of impurity" as they often termed their illegal actions in the guise of righteousness. They felt they were policing the community when the law in the city was unable to do so, and thought there was nothing wrong, and everything right, in it. Besides the police at the time would often blame the immigrants or resident Negros regardless of who was at fault and this helped reinforce the justice of his cause.

It was only when the draft law of 1863 was passed and beginning to be enforced that the war really came home to him and many of his fellow New Yorkers in Five Points. Most of them had never volunteered nor had any intention of doing so. The last thing they wanted was to prop up the Negro towards any semblance of equality with themselves. That was half the reason they went out at night in the first place. Their level of resentment was only intensified when they saw the great influx of new immigrants flocking into the Five Points, so many Irish, Dutch and Germans that the air fairly reeked with the smell of sauerkraut and corned beef, as they would say with scathing contempt.

Charles had a strong sense of his Americanism and was deeply pro-Union, as were many of his friends. It was his, and their upbringing of fear and hatred of social and economic upheaval associated equality with immigrants and negros that submerged their patriotism. He just couldn't see the point of making his already difficult life any harder by adding more competition, and the very thought of Negros and Irish being his social equals made him nauseous.

It was the draft riots in that same year that brought the war to him. He had never been much of a saver and while several of his friends had the $300 to pay for a substitute, and there were enough substitutes to go around, he didn't have that sort of ready cash. Even if he sold most of his meager assets, he wouldn't have been able to come up with it. It wasn't like his friends would have enough to loan him it either, many were barely able to scrape up the $300 in the first place, which for a lot of them was more than they made in half a year. He was vociferous in his denunciation of the "Rich Man's War, Poor Man's Fight", listened to many public speakers' pronouncements in the same vein, and was ready to make his protest known in more than just words.

This is what prompted him to join forces, at least unofficially with his hated foes, the Irish, in the draft riots that afflicted the city in the course of one hellish week in the summer of 1863. Charles knew full well his name was in the bin and could likely be drawn from it. He didn't take part in the raid of the draft offices that resulted in the lists and draft records being burned, but he played his part in other ways. He looted and burned several known Negro establishments, and was there the day the fabled VI Corps of the Army of the Potomac fired into the crowd to quell the rioters.

He wasn't hit, but that was the first time he saw the soldiers of the Republic. Five Points wasn't an area one would ever see any soldiers so seeing the uniformed infantry in their disciplined massed ranks was an intimidating sight to behold for the uninitiated. Even those who had seen it before felt a tinge of awe at such a spectacle. He ran helter-skelter like the rest of the mob and that quenched his desire for violent protests.

He took the wiser course and when the next draft came up, while his name wasn't called, he took the course of offering himself as a substitute and collected a fine bounty by one of the wealthier folk of the city and entered the army that same summer. Now just because he had joined the army didn't mean he had any intention to faithfully serve. He had learned soon after the draft, when he was first mustered into service that some of those were drafted, and even some substitutes wound up skedaddling and made off scot free.

Now Charles knew that if he did something like that he would become what was known as a deserter, and the penalty for desertion was death by firing squad, but he had already heard his fair share of horror stories of what was in store for him in a real battle, and already had the stark vision of what facing the enemy in a line of battle could look like and that was all the impetus he needed. He made off the first opportunity that came along and was able to get clean away with no fuss at all.

It then came upon him that with a simple name change and new locale, he could claim another bounty and do the same again when it came time to being mustered in and being sent to the army proper. So it was he forever changed his name to Charles, and became what was commonly termed, a bounty jumper, an unworthy occupation for all but a profitable one at that, as long as he got away with it.

He managed to get his second bounty pretty easily. He was in Philadelphia at the time of another draft and signed his name, well his alias, onto s substitute list and soon enough another wealthy lawyer came to him with a nice bounty of $1000 to become his substitute. Charles accepted with magnanimity and was soon mustered into service, again, and was marching off to war. He now had more money in his pocket than he had made over the last 10 years!

He knew if he didn't get out of his predicament he would likely never have the chance to spend it. So when he found his first opportunity he managed to wander off one night as his regiment passed a railroad. He jumped onboard an empty car of a northbound train and soon found himself back in New York. He got himself back into the Five Points, but didn't tarry there long. He didn't want to be recognized and be called out as a shirker amongst his friends. He only stood as long as it took to squirrel his money away with an old friend before he made his way out of Manhattan and into Brooklyn.

Voluntary enlistments in New York had dropped off significantly in 1863 so in order to meet its quota New York had another draft call, which suited Charles very well. He had signed up and once again was called in as a substitute with a bounty of around $500. The best part about his new company was it was merged with one of the Heavy Artillery Regiments that garrisoned the City of New York. Now he had the best of both worlds! A nice wad of spending money in his pockets, and a plush assignment as an honorable member of the US Army. Garrison duty was considered the best possible assignment since there was no chance that New York would ever be invaded, and due to his previous experience as a butcher, he had been tasked with helping prep food for his company so he was thoroughly enjoying his new regiment. Charles was looking forward to biding his time for the rest of the year then perhaps "jump" again come spring and do it all over again.

Charles figured at this rate he could do jump two more times and take himself, with his newfound wealth, out West and be free and clear of any draft calls and with a nest egg of a few thousand dollars he could set up a nice butcher shop, or even try his hand at something new. The opportunities were boundless!

Unfortunately, in early October his company was called into field service and transferred to Virginia. Charles's plans for a plush assignment were dashed, but he was nonplussed since he planned to jump anyway come spring. But it was now that trouble arose. His battalion had been joined up with several others, some from different states and were marching south as the trains had been requisitioned for supplies and wounded. One evening as he tried to slip out between the lines he was caught! A picket confronted him for the password.

He didn't have the pass that would have allowed him to leave, and the guards were none too pleased when he attempted to bribe them. They quickly brought Charles to the regimental commander. It was then that his luck turned from bad to good. The commander's cook had come down with a malady and the Colonel gave Charles a chance to redeem himself. He would be attached to the Colonel's personal valet and act as a cook until the Colonel decided what to do with him. This didn't allow

Charles any chance of escape, but it did keep him from the firing squad, at least for a time.

However, as fate would have it, Charles wasn't some sort of great chef, he was merely a butcher after all, so the Colonel soon became less than pleased with his meals. He was allowed to stay on as an assistant when the Colonel's original cook returned but when mid-May rolled around Charles was transferred again to fill out a regiment in the V Corps of the Army of the Potomac, which was decimated in the recent Battle of the Wilderness, under personal threat by the Colonel that if he tried to jump again Charles would be summarily executed for desertion.

This cured the itch of bounty jumping even though Charles didn't relish saving himself from a firing squad just to be shot by some Rebel. It didn't seem he had much of a choice, since deserting at this point could get him sent to a Rebel prison, which he heard was even worse than death, so he chose to live out his remaining days in style. He still had his bounty and spent that as many soldiers did, drinking, gambling and occasionally spending time with the ladies who attached themselves to the army as camp followers.

It was as a proud member of the late New Yorker Major General James Wadsworth's Division (later Cutler's) in Warren's V Corps that Charles served out his time in the Army. He took part in all the Corps' battles from Spotsylvania thru Five Forks. He was a bit luckier in war than he had been as a civilian. Though involved along the fringes of the horrendous 18 hour battle known as The Bloody Angle, and saw action at Cold Harbor, he didn't receive any wounds and was now a veteran with no thoughts of leaving his comrades. After what he saw he knew it would be a dishonor that would haunt him to the end of his days. He had matured greatly over the course of the last six months, and if he didn't forget his previous dishonorable actions, he no longer had the desire to repeat them.

His innate racism was cured somewhat after the Battle of the

Crater during the great siege of Petersburg. It was there he saw the gallantry of the Negro soldier for the first time, and what such gallantry cost them when faced against the hatred of the Southern rebels. He thought he hated the Negro but after what he saw he now knew what real hatred was.

He was a stretcher bearer for a bit during the truce after that disaster and saw firsthand the butchery inflicted upon black soldiers by the enemy in that battle. That opened his eyes to what blind hatred could do and he was amazed and awed by the steadfastness of the Negro troops that even after that battle they were willing to continue in the struggle for the Union, the struggle for their freedom.

He didn't hate the Southern man even then for he knew and shared their view that even though now he wanted freedom for the Negro he would never want them to hold equality with his own people. Being equal to the Irish was one thing, but not to upstanding good well-bred white folk. That was quite another thing altogether. But the Negro deserved freedom. They fought for it so they should have it. He wouldn't want to deny them that basic right.

He even got to glimpse that noble warrior, Robert E Lee, Mars Robert as he was called by the Rebels. He seemed a mighty man on horseback, but when dismounted he looked pretty average though broad shouldered and with a large well-formed neck. This was at Appomattox and soon after the surrender of the Army of Northern Virginia he found himself back in New York City being mustered out of service as an honored member of his company.

Prior to this he had heard of the cowardly assassination of President Lincoln, and it was this act and the President's lifelong quest to free the Negro that brought back into mind his earlier desire to visit the West. Now it wasn't an urge to journey there in order to escape the draft or live as a fugitive. Now his desire, or as the ancients' called it, his pothos if you will, was to visit the land where Abraham Lincoln grew up and became a man in order to understand more about him, and maybe through the great man's life, more about himself.

He felt akin to Lincoln, as did many of his comrades. He was a constant source of conversation. All had their own feelings and ideas about Honest Abe. Charles wanted to find out about the real Lincoln. He felt he wanted to write about him, of the great man of peace who led his country through its greatest trial and greatest war, a war he was an unwilling participant, but through it became a better man.

He didn't see how he could in the East. Lincoln only lived there a few years, though he died there. He certainly couldn't learn about him from anyone who met him. Most of those were of a social standing he could never attain so interviewing them about Abraham was out of the question. Besides so many stories were popping up about him and so many contradictions and myths there was no way to make heads or tails of them all from where he was.

Charles therefore found himself, soon after the war had ended, on his great odyssey that took him from New York City, to the backwoods of Kentucky, and from there through Indiana and into Illinois. He found many people who said they knew Lincoln, learned much but never enough it seemed and he often thought much of what he heard was, like the stories he had heard all too often back home, as much fiction as fact. But he did find himself after all his journeys. He found peace in a land of peace. Most of the journey to the West was on the railroads. They seemed to be popping up everywhere. The country was rich and prosperous and the great metal engines were a sign of this prosperity. It was the easy way to travel but even though these railways were becoming the norm, much of the country was still unconnected to this modern convenience. So he often found himself on wagons and some of his travels was by horseback.

It was at these times that he was most often at peace and found peace in his surroundings. The roads were often poorly constructed, but he was used to hard travel since his days in the army. Living in the country was nothing to him and it was far easier when there was no thought of being shot at out of the blue. He found many a home willing to take him in for the night if he didn't reach a town by dusk. Most of these had lost a loved one in the war, a husband, father, son or grandson. Some more. Some fought for the South, most for the Union. They were friendly enough and Charles thought they felt in him a bit of the one they had lost, though they were all too often sad while he was there and some were happy to see him leave, as if he brought up too many memories, happy and sad.

Charles never felt himself as much of a writer and he guessed that after all his biographical effort was more to appease the restlessness of his soul than it was ever for public consumption. He did enjoy the companionship when there was some. He often met other veterans like himself, and some from the South. They were all nice, as they all had a bond that could never be broken, even if they were once enemies. He never brought himself to visit Lincoln's near kin though he had found out where they lived. He felt it would be sacrilegious to ask of them about one who was so close.

Of all the people he spoke with who claimed to know Abraham Lincoln, two of them stood out. The first was an old bloke. Charles had forgotten the name and had neglected to write it down at the time. He hadn't expected to meet or speak with anyone that evening. He was dog tired from a long day in the saddle and wanted nothing more than to grab a bite and a drink before settling into bed looking forward the next morning for a look around the town of Decatur where he had stopped for he knew that Lincoln had once resided in a town nearby that had long been abandoned.

This old fellow was from the very town Lincoln had once lived, called New Salem. He was quite friendly and knew immediately

Charles was an easterner from his accent. After he found out the reason for being so far from home he opened up and even offered Charles a drink as he told what he knew of Lincoln. And he sure knew a lot!

"I wuz there the day ole' Honest Abe was formally introduced to both the New Salem gentry and The Clary Grove Boys in partikulur. We Clary's Grove Boys wuz a rowdy lot if I do say so myself. We wuz young and full of beans and generally had the run of the town, when we had the time and money to get ourselves down thereabouts. That wuzn't often but we sure tried to make the most of it."

"We had loads of fun those days, mostly on account there being no law to say. Hell we wuz the law in those days. It wuz a rough and tumble time and the toughest of the lot wuz the unes who said and did what we wanted, and well truth tell, the boys who ran the show wuz us Clary's Grove Boys. When the Boys wuz back in town there wuz no une who had any sense goin' to say anything when we wuz carousin', at least no locals that is. Any new blokes that might have a mind of tryin' to rein us in found out quite quick what it meant to cross the Clary's Grove Boys."

"We wuz some bad news but most of our fun didn't amount to much and since we wuz all locals and everyun knew everyun we didn't really try to hurt anyun too much. We just wanted to have our fun with no une to bother us is all. And fun in those days wuzn't meant to scare nune but when we had too much booze in us we might do some damage to a local store an' all. But then we would be sure to help the poor shopkeeper who wuz put out by us becuz we knew in our town when things went south we all needed to pitch in to help or nune of us would last a winter."

"New Salem wuz on the edge of the wilderness in those days. Things wuzn't like they are now. All peachy and such. Now everyun's all close together, stitched up and all. Back then we wuz spread out across the prairie wich wuz all dotted with patchuz of forest here and thar."

"Here and thar wuz a farm and it wuz patchwork land with muddy tracks that wuz our roads. We didn't know any better. It wuz all we knew and to us it wuz the world. We boys grew up with this, and those that didn't lurned soon enuff how to get by or thrive. Those that didn't kinda stuck to themselves. They didn't want to muss with us or the other boys that wuz a ruckin' around Springfield."

"Now this wuz a type of town that wuz typical of the West as it wuz then in those days. We didn't know any better but we didn't know any worse. It wuz how things were and that's that. Now with the Clary's Grove Boys there wuz just une who wuz King. He wuz the une who could do the whuppin' when time came and no une's going to stop him. He wuz a tough as nails and smart as a whip."

"That be Jack Armstrong. Jack wuz tough as tough is but he wuzn't some giant or nune. He wuz a small un. But he wuz thick as thorns he wuz. He wuz like a tree stump that you culdn't get the roots out of and wuz just stuck thar. No budgin' that un. That wuz Jack."

"But the thing wuz with Jack and nune do good in telling is that Jack wuz smart. He wuz as smart as smart is. Thar wuz nune smarter, not even Ole' Honest Abe hisself. That wuz the thing with ole' Jack, he wuz small but you just culdn't beat him. He knew everything thar wuz to know about wrasslin' and fighting so thar wuz no beating him. Jack had took on many boys itching to take him down. They all thought he wuz a sprite old boy but too small to hurt anyone. How could he lick them? They figure they could just pick him up and slam him down like they dun so many others and Jack would be licked. He culdn't stand that and culdn't get out of it no how."

"Jack though, he knew it all. Jack knew all the moves you could know and then he knew all the other moves. If you ever thought you had Jack licked he would show you how you didn't. I never saw Jack picked up 'cept une time only. Nobody ever could pick Little Jack up, nobody, 'cept une."

"I see'd many a bloke try to throw Jack. Maybe they move him off his feet for a second but you don't throw Jack. Jack always landed on his feet. He wuz like a cat. It just didn't happen. I see'n boys bigger than Lincoln try it and it wuz like tossin' a stump. Maybe you moved him from une place to another but there wuz no tossin' ole' Jack Armstrong, and Honest Abe wuld say the same."

"Anyways we come to the day ole' Honest Abe and Jack Armstrong came to wrasslin'. This day wuz a long coming to some. I mean if you hear about it that ole' braggart Offutt had be talkin' some about Abe for months. But you really don't know unless you know about Offutt."

"Now Offutt wuz a gasser He wuz the talker of Springfield for it's first few years. He had opened his shop against good advice and major competition. But Offutt wuz Offutt. He felt he culd get his goods for less and sell for less and make his shop lick his competitors. Plus he had Lincoln. When he got here nobody but Offutt knew Lincoln. Offutt only knew Lincoln from when he hired him to boat down to New Orleans for him. But Offutt knew a gold mine when he saw it. And Lincoln wuz a gold mine."

"But un thing Offutt didn't know how to do wuz shut up. He wuz a talker and how did he talk! He talked about just everything but the une thing he talked about all that first summer and winter wuz une thing. Lincoln. He made it seem like Lincoln wuz the second coming. Lincon this, Lincoln that. He made it seem that you just had to wait for it and Lincoln would part the Sangamon. That's just how it wuz with Offutt."

"Now Jack for his part wuz a kind fellow. That's why we wuz not so bad on our part when it came to russin' and rousin' others. I don't think if we had another leader we wuld have been so kind as when we had Jack."

"Now most people be thinking that Lincoln won the fight. I

know why they are thinking that. It's because Lincoln became the leader of us but all us Clary's Grove Boys know the truth. It wuz ole' Jack who dun won their match. It's all fine that others be thinking that ain't true. Don't matter nune really. What matters is we all became like brothers and loved each other for the rest of our lives."

"Now when the two came to a' fightin' there wuz no brawl and no fisticuffs. It was all plain ole' wrasslin' cuz that is what Jack wuz best at. He coulda been kickin' n' scratchin' and throwin' punches with the best of 'em but Jack wuz the smartest wrassler there wuz in our parts. He dun beat ever'un. Now with Lincoln, he wuz big and scrawny but his arms wuz those of a giant, made of iron and hardwood they wuz. His legs wuz steady too from all the cuttin', choppin' and haulin' he been doing since he wuz a wee lad."

"Jack wuz strong too and for his size there wuz nun so strong as Jack but Jack wuz nimble and just as steady as ole' Abe. Now the two came to squarin' off and they each wanted to get it over right quick so they grabs each other right off the bat. Now Abe wuz tall and all gangly so he didn't look so strong and since we all knows Offut is such a talker we wuz none the wiser about how strong ole' Abe really wuz. He just gone an' picked up Jack like he wuz a sack of potatoes and flips him right over!"

"You'd thought Jack be right done. He'd be square on his back and sputterin' for air and quite out his wits. Then Lincoln be jumpin' on his back and that'd be the end of it. But not ole' Jack. As I be sayin' he wuz not just quick when it came to thinkin' and jumpin' about but he'd land on his feet just like a cat! I'd dun think I never seen Jack be thrown off his feet and if Lincoln couldn't do it then nobody could. I'd wind up scrapin' with Lincoln in some of our games we played in those times and there wuz no une ever as strong as him, but like I be sayin' even he dun can't be throwin' Jack. No way no how."

"Lincoln kept tryin' to throw Jack. First to one side an' then to 'nother but Jack wouldn't be hearin' of bein' thrown like a bunch of meal in a bag. He wuz floppin' about all over the place. It did look right comical but that don't matter nune when it come to a wrasslin'. You fight to win or you got no business fightin' in the first place. So these two a keep flailin' about for a time and we Clary's Grove Boys start lookin' at each other.

Now we never seen nothin' like this before. We wuzn't sure who gonna come out on top. I think the two of them wuz thinkin' likewise since Jack suddenly latched onto ole' Abe right tight as can be, an Abe bein' an ornery cuss, well he just smiles and then lunges upwards like and twists his body as he begins to fall meaning to put all his weight on Jack and knock his breath out of him. Then he could pin him all easy like and that would be the end of that."

"But Jack wuz never un to be caught unawares an' all. He wuz always ready for anythin' and everythin'. Lincoln wuz une who had many fights but Jack wuz a bit older and he had even more. He just a start twistin' himself the same way Lincoln dun and the two of them doin' a half twist, pretty as can be, like they a couple of dancers on the stage. So when they lands it wuzn't Lincoln who ends up on top but it wuz ole' Jack, smart as a coon and nasty as a wolverine."

"After that they rollin' aroun' a bit all round the middle of the square an' everyun' is shoutin' an' cusssin' then the two of them stop an' restin' Jack still on top of ole' Abe and the both of them start laughin'. We all thought they wuz crazy an' maybe Jack dun hit his head or somethin' so we come a rushin' over."

"Lincoln he dun see us comin' and he gets up since Jack and him let go each other, an' Abe starts backin' himself in the corner like he wuz gonna fight us all at once. That boy, he sure had moxey and some! We dun do nothin' of the sort. We just rush over an' pick up Jack an' start congratulatin' him an' a couple of us boys go over to Lincoln to pat him on the back an' all. Let him know he's un of us now."

"That's how the story come round that it wuz Jack who lost the fight. That wuz how Offut saw it an' he went around tellin' anyune who'd listen and most who won't that Lincoln dun tossed Jack to the ground and run him round a bit before lettin' him up an' then we came runnin' over to save ole' Jack so Lincoln be the winner."

"We an' most of them over in New Salem knew the truth an' all but we wuzn't about layin' on against ole' Abe. He wuz un of us now and he kew whut wuz whut so no need for that. But since Lincoln went on to bigger things, well the biggest thing of all since he became the best o' men and President an' all, the story of Lincoln winnin' wuz the one that there stuck an' since no harm came to no un there wuz no need to be settin' the record straight like I'm doin' now. Besides we wuz all peas and carrots now an' since Lincoln wuz as big an' bad as Jack an' smart as a whip an' culd talk a rabbit out its hole, he naturally came to be leader of us all an' nune of us, least of all Jack cared un whit about who dun what to who. We wuz all kings of the town an' that wuz what mattered."

"We all stuck together, thru thick or thin. No matter whut we wuz friends for life and stayed that way. It soon came that Abe wuz lookin' to get ahead in ole' politicals. He could spin a yarn like no une else so that sort of work came natural an' all to him. An' with the Clary's Grove Boys he dun hit the jackpot."

"With Lincoln we wuz his posse. We made sure if a person wuz goin' to vote that they went an' voted right. That being voted for Lincoln. Now we really didn't rough anyone up or nothing like that. We didn't need to be doing that, at least mostly. We would just put in a kind word and remind them who Lincoln be and that wuz enough. It's why Lincoln always wuz winning big with the locals and in the towns nearby. Didn't do us as much good outside the county but well you can't be everywhere at once."

"Now Lincoln for his part wuz always helping us no matter what. We wuld just ask and he wuld be there. Whether it wuz helping to put up a fence, lay in a crip or harvest, Abe wuz always there for us. Even years later. That wuz especially with Jack. Abe and Jack wuz great friends. Jack went and moved away after a time with his wife but they still kept in contact. And even after Jack passed, God rest his soul, Lincoln went out of his way to help them."

"It wuz a time when Lincoln helped them the most and when there wuz no one that could help them but Abe. It wuz when Jack's son was accused of murderin' some bloke. I don't know too much about the particulars of the accusin' but I do remember how it wuz Abe who went all the way where they wuz living and set himself up as their lawyer for the trial. For free! That's the type of fella Abe wuzs. There wuz none like him and the best of friends to all of us.""

It took all of Charles's meager skill to jot down the monologue but he did the best he could. After this yarn Charles took his leave of the old fella and went up to his room, his head still spinning from the tale.

The next days he spent in the area but that last story kept replaying in his mind so he decided to take himself off to Beardstown and see if he could learn more about that legendary tale.

Now this part of Illinois that was bordering on the Sangamon river was still in a wild state of things. It was as if the woods were right up upon the river and Charles kept thinking there were a bear, wolf or even a mountain lion peering at him from amidst the trees.

It was a bit unsettling but the birds were chirping and the bugs were buzzing up something fierce which did lend a peaceful air to the countryside. He traveled for the next few days and each night someone had some yarn to spin about Lincoln and many knew of the trial of ole' Duff Armstrong, though each had a different spin on how it went. This made Charles even more determined to find out the actual events.

As he made his way to Beardstown he found the widow of Jack Armstrong still lived there. It was easy to find her since she was a bit of a celebrity due to her previous association with the President and all around knew about the trial and Lincoln's part in it. Thus it was that Charles found himself at her small but comfortable home one late spring day.

Hannah Armstrong was an elderly lady but still hale and comely. She was friendly enough when Charles came and asked to speak with her, but he could tell she had been through this sort of thing before. It wasn't that she didn't want to tell the tale, or that it was tedious for her but she seemed to have a bit of a script for it since she dove right in to it with little ado.

"Well Abe Lincoln was an old friend of Jack and I." She began and then lost herself in her own story, "He lived with us for some time. I used to wash and mend his clothes and when his socks or pants were too worn I would often go and buy or make them myself for him. I would just tuck them in his drawer since he was quite absentminded about his appearance and I don't think he ever did buy his own clothes."

"Why I think when he first came to me after hearing that little

Legends of Lincoln

Duff, who he used to put on his knee when the boy was little, had gotten into trouble, he was wearing a shirt I had once made for him. Bless his soul."

"Lincoln remarked to me in jest when he first arrived in Beardstown, Illinois where the trial was, that while this was his second time coming here it was the first time he actually arrived. When I pressed him what he meant, he was as polite as could be and said."

"When I was plying the river trade my first time down to New Orleans," he said. "we had wanted to make port here to rest on dry land and perhaps a soft bed for a change. The people here were not too keen on having us river rats come. They had enough of the gambling and rowdiness from so many other boatmen they gathered at the riverside and jeered at us so much that we just continued on our merry way rather than stop to enjoy more of their warm welcome."

"He then smiled warmly to me and continued, "I assure you that my leaving this time will be on far better terms than my coming or going the first go around.""

"He enjoyed a meal before heading to bed early since he was eager to get started on the case and needed to become familiar with all the particulars as soon as possible. He still enjoyed the dinner immensely as he always did, and it brought me back to happier times when he would spend a long evening with John and I weaving a tale or three. He was some talker so I reckon it was why he was such an able attorney."

"He stayed up later than I thought though I didn't mind of course, and we talked about many things during dinner and a bit after. I wound up doing most of the talking since Abe wanted to know all about John's time since leaving New Salem and coming here and he asked about every particular he could of my poor William."

"I reckon he was looking to learn more about the character of my son and how John brought him up for Abraham had not visited for a long time. I told him everything he wished to know and then some and it was a few hours before he took to bed."

"He was up early as he said he would be and after a short breakfast he took himself down to the court to find out about the charges leveled against my son. He spent most of the day and the next two out and about, I reckon mostly at the court. He hadn't much time to prepare for the case but never discussed it with me after that first night."

"Every other time we would talk he would discuss his family, he dearly loved to talk of his children. He spoke of Springfield, which, and he often spoke of his time in Washington when he was a Congressman. He described the great Daniel Webster and Henry Clay with such detail that afterwards I could have surely been able to point them out on the street or if I heard their voice. Even though I had never met either or heard them speak."

"Soon enough the day of the trial was at hand. The trial was quite the spectacle, for while my young Duff, that's what we called him, was of not much account, John had made his mark as he had everywhere he went. So the courthouse was packed that day. The prosecutor was full of fire and he made a bold and compelling account of the night in question. His questions put upon the witnesses were pointed and painted a lurid and deeply convincing argument in establishing the guilt of my son."

"The gallery was quite taken with Duff as guilty of the charge laid upon him even before Lincoln ever stood up to speak beyond his opening arguments which were scarcely more than a statement declaring he would be able to establish John's innocence beyond a reasonable doubt within 10 minutes of questioning the first witness. Most of the folk in the court had never met Abraham and knew little of him other than he was a politician who served one term in Congress and didn't seek re-election."

"Abraham certainly didn't do anything that day to make it seem he was confident or even competent as a lawyer who had been to the capital of America legislating laws for all. He made me a bit of a nervous wreck and I dare say my belief in him was becoming quite shaky long before he got up to stand for the defense of my son and beginning counter arguments."

"The entire time the prosecution was questioning the witnesses and establishing a timeline of the night of the murder, Abraham had been leaning back against his chair with his feet propped up on the table where his papers lay. He seemed oblivious to the proceedings going on around him and more than once I heard a bystander remark that the defense was sleeping! I didn't think Abraham was asleep, but it seemed he was more interested in counting the specks of dirt on the courthouse ceiling than he was of listening to the accusations of the prosecution."

"It was only when the defense was called that it became apparent he had been listening intently the entire time for he immediately popped up out of his seat and called his first witness. It was the man who declared seeing my boy Duff right before the murder. When he called him Abraham picked up a book on his desk and strode over to the judge. He presented the book, declared it was an almanac then showed it to the prosecution and asked if he could submit the almanac as evidence. The prosecution complied."

"After the witness was reminded he was still under oath, Abraham asked him again if he knew Duff. The witness said he did. Abraham then asked where he was the night in question. The witness answered exactly as he had when previously asked by the prosecution. Abraham then asked if he could identify Duff. The witness pointed over to my son. Abraham then asked if Duff was the person he saw that night. The witness said he was. Abraham then asked how it was he could identify Duff at night from such a distance. The witness responded again that the night was brightly illuminated by the moon."

"Lincoln then goes up again and asked for the court to refer to a page of the almanac he entered as evidence. He asked the clerk to read the account of the moon's phase that night. It was then determined that it was impossible for Duff to have been positively identified as the culprit by the light of the moon since there was no moon that night!"

"It was unbelievable! I went from the greatest depression to downright shock and joy in but a moment! Abraham had completely destroyed the prosecution's case in less than ten minutes."

"It only took a few moments for the prosecution to deliberate before the charges were dropped against my son. Abraham, being the gentleman he always was and dearest friend would not take any money or gift for the case. He only said it was gift enough to know he was able to help in anyway to seeing his great friend Jack Armstrong's son and family were free from harm or ill fortune and it was a bonus he was able to enjoy the wonderful cooking and delightful conversation of myself for an evening or two."

"He was such a man as only comes about once a century and I am happy that I had not only met him but was able to call him my friend."

Charles spent the rest of the day talking with her before returning to his room at a nearby hotel. Charles thought he learned the most important thing about Lincoln and why he felt he had to free the slaves and why he was reluctant to do it when he first became President. It was his sense of justice.

He was one of the greatest lawyers of all time. He knew slavery was wrong. Most slave owners admitted it was wrong before the eyes of the Lord but still they persisted in the evil. Abraham Lincoln knew it wasn't lawful for him to decide upon the issue by his own conviction. It was allowed under the Constitution therefore only by a process legal under the Constitution could it be undone. That's why he issued the Emancipation Proclamation, which was loved by some and loathed by many and scorned as the most nefarious document in the history of mankind by the Southern man.

It didn't matter because the great moral right was done and the great evil forever corrected by the might of the Union army and Charles was downright proud to have done his small part to help keep his great country together.

Charles never did get around to completing his biography of Lincoln. He had decided to go down to New Orleans and see Vicksburg and other great battlefields of the war on the way and eventually made his way back to his beloved New York City, but he didn't stay in Five Points. That area had only bad memories for him.

Charles had money and he had a new sense of freedom. He moved off to the northern part of the city and opened up a small butcher's shop there. He soon met a pretty lass and within the year he was wed. He had four beautiful children, three of them reaching adulthood. Two daughters and a son and by the time

Legends of Lincoln

the first Democrat was elected to the Presidency since the war, and he was blessed with the first of many grandchildren.

Charles was a Republican through and through by now. He voted for Grant twice and sorely wanted him to run for a third term. He was there when his old General was buried in the monumental tomb named after the illustrious Victor. His butcher's shop was close by and he would pass the tomb each morning on his way to work and each evening on his way home and whisper a prayer for the safekeeping of the Republic each time followed by a salute to his old commander.

Every year he would gather with many of his fellow soldiers and over time even some of his one time enemies, but they were enemies no longer. Now they were brothers. And though each year more of the Confederates would show up at these gatherings each year there were less and less of all as the sands of time took some away each passing winter.

Charles himself passed at the turn of the century very soon after Theodore Roosevelt became President. He was old and frail and lingered for a long time before he finally breathed his last but he died knowing that he had a warm loving family and satisfied that through the small part he played his beloved country lived and thrived as the greatest nation on earth.

*Lincoln did appear in or on the outskirts of Beardstown on at least one other occasion and likely more. The occasion in question was when he journeyed with a group of other young men in order to meet the boat called The Talisman which was coming up from the Mississippi River in order to prove the Sangamon river was navigable up to New Salem.

*Lincoln was more active during the murder trial of Duff Armstrong and did question other witnesses than Collier but his questioning was limited and from the perspective of a worried mother I felt it just to highlight his comparative lack of engagement in the proceedings compared with the prosecutor.

Michael John Joseph Del Toro

*There was a moon in the sky that night but it was low in the sky and was not full so could not be seen or provide the light needed to make such an identification possible. Hannah likely embellished a bit to emphatically imply her son was innocent, which Lincoln had already duly established in court. A mother can be overprotective that way, even years later.

THE INSPIRATION OF AMERICA'S MARTYR

I believe I am around forty or fifty years old. I think I'm that old because I'm starting to get gray hairs but some say that could happen as early as thirty. I'm not sure of my age. It is not something that was important to us. Getting food, keeping quiet and making sure we didn't get our masters angry. That was the story of my youth up until I began to get hair on my chest. I guess I must have been around twleve or thirteen years old but I was the size of an adult so I could have been much older.

It was then that my life changed though not necessarily for the better. I had been working out in the fields for years picking cotton. I didn't know it then but cotton wasn't a common crop where I was living. I didn't even know where I was living at the time.

My hands were already well calloused. I didn't mind so much since it kept them from bleeding. They bled a lot when I first began to be a picker. That was only natural.

Each night when I would get back from the fields one of the other slaves would put some salve on my hands and feet to help with the bleeding. I didn't know who the slave was other than her name, Rebecca. I knew she wasn't my mother. I was told I was bought when I was very young so I never knew my mother or father. All I knew was they weren't on the plantation. It didn't take long before my hands grew tough enough that I didn't need the salve anymore.

I also knew I lived pretty close to the city. Much later learned it was called Petersburg. I will tell you about that in a minute. Like I said when I grew older my life changed. I was called into a small cabin. It was a cabin I would up spending some time in. It was there I learned to read and write and learn my numbers. I was being trained to be the next overseer. I found out later this was because the previous one had been caught doing something and was sentence to a whipping. He was beaten so badly he almost died. Then he was sold. I never found out what he did other than it involved one of the master's children.

Later on I also learned that our master was considered enlightened. He only rarely beat us, and let us decide what to do with those of us who disobeyed. He had us decide by vote though he was what I learned was called the judge of us.

I was chosen because while I was quick in the mind but had never done anything wrong. This made me suitable as someone to watch over the others. I knew all the rules and I obeyed. That was all that was needed. I still slept in the same hovels as everyone else except those working in the house. I still ate the same meals and wore the same clothes. It also made the others dislike me some. I did have more freedom to move about the plantation but not much. The house and other areas were still strictly off limits and of course I obeyed.

I didn't like learning to read and write. I was never given anything other than a few books but it opened my mind. It gave me some sense there were better things out there. It was then I learned the word slavery and some of its history. It made me aware of my inferiority in ways I never would have before knowing numbers and letters. It made me not like myself. It also gave me a sense of time. It was then I started to count the years.

That was until a dozen years later in the year 1860, as I later learned. It was one summer day that I, while out on the fields, met the man who almost got me killed but wound up changing my life forever. The man proved to be an abolitionist, one of those looking to free all the slaves. He had bought and read the novel which was infamous in the south called Uncle Tom's Cabin and this has brought him south to research actual conditions there for campaigning in the north.

We met that day and the abolitionist was shocked to see a slave overseeing the work of other slaves. While I was much lighter skinned than the others my facial features were a dead giveaway of my race. He told me he believed I was a mulatto. I learned that day a mulatto was half white and half negro. I never knew of any such thing, but it mattered little to me. I was a slave and would always be a slave.

The man was otherwise astonished and after we spoke a bit he discovered I had been educated and knew my letters and such. It was then he offered me the book. I know not why but of course I took it. He warned me to keep it secret. Now I said earlier I had done nothing wrong since before I could remember but that wasn't really true. After I learned to read I couldn't help but want to learn more. That was the curse of reading. I had my own secret cache of some newspapers, old and decrepit that I would read from time to time, and that night I began to read the book over the candlelight I had smuggled for just such an occasion.

I realized quickly how this book would be the death of me if discovered. I was determined to keep it a secret but that was not to be. I knew I was very careful, but such was the life of a slave that one of the others was always jealous of the little privileges I had over them and resentful when I would force him to work. He knew of my stash and one day when he pleaded sickness I let him stay while we all went out for our daily work in the fields. He wound up showing the master my stash and upon discovery of the book he became enraged.

That evening I was confronted and beat almost to an inch of my life and left for dead. Luckily not all had resented me and misery always finds company. Some felt sorry for me and helped me. They gave me small bits of their food and tended me each evening. Slowly over several months I began to recover and though I could never walk without a limp and couldn't fully bend my left arm I was well enough to work again. I was not allowed to leave the confines of the house but did small chores and the one who told on me would often gloat over my reduced circumstances.

The war brought great dangers but also great opportunities. As I was no longer an important or even wanted member of his slaveholdings, but still had some limited value when my master went off to the war he lent me for a fee to do hard labor digging ditches around Petersburg and Richmond with many other slaves. This was work that the whites said was beneath them so it was left to us slaves to build their defenses. I think my master thought that due to my injuries I would soon die anyway. But that was not to be.

Being on the outer works daily led to opportunities and one day I took mine to wander off. I knew if I was caught I would certainly be killed but at this point death would be welcome compared to my miserable situation. My luck held and I was picked up by a cavalry patrol and brought into federal lines. I was declared contraband by the commanding general and put to work. Now I was building defenses for the "enemy" but now I had what something I never had before in all my years. Freedom.

The very air felt fresher. The sun shone brighter. Even the rain felt better as it washed the stench and remains of the bonds that were once over me. I was a new man. I was finally, a Man.

I spent the remaining years of the war around the Petersburg area that was under control of the Union. I heard many tales about free Negroes who were making names for themselves in the north. Some who had done so even before the war, like Frederick Douglass, Harriet Tubman, Hariet Beecher Stowe (the book I read was written by her) and one known as Sojourner Truth. I found them all so very interesting but none more than Sojourner Truth. Her story was so amazing that for many years I believed it was not true, just a story to inspire abolitionists and put fear in the hearts of southern slaveowners. They all made me wish that one day I could make others feel the freedom I felt.

Many of the officers, and sometimes politicians visiting the trenches, or ditches as the Rebels caked them, around Petersburg would deliver rousing speeches to inspire the troops. Sometimes these would be held just behind the lines, about a mile or two beyond range of artillery. On occasion a politician would ask to visit the trenches. I saw one do this when I was there repairing some part of the trench that had been damaged from cannon fire.

He came close to where I was standing with a shovel. Sometimes a picket or sniper would fire a rifle. We knew from experience if it was close or not. This happened when the politician was there. We knew from the sound that the shot was nowhere near him. He fell flat on the ground. His jacket and pants got very muddied and then he jumped up and scrambled out of the trench shouting, "Did you see that? One of them rebels tried to shoot me!"

We thought this was very funny. I bet he is still telling that story how he almost got killed when he was in the trenches around Petersburg.

I got a chance to listen to many of these speeches. It was the first time I got to hear White men speak formally. My only prior experience with public speeches were the few times I attended a Negro church that was built behind our lines.

Most of the speakers talked of latest Union victories and predicted future Union victories, staying steadfast to the cause and more and more frequently about how the Southern man was oppressive and deserving of their fate, especially the loss of their slaves. Many of the politicians were abolitionists and they sounded much like the ministers sermons I heard while attending church. It was the way they spoke and the constant invoking of the will of God and the divine that struck a chord with me.

Finally, the blessed day came when Petersburg fell. Robert E. Lee's invincible legions fled against the superior forces of US Grant and not long after finally surrendered to him. I knew little of that because my mind was caught on a chance meeting I had with the greatest American of them all.

Right after Petersburg fell, we Negroes were left with complete freedom. All the soldiers both north and south had moved off from the city and were fighting somewhere to the west. The city was left to just the residents and us Negroes. I was walking down the street. I had just had a nice meal I scavenged from one of the many abandoned homes. And out of nowhere a very small group of horsemen was approaching me.

They were surrounded by hundreds of my brothers and sisters. They were all shouting and jumping about and dancing jigs and holding their hands in the air screaming "Halleluah!". I didn't know what to make of it.

Then I noticed in the midst of the crowd, atop one of the horses was a very tall man who was made even taller by a stovepipe hat. Could it be? It couldn't! But as they came closer I could see him very clearly. It was! Abraham Lincoln! Everyone knew what he looked like by now. His photograph was everywhere. Even a simple Negro like me knew every blessed wrinkle on his face.

I was in shock and awe and found myself moving towards him. I had to get nearer to him. To be close to the Great Liberator. It was the only thought in my mind. I managed to get close to his horse and he even seemed to notice me for a moment. I then touched his foot. He was real! Tears were streaming down my face. It was the greatest moment of my life up to that time.

Michael John Joseph Del Toro

Everyone was sobbing and laughing and hugging each other. It was so amazing that I would never have believed it even seeing it with my own eyes if I hadn't touched him. I now knew he was real. Our salvation was at hand!

I spent some time there, made my way up to Richmond and very soon afterwards I found myself in Washington DC itself. It was then I learned of the most horrible thing in the world. Someone had shot the blessed Abraham Lincoln. He was dead. I was thunderstruck. I wondered what would happen to us now.

I had to see for myself. I found out that his funeral was scheduled for the next day so I decided to go. It was easy to go. Everyone was going. I was not able to get close but it didn't matter. I was close enough to see him. I knew. He was gone. There were thousands of people there. I never saw so many people, not even when I witnessed a battle. Everyone was crying. I think if there weren't handkerchiefs the tears would have made a river. I cried like the rest. How could I not? Father Abraham was gone.

I felt a hand near mine. I clasped it and the hand clasped mine tightly. I looked at the hand and then up at the same time the one holding me did likewise. It was then I saw her. The most beautiful sight I had ever laid eyes upon or ever would until my children were born.

I grew up on a small plantation located on the Louisiana side of the Mississippi river near Bruinsburg. My mother and father were both household slaves and I grew up playing alongside my master's children. My master had only ten slaves and we were all related.

Life was slow and easy for us and it wasn't until I was about six or seven that I ever understood that I was a slave. It was the day my friends, my master's children began schooling. I wondered why I didn't go to school. I was older than both of their children so I asked my mother.

She just said, "Hush child. We don't git no schoolin'. You best be keepin' them such thoughts to yourself and never you mind none."

Legends of Lincoln

I didn't understand but I didn't question my mother.

Over the next ten years the Mississippi flooded a few times and we had to move. This didn't sit well with the master and he needed to make ends meet. That became harder and harder. He had me start doing the chores my mother used to do. My mother now just did the cleaning and cooking and I attended the master's wife personally.

Once I became good at it I started to do some of the cooking and all the cleaning. One day when I was fourteen two of master's sons came in and took mother. I screamed but mother told me to keep mum, and one of the boys smacked me. I was so scared. I didn't know what to do. They just took my mother and left.

I wanted to ask my father but he was no where to be found. I later discovered they had been taken up to Vicksburg and sold. That was the last I ever saw of them. It was only a few years later that the War began. Things seemed mostly the same. We were many miles away from the Mississippi and my master didn't think the war would come near us. Both of his boys had gone off to fight and so it was just him and his wife, myself and three other slaves. The rest had been sold.

Then suddenly master heard that the enemy were coming closer. Each day more and more news came that northern troops were getting further and further south. We heard more Federal troops were coming up from New Orleans. Closer and closer. Then one day master told us to mind the plantation. He and his wife had to go up to Vicksburg. I never saw them again. Three days later the Federals were here.

When I first became free I had nothing except the clothes on my back. These happened to be my former mistress's best Sunday gown. I wore that when I first greeted the troops when they first entered town. My master and mistress were long gone by then so me and my fellow slaves had the plantation all to ourselves. We definitely made the most of t. The boys got all liquored up and took the master's clothes while we girls got spruced up in the ladies finery.

The troops took that in stride since they had become used to it. I and several other girls attached ourselves to a company for a time and did work cleaning or mending their clothing and cooking their food. It wasn't the one that had freed us but they were part of the same army.

They also took liberal privileges from us young girls. Now this wasn't to say the girls weren't unwilling. We were grateful to have our freedom and we thanked the lucky soldier in the only way we could, by giving ourselves freely to him. The point is that now we had the choice. Choice is what matters.

This had fringe benefits since the warm relations this created often gave us the opportunity to travel with the army as camp followers with easier pickings for food and clothing. But that situation couldn't last and eventually I had to make my own way.

I had to take my chance to leave the company. It was time. The army was seeking to abandon us. They felt we were an encumbrance since they had to feed and otherwise take from the supplies of the army. The commander was not an abolitionist. He didn't like us Negroes. I heard of this from one of the boys in the company. He said the commander privately termed us "useless baggage" and said it would be better off once he was rid of them.

Many wouldn't leave since they feared what may happen once they left the safety of the army so they ignored the general and stuck with the army, much to their later chagrin. Those that stuck with the troops found out he meant what he said for when he got the chance he made quick work of getting rid of them. This left many of them at the mercy of the locals who came swarming out in the wake of the army's passage. These vagabonds and bandits who had evaded the conscription officers were too cowardly to join the rebel ranks but they were brave enough against unarmed folk, especially women and children.

They took out their revenge against the depredations of the army on these helpless souls with a vengeance. Not much was ever spoken about the horrid encounters between roving raiders nipping at the heels of the army and the freedmen and women and children left in their wake, either at the time or long after, but the memory of it was embedded in the minds of the survivors for all their lives and lived on long after in the stories they told their children and their children's children creating a lasting enmity for between the races whether they or their ancestors had taken part in the atrocities or not.

I was far luckier. I found a chance to get aboard one of the many cars heading east and traveling a long distance by rail I eventually found my way to the capital. I didn't want to leave the army because I always lived with the fear of having my newfound freedom stripped from me but I eventually did and found my way to a hospital in Fredericksburg and became a nurse there. I had found my calling helping the wounded from the armies of the North and even some from the south.

I cared not where they came from for I had joined a local church and recommitting myself to the Lord I knew in my heart I was helping all America by helping both. I saw in their careworn faces that even the southern boys had no thoughts of slavery. Many of them never had slaves and cared little for the curse of the South.

Nurses were always in short supply and in this way I could still help the soldiers who gave me freedom, now with more dignity, and at the same time find room and board. I found that I was still too close to the fighting and I wanted no part of that any more so I left and walked to the capital itself and worked as a nurse there.

I found a new freedom in Washington on and even had chances to see the Great Emancipator himself on more than one occasion. This was always at a distance but even at great length he was surrounded by an aura of awe that was usually reserved for the Lord himself.

To me he seemed the most majestic and wonderful looking man who walked the earth. His humble and modest bearing epitomized what a true Christian should look like and I could see compassion written across his wrinkled visage and in the way he carried himself.

I spent over two years working as a nurse before Richmond fell. I knew that soon the war would end. Sure enough after a few weeks we heard of the surrender of the Army of Northern Virginia and the church bells rang and the cannons roared their mighty salute. It was a joyous time.

Lincoln was not only indirectly responsible for their freedom but was directly responsible for meeting my beloved, Roger. It was during Lincoln's funeral at the capital. I was in the section reserved for black citizens and since both of us had come to the somber proceedings alone we just happened to be standing next to each other. During one of the speeches in the late President's, honor the orator has read a glowing tribute to Lincoln and his Herculean efforts to free the slaves and we unconsciously clasped hands. Little did we know that this chance meeting would affect us so profoundly.

Roger blushed like a schoolboy as I smiled shyly up at him. He was much older than I but he was the handsomest man I have ever seen. Things led quickly to more emotional attachments. We were alone in a large city with no prospects and naturally we were attracted to each other. We had the mutual experience of bondage and long years serving the cause of freedom and unity. We told each other many stories, mostly of the years of our freedom. We did speak some of where we came from before the war. He had much more to tell than I since I was but seventeen when the war began.

We then settled down in a nearby town and open up a general goods shop. We prospered but did not display our wealth ostentatiously. Dear Roger voted regularly and always republican in thanks to their liberating him and his fellow black brothers and sisters.

After some time we sold our store and moved further north where we opened another one. We became rather wealthy and had many children who followed in our footsteps becoming a foundational family of the town. Several are now lawyers and doctors, while a few work in law enforcement. I am very proud of them all.

Our lot in life after civil war differed greatly than my brothers and sisters who remained south or were not as fortunate in their life up north. In many states there remained black laws, some called them Jim Crow laws. These were made to place blacks back into the servitude we fought so hard to escape. These laws were modeled on the institution of slavery and refined by the black codes found at the time in parts of Illinois, Indiana, New York, etc.

Our status differs in that we settled in a more liberal minded town and were able to establish ourselves and our business quickly and gained a modest success and we began to become pillars of the community and blacks in general as model citizens.

It was Roger who taught me how to read and write. I was a quick learner and soon became better than him at both. He didn't mind. He loved to listen to me read to him. He would sit back in his rocking chair with a smile and his eyes glistened as I read to him.

Roger always told me how proud he was the day he voted for the first time in his life. He was near 60 years old by then, maybe even older, and working as a laborer at a printing press and he never felt prouder as he cast his ballot for Ulysses S Grant in 1872. All thanks to Father Abraham, the Great Liberator he would say and of course I agreed, though I will add the Lord guides us all.

I never knew my father. I was born posthumously. Mother said he was a great man. I never knew him but all the neighbors agree that he was a good god fearing man who was a loving husband and father. I really wish I knew him, at least for a little while but mother told me stories about him all the time. That helped and it inspired me to live like he did.

He and my mother were always in my mind, from the day I could understand who I was, and who they were. My mother always strove to give each of her children all the opportunities to become whatever they wanted to be. That was the American dream, to reach their potential.

We were lucky to have two such wonderful parents. They gave us the chance to attend good schools, to give us the best education they could. As a colored woman, growing up in a land where in many places this would have been an almost impossible task, here we found ourselves in a community where we were not judged solely on the color of our skin, but on our worth to the community.

Things were not always this way. It was a constant struggle. It was a struggle my father and mother fought from the moment of their freedom. They didn't fight it with their fists. They fought it by using their minds. They fought it with their honor and their dignity. By proving each and every day that they were not limited by the color of their skin, or their gender, they showed everyone around them that a person should be judged not by their appear-

ance but by their worth to their community.

My mother was an important part of the movement that strove for decades to bring the right to vote to all Americans, not just men. She always told me that the War Against Slavery was just the beginning. The struggle could never be finished until every American, colored and white, man and woman, had equal rights not just in front of God but in the eyes of the Law.

Three days ago we achieved another milestone. For the first time since the end of Reconstruction a colored man was elected to the House of Representatives. Oscar Stanton de Friend said that day that it was due to the colored and white women who closed ranks and marched to the polls that we all reached this signal moment in history.

I stand before you to tell you that when I went to my mother on her sickbed and told her of our success, she wept. She wept and told me that this was the culmination of her long life and if the Lord decided it was her time, she was proud of the small part that she played in helping women everywhere to be able to have their voices heard.

She said she knew that this great moment was a precursor of more to come. Soon, maybe not in our lifetime, but someday in the future, we would see women take their rightful place alongside men as legislators. We will be creating the laws that govern all of us. She said we would one day we would preside over the courts, even the greatest court in the country, The Supreme Court.

She said that one day the United States of America would elect a colored woman as President. That one day having a female President and a President of any race and sex would become normal, so normal we would be amazed to think it was ever any different. Her words have always been prophetic so I see no reason these will not be any less true than any of her other beliefs.

I believed her words as much as I have always believed her. She has always told me the truth and said that as long as you believe, there is nothing you can't accomplish. When I look upon all of you here to pay your respects to my dear mother, I know that what she said is true and together we will see her words bear fruit.

I believe I speak to everyone here and everyone who could not attend but knew and loved my mother when I say, "Thank you

Mother. We will not fail you."

Pam stepped down from the podium that was set before the casket holding her mother's body. She turned and knelt at the pew and said a short prayer thanking the Lord for giving her such wonderful parents and helping them all in their time of need. Then she kissed her mother's forehead and walked over to the side and allowed her children to follow suit.

The church was full to overflowing, evidence of the standing of Pamela and the love she brought to everyone. White and black, they had sat mixed. There was no segregation today. They all sat as one to pay their respects to their neighbor and friend.

All with the dream that one day, in the near future, this would become the norm in this great nation and fulfill the greatest desire of the man who united the nation in the hope that the nation would be healed and truly united in mind, body and soul.

*the above story is not meant to reflect the truth of the state of the nation at the time of Pam's eulogy for her mother. It is rather a heady reflection of the times in that across the nation was held the belief that anything was possible. There was a spirit of the invincibility of the nation that was supported by the unparalleled prosperity. This was reflected in marked progress in civil rights from labor through social. It was a chimera, the edifice was fragile and the façade came crashing down within the year with the Stock Market plummeting, the impotence of the government and the reversal of the rights of the people across Asia and Europe, including America especially for African-Americans.

*Some say Lincoln was not religious as he had never joined a church. It may be that he did find some of the stories in the Bible a bit far-fetched, but he was certainly a god-fearing man and as there were few churches around at the time he never formally joined a church. He did go with his stepmother and was often chided afterwards for mimicking the pastor's sermon. This had fueled the irreligious speculation but was likely due to his playful and mischievous nature.

A FINAL WORD

In my opinion, absolute truth is a will o' wisp of perspective. Facts exist but interpretations of them as they relate to events vary from mind to mind and evolve over the course of time, even within a single person's mind. They are clouded by memory, additions of evidence and opinions, bias inherent in the environment through which the events are perceived, and the changing of one's own views through the effect of all the above.

I do not represent any of the preceding stories as unsullied facts or interpretations. On the contrary, I believe they only enhance myths, while cresting tangents of thoughts previously held on personages or historical events.

I hope the reading of these stories provide food for thought about the events and times of the past and perhaps be fruitful for the future in dealing with divergent perspectives.

In any event I hope you enjoyed it and it proves to be a helpful and entertaining resource for you on your life's journey.

SELECT BIBLIOGRAPHY

Abraham Lincoln: A Life From Beginning to End by Henry Freeman; Hourly History, 2016

Abraham Lincoln: A History by John G. Nicolay & John Hay;

The Young Eagle by Kenneth J. Winkle; Taylor Trade Publishing

The Eloquent President: A Portrait of Lincoln Through His Words by Ronald C. White Jr.; The Random House Publishing Group

Recollections of Abraham Lincoln in Illinois by David Kent Coy, the Looking for Lincoln Project

The American Presidents by David C. Whitney; Doubleday & Company

The Civil War: A Narrative Vol. 1-3 by Shelby Foote; Random House Inc.

Team of Rivals by Doris Kearns Goodwin; Simon & Shuster

Lincoln & Stanton by William D. Kelly; A Story of the War Administration of 1861-62; Big Byte Books

Lincoln & McClellan: The Troubled Partnership Between a President And His General by John C. Waugh; Martin's Press LLC

"New Light on Lincoln's Boyhood" by Arthur E. Morgan, The Atlantic Monthly, February, 1920; Vol. 125, No. 2 (p.208-218).

Herndon, William H. and Weik, Jesse W. – Herndon's Life of Lincoln – DeCapo Press, 1983

Made in the USA
Columbia, SC
14 November 2022